Anxiety and the Executive

Anxiety
and the Executive

Alan N. Schoonmaker

American Management Association, Inc.

Standard book number: 8144–5182–9

Library of Congress catalog card number: 77–78056

Second printing

To
Phyllis and Erica

Acknowledgments

MANY PEOPLE HAVE HELPED TO WRITE THIS BOOK. RUSSELL MOORE helped me get started. Elizabeth Marting provided several useful suggestions, and Mary Stanton read and corrected the manuscript. Danielle Marton typed the entire book in record time. Professors Stein, Bolman, and Siegel criticized early drafts and helped me revise them. My brother, Brian, gave me the benefit of his editorial experience and ability by reading the entire manuscript and criticizing it thoroughly. Most important of all, my wife tolerated my irregular hours and habits and helped me keep working. I thank them all; without them, I would never have finished.

Contents

CONTENTS

PART ONE

Introduction to Anxiety

1

"Anxiety in its milder forms is a universal human phenomenon."
—FRIEDA FROMM-REICHMANN, M.D.

The Hidden Problem
of Executive Life

IN THE POPULAR NOTION, EXECUTIVES ARE COMPLETELY RATIONAL MEN who ignore their own emotions, base their decisions entirely on the facts, and constantly strive for maximum profits and efficiency. As with most other stereotypes that attribute a standard set of traits to all the people in a given profession or occupation, this one contains some truth; but it is incomplete and misleading.

Because of their basic character and training, executives are more rational than most men, and they do have better control over their emotions. But this control is certainly not complete. Sometimes they can't understand their emotions; sometimes their emotions are too powerful to control, and then they act as emotionally and irrationally as other men. Some executives kill themselves by driving carelessly; others commit slow suicide by drinking, smoking, or eating too much. Many buy cars and homes that they don't need, and can't afford, in a frantic and obviously irrational struggle for prestige. Many are so busy "getting ahead" that they ruin their marriages and lose contact with their children.

Their emotions can even affect the way they act on the job. One executive lets his guilt feelings prevent him from firing an incompetent subordinate. Another postpones or avoids an important decision because he is afraid of making a mistake. A third is so anxious about uncertainty that he makes important decisions too hurriedly.

None of these actions is rational in the classic sense of the word, yet such actions happen every day. They happen because executives are as human as everyone else and cannot completely control or ignore their own emotions. And, of all these emotions, anxiety is the most common, the most powerful, and the least understood. Other emotions come and go, but anxiety is a relatively permanent part of our lives. We may not understand it, but we all know what it feels like. It is the official emotion of our age, the symbol of our era.

The bomb, the war, crime in the streets, the revolt of our young people, and all the other incomprehensible changes of our era have made most of us tense and anxious. The evidence of our anxiety is everywhere—the popularity of tranquilizers and psychoanalysis, the endless books, articles, and columns on personal problems, our frantic search for new pleasures and new escapes, our high rates of suicide, crime, alcoholism, and divorce. We live in an anxious age, and very few of us can escape the anxiety of our times.

Executives live at the leading edge of our society and receive more of the stress of modern life. Most people live under pressure, but the pressures on executives are unusually severe. Most people compete, but competition is often the center of their lives. Many people feel the anxiety of rootlessness, but they move every few years and may have no real roots. For all these reasons anxiety is a serious problem for many executives.

But it is a hidden problem, one which is rarely discussed. There are hundreds of books and articles on almost every topic in industrial psychology: training, decision making, supervision, communications—even handling *subordinates'* emotional problems—but virtually no literature on executives' anxiety and irrationality. Executives and the men who write for them have ignored these topics and focused on the rational side of executive life.

Executives and writers alike have ignored anxiety and its effects for the same reason that most other people ignore the subject. It is human nature to want to believe that we are rational men. We all want to believe this, but this desire is especially strong among executives. Their whole culture and their system of values emphasize rationality and minimize emotions. Executives are expected to ignore and control their own feelings and are ashamed to admit that they can't do it. They therefore deny their own feelings or try to ignore them.

Although this desire to minimize the effects of emotion is understandable—even laudable—to deny or ignore emotions has exactly the opposite effect. The simple, inescapable fact is that *anxiety exists*. It does influence a great deal of everyone's behavior—yours, mine, your boss's, your subordinates'—everyone's. Nothing can change this fact, and to ignore it is as foolish as to ignore friction, communism, or heart disease. It is a problem, a serious problem, and it won't go away if the person who has it pretends that it does not exist. Ignoring the problem of anxiety or hiding it behind a wall of rationalizations and denials may make a man more comfortable for the moment, but it prevents him from solving the problem.

However, although anxiety is a serious problem for some executives, it should not be thought that executives are more anxious and defensive than other people. On the contrary, the evidence suggests that they are less anxious and defensive—for example, they have more stable marriages, fewer divorces, better-adjusted children, and less mental disease. Our goal is therefore to make executives more aware of the problem and better motivated and able to solve it, not to argue that the problem is especially serious for them.

How to Recognize Anxiety

Now that a general idea of the importance of anxiety and the reasons for keeping it hidden have been stated, let us consider a few types of executives and see how anxiety affects them. On the surface they appear to be about as different from each other as people can be—an optimist, a pessimist, a gypsy, a drinker, a puritan, a conformist, a rebel, a tough guy, and a nice guy. But when we look beneath the surface and examine the causes and meaning of their behavior, we find that they have a great deal in common.

Each of these executives acts as though he had consciously chosen his style because it was appropriate for his job and career, but anxiety affects every one of them. There are certainly other reasons for their behavior, but each executive is trying in his own way to solve the problem of anxiety. Each is trying to reduce his anxiety and preserve his self-image as a rational man.

And each tries to solve the problem in ways that he has *learned*. He has found that certain kinds of behavior may relieve his anxiety, and he uses them even when they are inappropriate. We call this kind of behavior "defensive" because it defends a person and temporarily relieves the pain of anxiety. But, because it doesn't remove the causes, the anxiety returns. Some men defend themselves by drinking to excess; they have learned that alcohol blots out their anxieties and lets them relax. But drinking provides only temporary relief and can actually increase anxiety by ruining career, home, and health. The tough guy has learned to beat down his anxiety, and he is tough even when he alienates people. The puritan becomes very anxious when he yields to an impulse, and he has learned to repress impulses even though repression deprives him of many normal and healthy pleasures.

Each executive has also learned how to *rationalize* his behavior. Anxiety influences all of them, but they all try to ignore it and give rational reasons for their behavior. The tough guy is tough because he has to "get production." The rebel breaks the rules to "do the job better." The conformist follows the rules exactly to "prevent chaos." Even the drinker drinks because it helps him to "think better."

These rationalizations keep the executives from understanding how anxiety affects them, and that is exactly what they want to happen. Even though we all say that we want to understand ourselves, even though we are all proud that "we don't kid ourselves," we all rationalize. And very few of us really want to know the truth about ourselves. Even people in psychotherapy, paying $25 or $50 per hour to learn to understand themselves, work very hard at deceiving themselves. It is a basic human desire to want to preserve our self-image, and we all tend to ignore, deny, or rationalize information which conflicts with that image.

These tendencies create a very difficult problem. Most people are very good at rationalizing their behavior. They can come up with plausible explanations for everything they do, even though the explanations are incorrect. Since these rationalizations are plausible, and since almost any kind of behavior can be caused by a man's anxiety or his situation, it is far from easy to tell when a man is being defensive. An executive can be tough because his job requires him to be tough—or because being tough relieves his anxiety. A man can postpone a decision because he really needs more facts— or because he is unduly afraid of making mistakes. How, then, can we tell whether a man's behavior is rational or defensive? How can we know whether a man is responding to his situation or to his own anxiety?

This question is oversimplified. Usually, a man doesn't respond to one *or* the other. He responds to both. The question is, then, not whether his emotions affect his behavior, but how much effect they have. Is his behavior primarily rational or primarily defensive?

This question can be answered by asking two more simple questions. First, does this particular kind of behavior occur even when it is obviously inappropriate? (Is the tough guy domineering toward everyone—even his wife and children?) Second, does it have unpleasant consequences which he ignores? (Does the nice guy ignore the fact that some of his subordinates take advantage of him?) In other words, is this particular behavior rigid and ineffective? If so, it is primarily—but probably not entirely—a reaction to anxiety and his other emotions.

With these basic principles in mind, let us analyze a few fairly common executive types. These descriptions are, of course, extreme and oversimplified because we are trying to illustrate the principles. Very few executives completely match any of the types, but you will certainly see some of your friends here, and you might even see a little of yourself.

ANXIETY ABOUT PEOPLE

Everybody has problems relating to people. People need other people as much as they need food, water, or air. They want to get close to others but are afraid of being hurt. They need intimate, confidential relationships but are afraid to let other people come too close because they may reject or take advantage of them. These

17

desires, doubts, and fears are completely normal, and everyone has them. But some people have stronger doubts and fears than others, and such people usually behave rather rigidly.

Although the problem is the same for everyone, there are three very different ways of solving it: A man can move *toward* people (dependency), move *away* from them (aloofness), or move *against* them (hostility). Most people lean toward one approach but are flexible enough to use all three at different times. The people who are most anxious and rigid rely almost exclusively on one method, and these people form four well-known executive types. The tough guy moves against people. The nice guy moves toward them. And the gypsy and loner move away from them. Although they use different methods, they all began with the same feeling, and they all end with the same problem—loneliness.

The tough guy. This man is a tough boss and proud of it. And he is always ready to tell you why he is tough: "I'm not paid to be popular. I'm paid to get production, and I've got to push my men to get it."

We cannot assume that every executive's toughness is defensive. Some executives are tough because they have found that this is really the best way to get jobs done, but others act autocratically to relieve their own anxieties and then rationalize that they have to be tough to do their jobs.

We can find out what causes an executive's toughness by asking the two standard questions: Is he aggressive, domineering, and autocratic when these attitudes are obviously inappropriate? Does this kind of conduct cause problems with other people which he ignores? If he bullies everyone—his subordinates, his friends, his wife, his children—he is probably being defensive. Certainly, bullying his family is not caused by any rational desire to "get production." And his behavior has many unpleasant consequences: His wife will almost certainly dislike him and may even leave him. He may lose contact with his children. His home life will be unsatisfactory. His subordinates may leave the company.

The executive who bullies everyone illustrates very clearly the rigidity of defensive behavior. The defensively tough executive bullies everyone, even if by doing so he ruins his career or his home life. The rationally tough executive is much more flexible. He knows when to be tough and when to behave differently. He may be tough on the job but gentle with his wife and children, or tough when subordinates make mistakes but understanding when they have personal problems.

A defensively tough executive is trying to escape the anxiety he feels about people. Everyone needs people, and his needs are as strong as other people's, even if he won't admit it. He wants to be close to people, but he is afraid to let them come near him. He is afraid that people don't really like him and that they will hurt him if they get past his shell. So he hurts them first, to keep them away.

The tough guy pays a high price for this protection. His toughness protects him by keeping people away, but then he feels lonely. Because his defenses are not perfect and the need for people is so basic, he occasionally realizes how lonely he is; and this loneliness is so painful that he has to escape it. He may drink too much, or rationalize that he doesn't need people, or throw himself into his work. But he still can't escape it completely, and occasionally he lets someone get close to him, even if only for a moment.

Most of us can remember being surprised when a tough guy (who may have had a few drinks) told us how lonely he was and how he wished people liked him. You might have been touched and pleased that he had taken you into his confidence. But the next day he was the same old bastard! He let the barriers down momentarily, but he couldn't keep them down. He needs people, but he is too afraid of them to let them be close to him.

The nice guy. This executive likes his men, and they like him. He will tell you that people work best when they get along with each other: "My group gets good production because we work well together, and we work well together because we like each other."

Again, we must not assume that the nice guy is being defensive. Perhaps he is, but many nice guys have found that friendliness and cooperation increase efficiency. We can determine how defensive his friendliness is by asking the two standard questions.

The defensively nice executive will be friendly even when he should be firm or tough. He will avoid criticizing a subordinate who needs criticism, or let his desire for popularity reduce his unit's efficiency, or give overly generous performance ratings and salary increases, or retain incompetent subordinates. He will be nice

19

even when his people take advantage of him or external pressures require hard measures. His behavior is therefore as rigid, ineffective, and defensive as the defensively tough executive's.

His behavior is caused by the same basic problem—anxiety about people. The defensively tough executive relieves his anxiety by keeping people away from him; the nice guy, by bringing them closer to him. He is unsure of himself, unsure of whether people really like him. He needs reassurance that he is liked; he will sacrifice efficiency for reassurance and let his own need for affection blind him to the effects his behavior has on the company.

Paradoxically, he feels as lonely as the defensively tough executive. His needs for affection are so great that they can't be satisfied. And his demands for reassurance often drive people away rather than bringing them closer. People tire of proving that they like someone, and they lose respect for someone who is too eager to please. Furthermore, as we shall see in a later chapter, he actually feels hostile toward people who don't give him the affection he needs; and other people can sense this hostility. The net result of his behavior is that he obtains neither operational efficiency nor the affection that he craves.

Fortunately, the extreme type of "nice guy" rarely becomes an executive. The executive culture and promotion system prevent most men with these traits from attaining executive positions. Many executives, however, have some of these characteristics. Some executives can't criticize or fire incompetent subordinates. Others give overgenerous performance ratings. Many executives want to be a sort of symbolic father to their subordinates, and they feel very hurt when one of their men quits or behaves in ways that they regard as disloyal (even if this "disloyalty" is for the good of the company). In each case their behavior is caused, not by the demands of their jobs, but by their own anxieties. And in each case it has some unpleasant consequences.

The loner. The loner works hard and knows his job, but he doesn't mix with other people or work well with them. He isn't nasty or antisocial; he merely prefers to be left alone: "I can think better and get more done when I work on my own. Besides, I don't have time for office politics and gossip."

The loner keeps away from people because he is afraid of becoming involved, afraid that people will hurt or reject him. He doesn't really understand people or emotions, feels anxious when people come too close to him, and tries to keep them from touching him.

His aloofness protects him; it also makes him feel lonely. Usually he prefers loneliness to involvement, but sometimes his loneliness becomes so powerful that he approaches people. However, because he doesn't have much experience with people and doesn't know how to approach them, he feels awkward and uncomfortable and quickly returns to the security and predictability of being alone.

The gypsy. The gypsy is a good man and does a good job, but he is always changing jobs. He has had six jobs in the past ten years and has done well in all of them. "I know people say I move around too much, but each time I've changed jobs, I've moved up. And getting ahead is what this ball game is all about."

The gypsy is also aloof, but his style is a little different from the loner's. He doesn't keep away from people all the time; he just moves on when they come too near him. And he probably changes more than his jobs. Most gypsies, especially the very defensive ones, change many other things. Some have been married two or three times or have had several love affairs. Many change houses, cars, or hobbies regularly, and they are always restless with the present and ready to try something new. They are always running away from involvement and the anxiety it creates.

A gypsy is willing to become involved, but not too involved. He doesn't want anything or anybody to become too important to him, because he could be hurt very badly. So, whenever he finds himself becoming too attached to something—a job, a wife, a house, a friend—he becomes anxious and breaks away. He breaks away, but he can't stay away. Like all other men, he wants something and somebody to be important to him. He needs to be close to people and may even want to be deeply involved in his job. So he tries again. The next job, the next wife, the next house must be the one he has been looking for all these years. He starts off enthusiastically—this one is for keeps—but soon the same old anxiety hits him and off he goes. And the cycle is repeated. He is trapped in a vicious circle and can't get out.

Four very different executive types—the tough guy, the nice

guy, the gypsy, and the loner—are therefore trying to solve the same problem. They all want and need close personal relationships, but they are all afraid of allowing people to come too near them. This problem creates anxiety which makes them act rigidly and ineffectively. They escape from their anxiety temporarily but don't solve the underlying problem, and the anxiety returns.

The tough guy beats down his anxiety by aggressiveness against other people, dominating or attacking them. But people resent or reject him. The nice guy advances toward people to reassure himself, but people lose respect for him and reject his demands for reassurance. The gypsy and the loner go away from people and thus avoid deep involvement; they can't be rejected, but they obviously can't be accepted, either. In other words, anxiety interferes with the work and careers of all four types, and they all end up as lonely and anxious as they began.

ANXIETY ABOUT DESIRES

Freud felt that anxiety about desires was the basic cause of all anxiety and of the neuroses, which are extreme cases of defensive behavior. According to Freud, human beings consist of three parts—the id, the ego, and the superego—and conflicts among these three parts, especially between the id and the superego, are the basic cause of anxiety.

The *id* is the wanting part of man, our basic biological inheritance, a carry-over from our uncivilized past. Its slogan is "I want." It wants satisfaction, relief from pain, sex, power, money—and it wants them *now!* Its desires are unlimited, unreasonable, and uncivilized. It doesn't merely want power; it wants unlimited power, the power to take whatever it wants and kill anyone who frustrates it. It doesn't merely want sex; it wants unlimited, immediate sex, and, if it doesn't get exactly what it wants immediately, it only becomes more demanding.

We can see how demanding, unreasonable, and uncivilized it is by looking at a newborn baby, the closest thing we have to pure, uncontrolled id. A baby wants immediate satisfaction—food, water, comforting—and won't tolerate delays or excuses. If the baby is hungry, he cries—no matter what you say or do—until you feed him. He won't tolerate any delays, and he is not interested in any explanations; he just wants food *now!*

As the baby grows older, he slowly learns that he can't have everything he wants, that some things are prohibited. Slowly he accepts these prohibitions, internalizes them, and develops a conscience, a superego. The *superego* is the social part of man, the internalized rules and prohibitions of society. Its slogan is, "You can't." You can't take other people's property. You can't hit people. You can't touch your genitals. But the superego doesn't just prohibit actions; it also forbids feelings and desires. You shouldn't hate your mother. You shouldn't want to hurt people. You shouldn't have sexual desires. And these rules are usually as absolute and unreasonable as the ego's demands.

Some girls (and a few men) don't merely feel that sex is wrong outside of marriage. They feel that sex is wrong—period. Soldiers feel guilty about killing people, even in battle, because they have been taught "Thou shalt not kill," not "Thou shalt not kill except in battle."

The more rigid these rules are, the more they conflict with the absolute demands of the id. The id demands satisfaction of all of its desires, and the superego prohibits all of these desires and the actions required to satisfy them. This conflict is, according to Freud, the basic source of our anxieties. The id wants, the superego forbids, and the person feels frustrated, guilty, and anxious.

The rational part of man, the *ego*, helps reduce this conflict and its anxiety. The ego also develops from the child's frustrations —not the ones caused by social rules or other people, but the ones caused by reality. A child wants to pick up the sofa, or reach the cookies, or turn on the television set, but he can't do it. He learns from this frustration and becomes more realistic and rational. He learns what the world is like and how to deal with it.

This realistic approach is essential because the ego has to moderate the conflict between the id and the superego, between desires and prohibitions, and help the person adjust to reality.

If the slogans of the id and the superego are "I want" and "You can't," the slogan of the ego is, "Let's compromise." The ego compromises between the id, the superego, and reality and enables men to survive and act intelligently.

If, however, the ego is weak, if the other parts are too strong for it, the conflict between desires and prohibitions dominates a man, paralyzes him, and makes him unable to enjoy life or act rationally. The puritan is ruled by his superego, the rebel by his id.

The puritan. The puritan arrives at work early every morning and leaves late every night. He never drinks, swears, or wastes time on the job, and he doesn't like people who do: "I am paid to work, not to fool around. If other people would take life more seriously, we would all be better off."

The puritan handles the conflict between his desires and his conscience by completely yielding to his conscience and denying that he has any "improper" desires. He has, of course, the same desires as everyone else, but he is so ashamed and afraid of them that he pretends they don't exist. And he doesn't pretend only for other people; he tries to delude himself as well. He represses these desires and pushes them completely out of awareness and into his unconscious. But, since his desires are too strong to be kept there by repression alone, he overreacts and tries to keep them unconscious by acting in a way exactly opposite to what his desires tell him to do.

These desires are often sexual, but he may not be able to accept his other desires even if they are acceptable to other people. He would like to loaf once in a while, or gossip with the boys, or have a drink, but his conscience won't let him.

He is a prude, a complete prude, for himself and everyone else. He acts as a self-appointed censor and is always ready to preach a sermon on morality and self-discipline. By acting as a conscience for other people he keeps from recognizing his own unacceptable desires.

The puritan is, then, a man at war with himself, constantly fighting his own desires and weaknesses. He can never relax, because the desires are always there and they are always so powerful. If he relaxes, if he realizes what he is, he will feel guilty, ashamed, and anxious.

The rebel. The rebel breaks every rule but somehow, usually, does a pretty good job. "Rules aren't sacred. If I can do my job better and help the company by breaking a few rules, I'll do it."

Rules are as important to the rebel as they are to the puritan. For both of them rules are not just guides to action; they have an emotional significance all their own. Following or breaking them is emotionally important, regardless of the costs or gains of doing so.

24

The puritan is dominated by his conscience, the rebel by his desires. His conscience is a nuisance, and he tries to beat it down because he needs to feel free. Rules, whether imposed by society or by his own conscience, make him feel trapped and anxious, and he has to keep breaking them to prove that he is free.

But the rebel is not free at all. He is as thoroughly trapped by the rules as the man who blindly follows them. He is in a different box, but he is trapped just the same. He has to break the rules, and so the rules dominate his life as surely as if he had to follow them. He is not free to choose, to follow or break them as he sees fit. His anxiety about being free forces him to break all the rules, and so he is not free at all.

Of course, none of us is completely free from this conflict. We all have desires that we don't accept or admire, and we are all bothered by our consciences. But, unlike the puritan and the rebel, we try both methods for reducing this conflict and its anxiety. Sometimes we yield to our impulses, sometimes to the rules and our consciences. But yielding to either is not rational in the classic sense of the word. Yielding is an emotional reaction to our inner tensions rather than a rational response to our objective situation, an attempt to relieve anxiety rather than a realistic attempt to solve the underlying problem.

ANXIETY ABOUT DECISIONS

Everyone feels anxious at times about making decisions. We don't like the uncertainty of not knowing what to do, and we are afraid of making mistakes. Sometimes we avoid the anxiety of uncertainty by making decisions too hurriedly; at other times we are so afraid of mistakes that we avoid making any decision. Either type of behavior is irrational and can cause serious problems.

Since decisions are such an important part of their jobs, anxieties about decisions are probably more important for executives than for most other people. Executives are constantly confronted with the need for decisions and often have to act with very little information —when a delay or mistake can be very expensive. Despite the popular impression, very few executives are completely rational in their approach to decisions. Most of them vacillate. Sometimes they avoid or postpone important decisions; sometimes they make decisions too hurriedly. A few executives develop rigid patterns which relieve their anxieties but cause some very serious problems.

The optimist. The enthusiasm of the optimist has helped him solve some tough problems; but he is always getting into trouble because he rushes into things, hoping they will work out. In his own opinion, his optimism is a virtue. "I may make some mistakes by being optimistic, but it is the only way to be. It helps me to solve problems other men wouldn't even touch, and it keeps up my group's morale."

The optimist can't stand the anxiety of uncertainty. Whenever he has to make a decision and doesn't know what to do, he becomes very anxious. His anxiety—not the need for a decision—takes over, and he just wants to get it over with. He knows that he should think more about his decision, but he is too anxious to think clearly. He acts impetuously to escape from uncertainty and anxiety. He jumps into a course of action and hopes that "things will work out."

The optimist knows that he makes some avoidable mistakes, but he prefers mistakes to the anxiety that he feels when he thinks carefully about his decisions. His superiors, who are much more concerned with good decisions than with his psychological problems, may have threatened and lectured him about thinking carefully before acting; he may even have taken a course in "scientific decision making," but he hasn't changed. Lectures and threats and courses can't change his behavior, because it is not caused by the rational desire to make good decisions or to please his superior. It is caused by the anxiety he feels when he doesn't know what to do.

The pessimist. The pessimist always expects the worst and plans accordingly. He prefers to avoid decisions, and he won't make one until he has all the facts, even if the facts are not available in time. He makes few mistakes but misses some good opportunities. He feels, however, that on balance he is better off: "I think people should be more careful. Most men make mistakes by rushing into things without even knowing what they are getting into. I have saved the company a lot of money by being careful."

The pessimist feels so anxious about making mistakes that he avoids making decisions. He is so afraid that he will make the wrong decision that he thinks things over, stalls, thinks again, and does everything possible to put it off. If he absolutely must make a decision, he picks the most conservative alternative. By not taking any chances he escapes the anxiety he feels about making mistakes.

To take no chances may of course be the biggest mistake that the pessimist could make. A man who won't make decisions, or won't take chances, probably should not be an executive. Executives must take chances to do their jobs. His superiors have told him that, dozens of times; but what they said never convinced him—couldn't convince him—because his behavior is not caused by a rational analysis of what an executive should do. It is caused by the anxiety he feels about making mistakes.

Although the books on executive decision making do not discuss anxiety, all executives let their anxieties influence some of their decisions. They are men, not machines, and they cannot completely ignore their own feelings. Sometimes they act like optimists, sometimes like pessimists. When the decisions are very important, the pessimistic side dominates; the executives are so afraid of making mistakes that they procrastinate or avoid making necessary decisions. At other times, they feel so anxious about not knowing what to do that they act impetuously. The way to reduce this erratic behavior is not to give courses in executive decision making or to ignore anxiety, but to understand anxiety and its effects.

GENERALIZED ANXIETY

The kind of anxiety that is driving the executive types previously described can be deduced from their behavior. The optimist avoids uncertainty; the pessimist is afraid of mistakes; the nice guy needs reassurance that people like him; and so on. But we can't say what kind of anxiety the drinker, the conformist, and the go-getter are running away from, even though their rigidity and defensiveness show how anxious they are.

Some of the men in each group are running away from general feelings of inadequacy; they don't think much of themselves, and they drink or try frantically to get ahead in order to relieve their self-doubts. Others are afraid of people or uncertainty or their own

27

desires and use alcohol, conformity, or their careers as a general antidote for their anxiety. We can't be sure what kind of anxiety they feel, but their behavior leaves no doubt that they are running away from their anxiety—and from themselves.

The drinker. The drinker works hard and is usually all right in the morning, but he has a couple of drinks at lunch and is drunk nearly every night. Yet he still expresses confidence in his control of the situation: "Don't worry about me. I can hold my liquor. And a couple of drinks help me think better."

We may have been deceived by the rationalizations of a tough guy or an optimist, but a drinker's are transparent; we know that he is anxious and uses alcohol as a crutch. Nor are the chronic heavy drinkers the only people who use alcohol to relieve their anxieties. Lots of "social drinkers" depend on it when things get tough at the office or they have problems with their wives. Unfortunately, alcohol doesn't deal with the causes of anyone's anxieties; it only deadens the pain and makes them less aware of their anxiety and problems. As soon as the effect of the liquor has worn off, the anxiety returns and may be even stronger than before. This, of course, is true for all kinds of defensive behavior. Being tough or puritan or overly ambitious doesn't solve anything. It merely relieves the pain of anxiety temporarily.

The conformist. This executive does everything "by the book," knows the rules inside out, and obeys them without question. Even his clothes and personal habits come under the rules; he tries to look and act like everybody else. "I follow the rules because, in a company like this, there would be chaos if everyone did what he wanted to do."

Superficially, the conformist and the puritan are quite similar. Both care a great deal about rules and feel anxious and uncomfortable when they break them. The puritan, however, carries the rules around in his head, but the conformist accepts the rules for whatever group he happens to be in. The puritan would stand out in a crowd which behaved in ways that he felt were improper, but the conformist would blend right in. This distinction shows that their anxieties come from different sources. The puritan's come from conflicts between his desires and his conscience, but the conformist's anxiety is much more general. He can't make his own decisions, or relate to other people, or develop any real core of permanence and identity.

The conformist cannot tolerate the uncertainty of being alone or having to make his own decisions. He needs to lean on someone, because to him the freedom to make his own decisions is not an opportunity but a threat. It means doubt, uncertainty, and anxiety. He therefore tries to escape from freedom by becoming like other people, by letting them tell him what to do. He lets them dictate his work habits, his tastes, even his morals. He escapes from the anxiety of freedom to the security of conformity. But he also escapes from himself.

His conformity relieves the anxiety of uncertainty, but it costs him his identity. He is not a man in his own right, but a reflection of the people around him. He is a man without a core, a hollow man, standing for nothing and meaning nothing. His conformity relieves the uncertainty of not knowing what to do, but it creates a greater and more frightening uncertainty: he does not know who he is or what his life means. If he is absolutely without this knowledge, his life is intolerable and his anxiety is overwhelming.

The go-getter. The go-getter is the ideal executive—ambitious, hard-working, conscientious. He is always willing to work late, and he never complains about difficult assignments. He will go wherever the bosses want him to go and do whatever they tell him to do— just as long as it helps his career: "When I entered the business world, I swore I would make it to the top, and I'm not going to let anything stop me."

The complete go-getter, the excessively ambitious executive, is an American ideal. He should be an ideal: That's the kind of man who builds this country, and we owe such men a debt of thanks. Unfortunately, the public usually doesn't realize how much of a sacrifice they have made for their success, what they are really like, what they are really trying to do, what is really driving them. American books, articles, and general folklore portray them as the epitome of rationality—men who know what they want and who have the courage, independence, and self-confidence to go after it. But this idealization has created a myth; the go-getter really deserves pity rather than admiration or envy. He is not rational, confident, independent, or courageous; in fact, he is a lonely, anxious, and unhappy man.

The go-getter is not rational, because he pays more for success and receives less from it than he expects. He sacrifices friends, family, leisure, satisfying work—perhaps even his health—to get ahead, but usually finds that getting ahead provides very little and very temporary satisfaction. And, when he realizes this, it is usually too late. He has sacrificed everything to win the game, but it wasn't worth winning.

The go-getter is not confident, either, even though his ambition and drive make him look very confident. In fact, he feels quite inadequate and has very little faith in himself. He drives himself, not because he is confident of obtaining what he wants, but because he must keep proving himself. He has to prove that he is a good man because he doesn't really believe it.

Nor is the go-getter independent, because his obsession dominates him. It takes away his freedom to choose; he has to get ahead. To fail would confirm his suspicions about himself and completely destroy his self-image. So he tries frantically to get ahead but loses control over his own life and decisions in the process. He may look free, but he has lost his freedom of choice because he has no real choice to make.

Finally, he is not courageous, because he is using his career as a crutch, as a narcotic, instead of honestly facing himself and his feelings. His career and the drinker's alcohol serve the same purpose —to deaden the pain and let them escape temporarily from themselves and their anxieties. The drinker's fear is much more obvious than the go-getter's, but the principle is the same. Neither can face himself, and both are running away from their anxieties. The complete go-getter, then, is not really running toward the top; he is just running away from himself.

2

"Studies have shown anxiety, worrying, and brooding to be far more common among highly placed businessmen than among the public at large." —Dun's Review.

Understanding Anxiety:
The Basic Principles

THE PURPOSE OF THIS BOOK IS TO HELP YOU SOLVE THE PROBLEM OF anxiety. Anxiety is a problem for all of us, and we all have solutions for it. We drink too much, or avoid decisions, or struggle frantically to get ahead, but these solutions don't work very well. They relieve the pain and awareness of anxiety temporarily, but they don't solve the problem permanently. They reduce the symptoms but don't touch the causes, and the anxiety always returns. Our intention here is to provide better solutions than you have now, permanent ones which will reduce both your current anxiety and its causes.

To help you solve the problem for yourself is our main purpose, but this book may also help you deal with other people's anxiety and defensiveness. It may also help you advance your career or increase productivity, efficiency, and profits, but these would be incidental and rather infrequent benefits.

We are certainly not implying that advancing your career or increasing productivity, efficiency, and profits is an undesirable or irrelevant goal; we do realize how important these goals are, both to you and to our society. But our society has done a superb job with these goals, and there are hundreds of books that can help you reach them. If you are like most executives, nearly all of your serious reading is related to your career, and you need much less help with it than you do in reaching goals which our society minimizes— developing a clear sense of identity, personal integrity, self-understanding and self-confidence, and the ability to live with yourself and other people.

Most executives are much less successful at reaching these goals than they are at producing things or advancing their careers. The goal of this book is therefore to help you become not a successful executive but a successful human being, a man who can live with himself and other people, who knows who he is and what he wants.

Because anxiety is a major obstacle to reaching these goals, we try to help you understand and deal with it. In Part One we describe anxiety and show how important it is. In Part Two we analyze its causes and show how the stresses of executive life can create a great deal of anxiety. In Part Three we analyze its effects and show how it harms executives' health and lives. In Part Four we present some solutions to the problem of anxiety and show you how to deal with it.

The understanding you gain from Parts One, Two, and Three will not completely solve your problem, but it will help you in several ways. It can help you make sense out of a great deal of behavior that confuses and frightens most people—riots, status-seeking, smoking, alcoholism, tyranny, paternalism, conformity. If you can understand these things and put them into perspective, you can cope with them more effectively.

This understanding can also help you to resist manipulation. Many psychologists, ignoring their ethical responsibilities, have developed techniques which build your anxiety, undermine your independence, and put you under subtle pressures. They have made it possible for politicians, advertisers, and your superiors to manipulate you without your understanding what they are doing or being able to resist effectively.

Politicians have learned how to sway public opinion and win elections by using the anxiety people feel about riots, crime, and national defense. They can also play on the general anxiety of our times and offer us expensive, often nonsensical schemes which provide psychological but not substantive relief.

Advertisers use our anxiety about people to sell mouthwashes, toothpaste, hair creams, and deodorants. They tell us we are lonely, unpopular, and unsuccessful because we smell bad, our hair is messy, and our clothes aren't right. They also use our status anxiety to sell us cars, boats, even gasolines and beer. ("Is today the day you move up to . . ." "For the one man in seven . . .")

Some corporations have the reputation of being skilled at manipulating their executives and other employees, making them anxious so that they will work harder and using their anxieties about being accepted in order to stifle dissent and independence by means of pseudo-democratic leadership. We shall discuss this topic extensively in several sections of Part Two.

But you can't be manipulated if you can recognize the attempt. You can see through the politicians, advertisers, and others who would try. You can resist them and act freely and in good conscience for your own interests.

Understanding anxiety can also help you to realize that other people have the same doubts and fears that you have. Everybody is unsure of himself; everybody has doubts about himself; everybody feels lonely and anxious at times. Most of us, however, look at the masks that people wear and decide that those people are more self-confident and secure than we are. These unfavorable comparisons make us feel worse. A major step toward living with yourself, therefore, is learning that you are not alone, that other people—even people who look very confident and happy—feel the same way you do. When you realize this, it is much easier to be honest with yourself and face your own anxieties.

Being honest with yourself, learning who you are, is the most important benefit of understanding anxiety. We all need an answer to the most common question of our era: "Who am I?" Unfortunately, some executives are too busy with their careers to learn that answer. They don't really know who they are; no amount of money or prestige will tell them, and this uncertainty causes a great deal of anxiety. The first step out of this vicious circle is to understand anxiety and ourselves; and this, of course, is one of the basic purposes of this book.

But even though this understanding is very important, it is not enough to solve the problem completely. We also need specific techniques for handling anxiety and building a sense of identity and security; these techniques, these solutions to the problem of anxiety, are described in Part Four.

THE NATURE OF ANXIETY

It isn't hard to define anxiety. We have all felt it, and we all know how unpleasant it is. It hurts, both physically and mentally. It makes our bodies feel tense, our hearts pound, our palms sweat, and our stomachs sink. Even worse is its effect on our minds: We know that something is wrong, and we feel confused and helpless.

Although anxiety is similar to fear, it is not exactly the same. It has the same general effects on our bodies but different and much more unpleasant effects on our minds. There are five major differences between anxiety and fear.

1. Fear is caused by a specific, external danger, but anxiety is much more general and is a reaction to an *inner* danger. When we are anxious, we have all the symptoms of fear—all of its unpleasant sensations—but there is nothing out there to be afraid of. We feel tense and frightened without knowing what we are afraid of.

2. Fear therefore appears to be a rational reaction, but anxiety an irrational one. It is reasonable to feel afraid in an obviously dangerous situation but unreasonable to feel afraid when there is no danger. For example, if your car goes out of control, your stomach may sink, your heart pound, and your whole body break out in a cold sweat; but you would know why all of these things were happening. In a state of anxiety the feelings would be about the same, but there would be no apparent reason for them. When you are in danger, these feelings are a rational and understandable reaction. But, when you can't see any danger, the same feelings seem irrational and incomprehensible. You wonder, "Why do I feel this way?" —and when you can't answer this question, you become even more frightened.

3. If these terrible sensations are not caused by some external danger, we think they must be caused by something wrong within

ourselves. We don't want to think that something is wrong with us, especially not a mental affliction. We want to believe that we are all right, that we are rational—yet here is this obviously irrational feeling. The doubts it creates about ourselves are one of the more painful aspects of anxiety.

4. Because there is no specific danger causing anxiety, we feel helpless and confused. If we were faced with some specific danger, we could act. We could avoid it or fight back. We could take intelligent steps to solve our problem. But we don't know what to do with anxiety. We can't avoid it, because it is within us. We can't fight back, because there is nothing to fight against. We don't know what to do, and nothing we do seems to work. These feelings of confusion and helplessness are another very painful aspect of anxiety. Dr. Rollo May has written in *Man's Search for Himself*:

> This is what anxiety does to a human being; it disorients him, wiping out temporarily his clear knowledge of what and who he is, and blurring his view of reality around him. This bewilderment—this confusion about who we are and what we do—is the most painful thing about anxiety.[1]

5. For all of these reasons, anxiety is a great deal more painful than fear. In addition to creating all the unpleasant sensations of fear, it raises doubts about ourselves and makes us helpless and confused. The net result is an extremely painful state, perhaps the most painful state a person ever experiences. Dr. Karen Horney, a well-known psychiatrist, has stated: "Intense anxiety is one of the most tormenting [emotions] we can have."[2] Dr. May goes even further: "In its full-blown intensity anxiety is the most painful emotion human beings experience."[3]

Of course, most people don't experience such extreme states of anxiety. Few become completely confused and disoriented, because most people can control their feelings—and executives generally have better control than most people. But no one can completely avoid feeling anxiety, and even mild attacks are very painful.

[1] Rollo May, *Man's Search for Himself*, Norton, New York, 1953, p. 44.
[2] Karen Horney, *The Neurotic Personality of Our Time*, Norton, New York, 1937, p. 46.
[3] May, *op. cit.*, p. 40.

Even though they have excellent control over their emotions, some executives experience extremely painful anxiety. They like facts, clear thinking, and rationality, but anxiety is obviously irrational. These executives tend to be intolerant of personal emotions and weaknesses—especially their own—but their anxieties clearly imply that something is wrong with them. They like to control themselves and their environment, but anxiety makes them feel helpless and confused. Anxiety may therefore be especially painful for them.

The Anxiety Sequence

Anxiety is, then, a very painful emotion which is similar to but not exactly the same as fear. Once its nature is known, its cause and effects can be analyzed.

Usually, it is easy to analyze cause and effect because they occur in a clear, unambiguous sequence; cause must precede effect, and the two can be clearly separated. Anxiety and other mental states, however, do not break down so easily. Some conditions are clearly cause and others are clearly effect, but the process is frequently circular, with an effect of anxiety becoming a cause for even greater anxiety. For example, a man drinks to reduce his anxiety about his career, but he is passed over because of his drinking and becomes still more anxious about his career. Another man constantly asks people for assurance that they like him, because he is anxious and insecure; but his need for reassurance drives them away and increases his insecurity and anxiety.

Although the process is thus sometimes circular, the anxiety sequence can generally be described. Some conditions in the environment or in the person himself create stress. Anxiety is a response to this stress. Because this anxiety is very painful the person tries to escape it, usually by acting defensively. Sometimes this defensive behavior changes conditions and creates *more stress* to start the process all over again.

The conditions which create stress have a wide range. Anxiety may arise from feelings of personal inadequacy, political and social changes, and the pressures of executive life. In Part Two the focus will be on certain aspects of modern executive life which create stress and anxiety. Rapid economic and technological changes, for example, cause uncertainty. Bureaucratic policies, unions, computerized information systems, and pressure techniques make many executives feel powerless. To be passed over or fired can create a sense of failure. All of these conditions, therefore, create stress which can cause anxiety.

Anxiety is a response to certain kinds of stress, especially *threats* to security, identity, integrity, values, or habits. Like fear, it is both a physical and psychological response, but unlike fear, it is caused by a psychological rather than a physical threat. When body or life is in danger, there is fear; but when self-image, values, or habits are threatened, there is anxiety. Take as an example the discharged employee: Even if he is not in any danger of starving, to be fired makes a man anxious because it makes him lose face, change his habits, and re-evaluate his own worth.

No matter what causes it, anxiety is always very painful. The first reaction to it is usually to try to get away from the pain. Part Three will analyze some of the methods we use to accomplish this escape, but nearly all of them deal directly with the pain, to the exclusion of its causes. People defend themselves against anxiety by drinking, or developing ulcers, or living in safe and predictable environments. But, as shown in Chapter 1, this kind of behavior provides very temporary relief, and the anxiety and pain soon return.

This common tendency to avoid or deny anxieties has a very confusing side effect; countless investigations have shown that there is no relationship between the awareness and the amount of anxiety. A man may be very anxious and not realize it, and another man may feel very anxious but have less total anxiety than the man who appears to be relaxed and confident. For example, certain kinds of neurotics and psychotics (who have become "sick" to solve the problem of anxiety) are almost completely unaware of their anxieties, and we can only tell how anxious they are by observing their behavior. *It is therefore completely incorrect to assume that one man is more anxious than another merely because he looks or feels more anxious, nor should you assume that you do not have anxiety problems merely because you do not feel very anxious.*

The key to understanding anxiety is not what the person feels, but what he does. If his behavior is very rigid, repetitious, and ineffective, he probably has a great deal of anxiety, whether it is conscious or unconscious.

Many executives reject the idea of unconscious anxiety and insist that they are not anxious. A few have even become angry when it was suggested that anxiety was a problem for them and have vehemently insisted that it might be a problem for a crazy psychologist, but not for mature executives. But the more loudly they protest, and the more angry they get, the more certain it is that they have a serious anxiety problem that they are trying to deny. In Shakespeare's words, they "protest too much," and their protests show how important it is for them to keep their anxiety buried.

Their protests are, in fact, defenses which keep them comfortable but prevent them from solving the problem. We shall therefore try to bring these feelings out into the open so that the problem can be solved. The discussion of anxiety and some of its serious effects—drinking, ulcers, and heart disease—will, we hope, motivate some executives to look more closely at the problem and try to solve it.

A WARNING

Although the problem of anxiety can be solved only by bringing it into the open, the process of doing so will not benefit everyone and may even harm certain people who have learned how to deal with their anxieties; this book can undermine their defenses. Everyone needs his defenses, and undermining them can do more harm than good; its effect can be likened to that of taking alcohol away from an alcoholic. Alcohol was slowly destroying him, but it did make him more comfortable. Without it he feels more anxious and uncomfortable, and to take it away without putting something better in its place is a useless and irresponsible act.

Here is the same kind of situation. This book may take your defenses away, or reduce their effectiveness and increase your anxiety and discomfort. Hopefully, it will provide something better in their place, but you have no guarantee of that. After reading it you may find yourself more anxious and uncomfortable than you are now.

It is therefore recommended that you put down this book if you: (1) are comfortable the way you are; (2) feel that anxiety is not a significant problem; (3) prefer to avoid discussing emotions and psychological problems; or (4) want immediate and tangible benefits from everything you read.

This book may be useful if you: (1) feel that anxiety is a significant problem; (2) are willing and able to examine your own emotions; (3) want to understand the causes and effects of these emotions; and (4) realize that the problem of anxiety cannot be solved quickly or easily.

PART TWO

The Causes of Anxiety

3

Basic Causes
of the Anxiety Sequence

IN THIS AND THE FOLLOWING THREE CHAPTERS THE FOCUS WILL BE ON the first part of the anxiety sequence, the conditions and stresses that make executives anxious. A wide variety of topics—social changes and norms, organizational pressures, even political and legal developments—will be discussed, but the emphasis will always be on the way these conditions make executives anxious and uncomfortable.

Occasionally, other parts of the anxiety sequence will be examined in this chapter to prove that these pressures and stresses really do cause problems, because executives are so good at disguising their feelings; they may be very uncomfortable and defensive but appear calm and self-controlled. In those cases indirect evidence will be introduced to show how much impact these conditions really have. Their impact depends, of course, on the individual. Some men are more vulnerable to certain stresses. For the sake of simplifying the analysis, these individual differences among men will not be examined here; but they are very important.

All the conditions that will be considered have been described by many other authors, and most executives are well aware of them.

Our description will therefore be very brief, and we shall devote most of our attention to showing how they create anxiety. Since our emphasis is on the effects rather than on the conditions themselves, these chapters will be organized by psychological principles and problems; we shall describe certain psychological problems and see how various conditions create them. Furthermore, because we are primarily interested in their effects, some conditions will be discussed in several places. For example, the limited power of executives to influence decisions about their careers is discussed under the headings of "uncertainty," "powerlessness," and "failure" because it can create any or all of these feelings.

Although these chapters are organized by feelings, we shall not be overly fastidious about the fine distinctions between them or their exact relationship to anxiety. Their definitions are overlapping, contradictory, and confusing; what one man calls "psychological stress" another calls "guilt," and a third names it "anxiety." We shall briefly discuss the relationship between these different feelings and anxiety, but all these feelings make executives uncomfortable and defensive, and we are more interested in the way they accomplish this result than in the fine distinctions between anxiety, frustration, stress, guilt, and shame.

These feelings are caused by two types of pressures: those that everyone faces—the possibility of nuclear war, crime in the streets, rapid social changes; and those that are particularly important for executives—overwork, relocation, union restrictions, and government regulation. We shall discuss both types but focus on the pressures of executive life, for they are added to the pressures that everyone faces, and the ability of executives to withstand them is impressive evidence of their mental stability. Because of their stability, personality, and background, they can live under more pressure than most men could tolerate and still maintain their equilibrium and effectiveness.

The psychological strength of executives, of course, is not the only reason for their stability. They have many other advantages to shield and support them—money, power, prestige, comfort, and so on. They don't have to worry about sheer economic survival, and they are protected from many irritations and frustrations by secretaries, assistants, and their own power and prestige. Nevertheless, the extent of their ability to withstand the pressures of executive life is rather impressive.

By focusing on the pressures and ignoring the privileges, this book presents an incomplete and unbalanced picture of executive life. This imbalance is intentional: To discuss executives' privileges is unnecessary, because everybody understands them (and most people want them). But relatively few people understand the pressures of executive life, and even fewer people could endure them. Besides, the objective here is not to present a complete picture of executive life; it is to analyze and solve the problem of anxiety.

The remainder of this chapter lays a foundation for this analysis and solution by describing four basic concepts: perception, emotions, conflicts, and uncertainty. These concepts will be used to analyze executive life in the chapters on rootlessness, powerlessness, and failure.

PERCEPTION

Next to assuming that men are rational beings, the most common and serious mistake that executives make is to assume that reality is the same for everyone, that everyone sees things the same way, that facts speak for themselves. When we think about it, we can all see that this assumption is incorrect, but we act on it again and again. Forgetting that people see things differently, we think that we have agreed on something, only to find later that we completely disagree. We assume that people have heard what we have said but find that they didn't understand us at all. We see people do strange things, and we throw up our hands in surprise and confusion. How could they act so stupidly? The facts are obvious; what's wrong with those people?

But facts are not obvious except as facts, and facts alone have no meaning for people. It is perception of the facts that counts. People respond to their perceptions, not to facts or realities. We live in the worlds we perceive, not the worlds of fact. In the terms of our perceived worlds, most actions make sense, even if they appear incomprehensible and unreasonable to other people.

Alcoholics confuse us, because their drinking destroys their careers, their health, and their families. But in terms of their world, in terms of the pain they feel and the relief they obtain from alcohol, drinking makes sense. We are disturbed and confused by violent crime; but when a man kills five or six strangers "for no reason at all," he actually does have a reason: He thought they were going to kill him and he acted in self-defense, or he was ordered by God to do it, or they were all Communists or spacemen who were taking over the country.

The same principle holds true for "normal" people. No one responds to facts alone; everyone lives in his own world and sees things differently. Two executives may be asked to address the board; one sees it as a threat, the other as an opportunity. The first sees the negative aspects of the situation: He may make a mistake; they may criticize him; he is not sure of his facts; and so on. The second feels that he can win their support for a pet project or at least make a favorable impression.

Anxiety, learning, and perception. The relationship between anxiety, learning, and perception is complex and circular: Our past experiences and anxiety influence the way that we perceive situations; we develop habits which provide the facts we fear, and our perception then reinforces and confirms our feelings and habits. There is so much information in most situations that we can find whatever we look for. If we expect and fear rejection, we will find plenty of evidence that people are rejecting us. If we want and expect acceptance, or a raise, or a new assignment, we can easily find evidence that we will get it. (Every boss has heard men complain because he failed to deliver on "promises" he had never made.)

This intimate relationship between perception and anxiety (and other emotions), together with the general refusal to discuss feelings, is the primary cause of the most frequently discussed and most rarely solved problem in management—poor communication. Virtually every firm has a communication problem, and these problems are almost never solved. They cannot be solved by any of the usual methods (house organs; suggestion boxes; reading, speaking, and writing courses) because they are caused by the natural human tendency to see what we want, or fear, or expect to see. There are ways to reduce these problems, but the problems themselves are inescapable parts of the human condition and will exist as long as men want, fear, and expect different things.

The complex and circular relationship among anxiety, learning, distorted perceptions, and poor communication causes or aggravates conflicts, emotions, and uncertainty and is a major factor in developing feelings of rootlessness, powerlessness, and failure.

Memories and anxiety. Memory is another aspect of perception. Memories are essentially internal perceptions, perceptions which the situation alone could not cause. Sometimes we recall things without any external stimulus at all, but usually something in our present situation reminds us of our past experiences. Regardless of what causes us to remember something, we frequently feel the anxiety and other feelings that we had during the original experience. Sometimes we don't consciously remember the experience, but we still feel the anxiety. We are anxious and uncomfortable but don't know why.

To illustrate this particular phenomenon: We have all met people who make us vaguely uneasy, but there is no reason for our feelings. Something about them just bothers us. Sometimes we may have even stronger feelings; we dislike or fear someone "for no reason at all." But there is always a reason for human feelings or actions, and there is a reason here: Something about this person—his eyebrows, voice, or gestures, perhaps—reminds us of someone who hurt us in the past, someone we hated or feared. We don't remember who it was, but we do remember the feeling. (Under hypnosis or after extensive therapy, we might also remember the person.) The feeling is unpleasant, and it is especially unpleasant because we don't know what causes it.

Because memories and their feelings can be so easily triggered, we may feel anxious in completely harmless situations. Something which is harmless in itself stirs up our memories and brings back old fears. Some people, for example, become extremely anxious when they are in bed for a few days with a minor illness. They may even delay their recovery by getting up and "proving" that they are not helpless, because being helpless—even temporarily—brings back the anxiety we all felt as helpless infants. They don't understand this, of course; they only know they become "edgy" and "restless" when they can't act independently.

The fact that harmless situations can trigger memories and anxiety creates some serious problems, and these anxieties are very hard to understand or deal with because people don't know what causes them. The following chapters will include many examples of this kind of anxiety.

EMOTIONS

Some emotions are intrinsically painful; they are related to anxiety and have similar effects—loneliness and feelings of inadequacy, for example. Others—anger, sexual desires, or dependency feelings—are not painful in themselves, but we may feel guilty or ashamed because of them. Guilt and shame are painful in their own right, and either can cause anxiety. We shall analyze both kinds of emotions here, beginning with the intrinsically painful ones.

Inadequacy feelings. Feelings of inadequacy are very common in America; paradoxically, they are often caused by one of the greatest virtues of democracy—the freedom to rise or fall on our own merits. In theory, each American is responsible for his own fate and is respected for his accomplishments rather than his ancestry. These ideals, unfortunately, are not applied universally even in America, and the race or religion of some men is held against them. Most Americans, however, are judged by their worth, not by their birth. In most other countries the pattern is very different: A man's birth determines what he will do in his entire life. The landlord's son becomes the landlord and the peasant's son will be just another peasant, regardless of their abilities. Our belief in individual responsibility and our competitive society have helped us to become strong and rich. They bring out the best in most people: Our rich men work, and our poor men can compete and contribute.

But no society is perfect, and we pay for our opportunities, freedom, strength, and affluence. The freedom to succeed includes the freedom to fail. In a society that worships success, that measures each man by his own success, this freedom and individual responsibility create some severe psychological problems. Everyone feels some doubts and uncertainties, and they can be very painful.

We have to make our own decisions, and we may not be sure what to do. We are responsible for our own fate and accomplishments, but we sometimes wonder how good we really are. We worry about our careers, abilities, personalities, sexual attractiveness, and so on because we can't be sure of anything in our competitive society. The peasant's son had no chance to be a landlord; so he didn't worry about it. His position was clear and came from no fault of his own. But our positions are unclear, and we are responsible for them. We can rise, and if we don't rise as high as we think we should, we can feel personally responsible for our "failure."

Several chapters in this book will show how the executive system increases these doubts and feelings of failure, but for the moment the focus is on the doubts themselves. They are painful in their own right and can create a great deal of anxiety. We want to believe that we are good men—smart, attractive, potent, popular—but these doubts threaten our self-images. A threat to our images creates anxiety in exactly the same way that a threat to our lives creates fear. To build our images and get away from this anxiety, we compare and compete with each other.

We wonder—for example—how much our associates earn, and we become very upset when we learn that someone is paid a salary higher than ours. We meet men with whom we went to school, and we try to find out whether we are "ahead" or not. We buy expensive cars, clothes, and homes, not because we need them to live comfortably, but to proclaim our success. We try to build up our departments, companies, communities, and country, and we resent unfavorable comparisons. Within limits, this competition and comparison are relatively harmless (and they are certainly good for the economy), but some people overdo it.

Such people are so unsure of themselves that they have to keep pushing down their doubts. They may build themselves up by boasting, or surround themselves with yes-men, or always compete with others. They have to win in business, at golf, and at cards; their children must get the highest marks; their homes and cars must be the biggest and best. This degree of inadequacy feelings (some people call it an inferiority complex) is not caused by the competitive nature of our society. It is a basic part of their personality and will not be relieved by any amount—no matter how great—of success or reassurance. They carry their doubts and problems inside of themselves and will not feel comfortable until they obtain professional help. However, the very doubts that make some men miserable can also make them very successful. They keep trying to prove themselves and end up as successes, even if they don't think so. In fact, some of the world's most successful businessmen, politicians, artists, and athletes have been compensating for an inferiority complex.

Inferiority complexes and the competitive system are not the only causes of inadequacy feelings. There is one cause that none of us can escape: aging. We are all growing older and slowly losing our strength, sharpness, energy, and virility. Some men don't mind growing old, and they do it gradually and gracefully, but others fall apart when they realize that their lives, opportunities, and bodies will never be the same again. They have refused for years to notice the slow changes, but suddenly they know that time is short, that they won't fulfill all their ambitions, that their bodies are not as strong or durable as they once were. They notice that they are no longer attractive to younger women, see younger men pass them, and feel that they won't go any higher in the corporate pyramid.

This sudden awareness can be especially painful for hard-driving executives whose lives are built around their jobs; retirement will take away the core of their lives. Their self-confidence was built by successful competition, but suddenly they realize that younger men have overtaken and passed them. They are proud of their abilities but see these abilities declining. They have never worried before about the possibility of losing their jobs, but now they feel terribly afraid when a friend of the same age goes without work for six months and then takes a low-paying job.

Loneliness. Loneliness is another emotion which is both painful and anxiety-provoking. It creates the same sort of pain and defensiveness as anxiety, raising self-doubts and fears. Indeed, according to Dr. Frieda Fromm-Reichmann some psychiatrists often use the terms "loneliness" and "anxiety" interchangeably. We have all been lonely and know that it is not the same as being alone. We can feel lonely in a crowded room and comfortable by ourselves. Loneliness is a need for people who aren't there, an acute hunger for personal relations, perhaps with a certain person, perhaps with anyone. We can feel lonely even if the people we need are right beside us. It is the relationship we need, not the physical presence, and loneliness can be most acute when we try to communicate with someone and realize that we can't get through to him, that he doesn't understand us.

The amount of loneliness that we feel depends on four factors: the objective situation, our perception, inadequacy feelings, and ways of handling anxiety about people. Chapter 4 will show how parts of the executive system create loneliness, but the focus here is on the other three factors. Perceptions and inadequacy feelings go together: People who feel inadequate perceive things differently, and this perception makes them feel more inadequate. They are more sensitive to signs of rejection—may even misinterpret innocent comments and gestures—and they overreact to these signs. They feel cut off, rejected, and alone even when other people are trying to get through to them.

Because of defenses, however, the amount of loneliness is not the same as our awareness of it. Some defenses are stronger than others, and certain types of defenses make people more aware of their loneliness. Generally, dependent men are more aware of their loneliness than aggressive or aloof men. They need reassurance and are more sensitive to signs of rejection; aggressive or aloof people may be equally afraid of rejection but prefer to keep people at arm's length. Aggressive or aloof men may therefore be as lonely but not feel their loneliness as keenly.

Regardless of its source and of the way a man deals with it, loneliness can be extremely painful—perhaps as painful as anxiety. It is so painful that people will go to great lengths to escape it. They will buy cosmetics, deodorants, and breath purifiers; agree with ideas that they privately feel are ridiculous; talk to people who bore them; watch television by the hour; buy over 35 million copies of *How to Win Friends and Influence People;* take worthless courses in popularity techniques; and even have sexual relations with people whom they don't like. They do these things to escape—at least momentarily—from the terrible pain of loneliness. We shall encounter this pain again and again; it is a recurrent theme in this book and a major problem of our era.

Guilt and shame. The relationship between guilt, shame, anxiety, and other emotions is complicated and confusing, but it is crucially important. The fine details will not be discussed here, but this re-

51

lationship must be understood if any sense is to be made of human behavior. It is crucially important because guilt and shame are very common emotions, and they operate in a way that violates all the rules of our legal, moral, and economic systems. In our country, people are held responsible only for voluntary actions; we are responsible for what we do but not for what we think or feel. Our courts recognize that our thoughts and feelings are not within our control and are therefore not punishable. But our consciences (superegos) do not distinguish between voluntary and involuntary, between feelings and actions, and we often feel guilty and ashamed about our feelings—even if we don't express them.

We can be ashamed of our sexual desires or feel guilty about experiencing anger, even if we don't do anything wrong. We have learned that these feelings are evil, and we punish ourselves with guilt and shame. In turn, guilt and shame can be very painful and often cause anxiety and defensiveness.

Guilt about sexual desires was Freud's primary interest; he found that it caused many psychological problems, especially in women. These problems were particularly severe during his era, because in the public mind sexual desires were dirty and shameful. Today, these desires are accepted as natural and healthy, and there is much less guilt about them. Sex is still a problem for many people, but it is not as severe or as important a problem as it was in Freud's time.

Guilt and shame about dependency desires and aggression are much more common today. Independence is a cherished ideal in America, especially for executives. We are supposed to stand on our own two feet and make our own decisions. We therefore feel ashamed of any desire to lean on other people. Unfortunately, this desire is a basic part of human nature, and everyone feels it from time to time.

Some people accept this desire as natural and feel little or no shame about it, but many others believe it to be a shameful sign of weakness and try desperately to deceive themselves and other people. They present an extremely independent façade: They can't take orders, reject suggestions and advice, and insist on having their own way in everything. By means of these actions such people may conceal their dependence, but they pay a terrible price for their self-deception. They have to keep deceiving themselves, can never relax or take advice. In many cases, they actually ruin their health. This is the classic ulcer personality type, and people of this temperament develop many diseases besides ulcers.

Guilt because of anger is also quite common and—as we shall see in Chapter 11—can cause heart attacks, migraine headaches, cerebral hemorrhages, and many other health problems. As children, we learn that anger is bad. We are supposed to love people—our parents, brothers, sisters, and friends—and not express hatred or anger. But pure love is an impossible ideal, and we always hate the very people we love. We do love our families and friends, but we also hate them. Love and hate are inseparable because everyone we love hurts and frustrates us, at least occasionally. Pain and frustration naturally lead to resentment; and the more we care about a person, the more painful the frustration and the greater the resentment.

Anger, resentment, and even hatred are therefore as natural as love and kindness, an inescapable part of human nature. But most of us don't realize that; we have learned that they are wrong and feel guilty about them. These hatreds are especially powerful toward our families, and we feel most guilty about them. The taboos are the most severe, but the feelings are also the strongest. This combination of very strong feelings and very strict taboos creates extremely severe guilt, indirect expressions of hostility—criticism, complaints, nagging, rejection, and the like—and occasional blow-ups. (Most commonly, murders involve husband and wife.)

These feelings are also important in business. Because executives' emotions have generally been ignored in the past, relatively little is known about these feelings in the business world, but Dr. Harry Levinson has done some work on "management by guilt." [1] He notes that "executives frequently make decisions in such a way that they can deny their anger and appease their consciences." This anger and guilt often refer to incompetent subordinates, especially long-term employees, and denying feelings leads to unpleasant consequences for everyone: (1) "The subordinate's occupational opportunities are either impaired or destroyed in the name of kindness."

[1] "Anger, Guilt and Executive Action," *Think*, March–April 1964.

(2) "Executives hurt each other as they transfer the subordinates from one to the other, each feeling guilty about unloading him on the other." (3) "The company suffers because the subordinate often draws his salary for years without producing adequately."

Many other aspects of executive life create anger, guilt, and shame. Organizations inevitably frustrate their executives by restricting their freedom. The executives may seem to submit passively to the organization's domination of their lives, but underneath they all resent it, and some men feel guilty about their so-called ingratitude. They may bury their resentment beneath a facade of unswerving loyalty, but the anger and guilt are there and will be expressed, indirectly, in physical symptoms, oblique criticisms, absenteeism, or poor work.

This kind of anger is only one result of the conflicts between human needs and organizational demands. These conflicts have been ignored by most of the writers on organization life; we have repeatedly been told that "what is good for the organization is good for everyone," and that apparent conflicts are merely the results of "poor communication" and "misunderstandings." Such statements are patent nonsense; we cannot begin to understand the impact of organizations upon individuals unless we clearly recognize that there are some basic, inescapable conflicts between the needs of a healthy individual and the demands of his organization. There are also, of course, many common interests, but we shall emphasize the conflicts because they cause the anxiety.

Conflicts

In the following chapters many of these conflicts will be discussed: conflicts between the individual's needs for freedom and the organization's need for control; between high salaries and low costs; between the desire for interesting work and the need for standardization; between the desire to reach the top and the pyramidal organizational structure. Here, we shall simply analyze the basic types of conflicts and their impact on people.

A person experiences a conflict when he must deal with two or more incompatible demands. Some of these demands come from within him, from his own needs; and some come from outside, from social rules and harsh realities. Three kinds of conflicts are therefore possible: between internal and external demands, between two external demands, and between two internal demands.

In our affluent society the least painful conflicts are caused by two internal demands. People rarely have to choose between eating and drinking, or between food and shelter, because they have enough money for both. Sometimes people may have to choose between a desire to finish a book and a need for sleep, or between sex and a steak, but they can usually handle internal-internal conflicts without much trouble. Internal-external and external-external conflicts are much more serious.

Several of the problems already discussed are caused by internal-external conflicts. People have strong sexual desires, but society imposes stern constraints. Men want freedom and variety, but their organizations dominate their lives and demand routine. People become angry but are required to be calm and reasonable. These conflicts are an inevitable part of life, and they create uncertainty, frustration, guilt, and anxiety.

External-external conflicts also create serious problems, and they are very common in our complex society. People who live in simple societies have few of these conflicts because their rules of conduct are generally consistent and they can follow tradition. We, on the other hand, constantly face conflicting rules and demands: We are told to be good fellows but hard competitors; practice the golden rule but remember that business is business; exercise our freedom of speech but refrain from destructive criticism; let our subordinates participate in decisions but make sure that they make the right decisions; turn the other cheek but be firm against aggressive tactics. These incompatible demands pull us in several directions and make us very uncomfortable.

Because all kinds of conflicts make men uncomfortable, they try to avoid them. They may ignore some demands, worry about which demands are most legitimate and important, try to compromise between conflicting demands—usually, without much success—or avoid the situation entirely and take no action. These strategies usually work; but some conflicts are so severe and the demands are so important that they cannot be avoided, and any solution is wrong. We may like a certain man who isn't producing, but we recognize our responsibilities to our organizations. We know that our families deserve more attention, but we have to travel and work long hours. We want to say what we feel, but our superiors won't tolerate dissent. We dislike company politics but have to play politics to survive and be successful. Because they are so common and create so much discomfort, conflicts will be a major subject in the next three chapters.

UNCERTAINTY

Conflicts make men uncertain about what they should do, but they are only part of the uncertainty of this era. For the first time in history, mankind and civilization can be destroyed in a few moments, and no one is sure that he will survive. Even if the war doesn't come, the world is changing very rapidly; and people are uncertain where they are, where they are going, and what they believe.

The impact of uncertainty. Regardless of the cause of uncertainty—conflict, the bomb, social change, or business problems—it produces anxiety. If the uncertainty refers to important issues such as our lives, family, or reputation, this anxiety can be unbearably painful. "People have been known to leap out of a lifeboat and drown rather than face the greater agony of continual doubt and uncertainty, never knowing whether they will be rescued or not." [2]

Leaping out of a lifeboat is a rather extreme case, but we have only to look about us to find countless examples of people who have committed irrational and costly actions to avoid feelings of uncertainty.

Superstitions. Tens of millons of people read horoscope columns, and newspapers invariably receive violent complaints if they try to discontinue the column. Palmistry is a flourishing business. Ballplayers and sports fans take jinxes and lucky charms very seriously. Nearly all gamblers try to ride "lucky streaks" and leave the game before their luck turns. Some gamblers even talk to dice or squeeze their cards for luck.

[2] Rollo May, *Man's Search for Himself*, Norton, New York, 1953, pp. 40 f.

These are all superstitious and irrelevant acts which make people feel that they are learning about the future or controlling the uncontrollable. They don't accomplish anything and may be quite costly, but they make people think that they are reducing uncertainties—that is, they reduce subjective, not objective, uncertainty.

Most executives laugh at astrology, palm reading, and similar attempts to control the future—even if they squeeze their cards in a poker game—but some common business procedures fall in the same general category. These procedures look sophisticated and make executives comfortable, but they have little or no objective value.

Perhaps the clearest example of "sophisticated" superstitious behavior is technical analysis of the stock market. Thousands of executives believe in it, and many pay huge fees for advisory services, even though dozens of published studies have shown that future prices cannot be predicted from the pattern of past price changes. Syndicated financial columnists have reported these studies to the public, and their reports are readily available to anyone who wants to read them; but many hardheaded executives and other investors base extremely important decisions on irrelevant and expensive advice. They do so, says Paul Cootner, the editor of *The Random Character of Stock Prices* (which contains many of these studies), because they want to reduce their feelings of uncertainty; they want to believe that they know what will happen in the future. Technical analysis of the market, therefore, has exactly the same value as astrology: It makes people think they can predict the future.

Decisions. What has been said here does not mean that executives are no better at dealing with uncertainty than other people. Because they are human, they dislike uncertainty and act superstitiously at times, but they can obviously handle uncertainty much better than most people. In fact, their entire system selects and prepares men to deal with uncertainty because it is an essential part of executive life.

Executives are men who make decisions, and decisions always involve uncertainty. When a man makes a decision, he may have a fairly clear set of expectations, but he does not know what will happen. (If he does know what will happen, he has not made a real decision; he has simply been a part of some routine.) Most acts that look like decisions are, of course, routine, but every executive occasionally confronts situations which are so new and complex that he does not know what to do or what will happen. This is the moment of truth, the moment the system has prepared him for, the time when he shows whether he is an executive or a clerk. The clerk does the routine things or passes on the responsibility to someone else, but the executive accepts the responsibility and uncertainty and makes the decision. Thus the responsibility for making decisions adds another dimension to the impact of uncertainty. Uncertainty is painful, but uncertainty plus decisions can be even more painful.

We have all heard stories about decisions causing ulcers; and these stories are not merely old wives' tales. A classic study has shown that making a decision can cause ulcers even if all other factors are kept constant. Two monkeys were strapped in seats with a light and a lever in front of them, their feet on an electrified rod. Every 20 seconds the light flashed, and, unless the "executive" monkey pressed his lever, both got a shock. The other monkey had a dummy lever, but he soon ignored it. Both monkeys therefore received the same number of shocks, but one was completely helpless to control them and the other had to make the decisions (push the lever). Although all other conditions were equal, the "control" remained in excellent health but the "executive" monkey died on the twenty-third day, the apparent victim of an ulcer.

Role, career, and performance uncertainties. Executives must also deal with much more uncertainty about their roles, careers, and performance than most other people. Most white collar workers know what they are supposed to do, but many executives are never told what their jobs really are, what their superiors really expect, or how their work is evaluated. Workers have clear promotion ladders and relatively unambiguous criteria for advancement (examinations and seniority, for example), but most executives have neither. They do not know whether they are promotable, what job they will get, or why they will be promoted or passed over. Because all of these issues are important to such men, uncertainty about them creates a great deal of anxiety, and we will encounter them several times in following chapters.

Identity. One reason these uncertainties are so painful is that

58

they refer to our opinions about ourselves, our identities. A man's identity is the core of his personality; he can't live sensibly or effectively without a clear picture of himself. But it is very hard to get this picture because of social changes, conflicting standards, incompatible demands, and buried feelings. We therefore need honest feedback from other people, but our entire system prevents them from giving it to us.

We need to know how people feel about us; but they aren't supposed to tell us, because it is rude to do so. We are afraid to be honest about our feelings and have developed rules and customs which prevent honest and meaningful communication: "Don't make personal remarks." "If you can't say something nice, don't say anything at all." "Look for the best in people." "Think positively." "Be constructive."

These rules are especially restrictive among executives. Talking about feelings is not just bad manners; it is also unbusinesslike, and very few executive groups will tolerate it. These restrictions are partly caused by the guilt and fear we have already discussed, partly by the businessman's natural preference for orderliness and reason. However, as we shall see again and again, the rules only create the appearance of order. To ignore feelings does not make them go away, and it does have several undesirable effects, including the creation of identity problems.

Executives have to face such a bewildering mass of conflicting demands and uncertainties, and get so little honest information about themselves, that identity problems are inevitable. These problems are not as severe as other people's, because executives are generally older and more stable, but they do exist and they do hurt. Most executives would disagree with these statements and insist that only teen-agers and mixed-up adults have identity problems. But their protests are a little too loud to be taken seriously, and the evidence is too consistent to disregard. This evidence appears in dozens of places in this book, but at this point it will be simply noted that the most common question of our time is, "Who am I?" Many books for and about executives try to answer it—among them, *The Organization Man, The Young Executives, The Man in the Grey Flannel Suit, The Executive Suite, Cash McCall,* and *The Uncommon Man.*

PROMOTIONS

Now that the basic concepts have been described, it is possible to analyze the conditions which make executives uncomfortable. The next three chapters cover the major causes, but promotions will be considered briefly in this chapter to illustrate the application of those concepts.

Promotions are generally regarded as unadulterated blessings, the best thing that could happen to a man. This description is usually fairly accurate; most people want promotions and are glad to get the greater challenges, opportunities, pay, status, and power. But some promotions cause so many problems that the recipients would have been better off without them. They may aggravate problems that people already have or create new ones; but the net result can be dissatisfaction, poor performance, and, in a few cases, a "promotion neurosis." A few men respond to promotions by becoming very anxious, disliking their new job, doing poor work, having family problems, and developing ulcers or other diseases.

These unusual reactions can't be understood if we view promotions in the conventional way, because the people in the situation don't see them in that way. They are overreacting to some of the negative aspects of promotion, and to understand their reactions we have to focus on these aspects. The psychological problems of promotion are very severe for a few people, and they worry many other people who really wanted and do enjoy their promotions. These problems are related to a man's perception of his job and divide neatly into the other three categories discussed—uncertainty, conflicts, and emotions.

Uncertainties. Promotion can increase dramatically the amount of uncertainty that a man must deal with. Some men enjoy this uncertainty; they regard it as freedom and opportunity, but it can easily upset a man. He has left a job that he understands; he must face new demands and challenges. Decisions become more difficult and more important, and he may have less information on which to base them. His superiors give him less direction; they expect him to act independently. He may have to change his entire pattern of activity: He stops working as a salesman, scientist, accountant, copywriter, or engineer and becomes an administrator. This change can cost him his professional identity, and the different skills and personality traits required by the job can create personal identity problems as well. He can't be sure of his performance because the standards are more ambiguous, and he is further from the point at which the actual work is done. He is more dependent on other people and becomes responsible for work that he can't really control. Segments of the job grow larger and require more time, and he can't tell how well he is progressing. Competition becomes stronger, and in consequence he is more likely to fail. There is a further possibility: Some promotions raise men to income and social levels so far above their background that they don't know how to conduct themselves with the people in their new environment.

Conflicts. Promotions also create many conflicts—which, however, vary with the person and his situation. Promotions change a man's situation in many ways, and each man emphasizes the things that are important to him. Some men want to move up but don't want to become administrators. Some want higher pay and status but don't welcome greater responsibility, or they desire to spend more time with their families. Some dislike the loneliness that comes with power and status. They don't want to drop their old friends. Many executives are glad to become more independent of their superiors as they move up, but dislike their increased dependency on subordinates.

Emotions. Usually, men are glad to be promoted. They appreciate the confidence that has been shown in them, enjoy their new status and independence, and look forward to having more money and authority. But almost everyone has some doubts and fears, and they can be rather painful. Inadequacy feelings are quite common, at least early in the new job; men wonder whether they are ready, whether they are really good enough to handle the job, whether they have the talent and drive to do top quality work.

More intense emotions are less common but very painful. In fact, they can cripple a few kinds of men and make it impossible for them to succeed in their new jobs. A few men, afraid of the increased responsibility, try to avoid it. They are so fearful of making mistakes that they avoid decisions. Some men are disabled by their loneliness. They don't know how to act with their new associates and can't mix comfortably with their old ones. This is usually a temporary problem, and most men learn how to fit in at their new level. A few, however, always feel left out, and they live lonely and miserable lives. They have risen too high to mix with their old friends but don't fit in with their current associates. This problem is even more serious for their wives and will be discussed in the next chapter.

4

Rootlessness
as a Factor in Anxiety

M AN IS UNLIKE ALL OTHER ANIMALS. ONLY HE KNOWS THAT HE
was born alone, lives alone, and will die alone. This knowledge is a basic source of his anxiety. Erich Fromm has summarized
this feeling eloquently in *The Art of Loving.*

> This awareness of himself as a separate entity, awareness of his
> own short life span, of the fact that without his will he is born
> and against his will he dies, that he will die before those whom
> he loves or they before him, the awareness of his aloneness and
> separateness, of his helplessness before the forces of nature and
> of society, all this makes his separate, disunited existence an
> unbearable prison. He would become insane could he not liber-
> ate himself from this prison and reach out, unite himself in
> some form or other with men, with the world outside.
>
> The experience of separateness arouses anxiety; it is, indeed,
> the source of all anxiety. . . .
>
> The deepest need of man, then, is the need to overcome his
> separateness, to leave the prison of his aloneness.[1]

The only way out of this prison is to build firm roots and rela-

1 Erich Fromm, *The Art of Loving*, Harper & Row, New York, 1956, pp. 8 f.

tionships—with family, friends, neighbors, associates, company, work, and society. These relationships give men a sense of belonging, certainty, and security. They help men know who and where they are and let them escape—temporarily, at least—from their essential aloneness and its inevitable anxiety.

Modern executive life, unfortunately, weakens these relationships for some executives. The pressures on them, combined with their attitudes toward life, prevent them from setting firm roots in any community, or developing close friendships, or giving themselves to their families, or relating themselves to their society. They are therefore terribly alone, cut off from their roots, isolated from themselves and from each other. Usually, they can disregard their isolation and concentrate on their careers; but sometimes it strikes them, and they feel the full impact of their aloneness. It may last only a moment, but at that moment they know how alone they are, and they feel the full force of the anxiety they have been running away from.

THE PRICE OF UPWARD MOBILITY: TEMPORARY FRIENDS, NEIGHBORS, AND ASSOCIATES

Because they are so thoroughly committed to their demanding careers, many executives cannot develop close friendships in any community. They work long hours, travel all over the country, are hungry to move up, and relocate every few years. Long hours and company travel cut down the time they have to relate to a community, and moving up or relocating breaks up their friendships.

Relocation means that the executive and his family have to start all over again somewhere else, and it occurs again and again. Many executives move more than ten times during their careers, and some companies transfer their executives every three or four years. As previously noted, this frequent moving makes it very hard to develop real ties in any community or form any close friendships.

Promotion also can destroy roots and friendships. New circumstances and pressures make it almost inevitable that the promoted executives will stop seeing their old friends when they move up. These pressures, together with their own status consciousness, can even disrupt relationships with friends who do not work for the same company. Some companies may want their executives' homes to match their status; many executives are eager to change houses, even in the absence of any encouragement to do so. Moving up— especially to the highest levels—can therefore mean buying a more expensive home. In older communities which have several kinds of houses and neighborhoods, an executive may buy a new house a few blocks from his old and still see his old neighbors occasionally. But he cannot do that in most of the better suburbs, because generally all the houses are in the same class or price range. To get an adequately prestigious home, an executive may have to move several miles to a new community. Moving up in his company can therefore have almost the same effect as a transfer. He breaks his ties with old friends and neighbors and starts again in a new community.

This constant moving has an even more serious effect: It prevents some executives from developing close friendships or real roots in any community. Because they know they will be moving again someday, they keep themselves and their families mobile. They don't become really involved in any community or get too close to anyone in it. They don't want anything to hold them back when they have to move next time. They therefore pay little attention to their communities and form cordial but superficial relationships. Their friends are usually people like themselves—families on the move— and everyone follows the same rules in these friendships. The principle may be stated as: "Be friendly, but not too friendly, because someday you will have to say good-bye."

Their mobility is not the only factor that isolates some executives. Their basic attitudes toward other people and their own careers are at least as important. Completely concerned with their own careers, obsessed with production, efficiency, and advancement, they treat people as things rather than as human beings.

These executives don't treat people as beings who are intrinsically important; they use them as means of increasing production or advancing their own careers. Friendship, to them, is a tool for getting ahead; they manipulate their subordinates, cultivate the right people, and drop the wrong ones. They look at personal relationships in terms of what they can get out of them rather than what they can put into them. This attitude advances their careers but makes genuine friendship impossible. Their superficial relationships, shallow roots, and noninvolvement keep them mobile and advance their careers but also create loneliness and anxiety.

FAMILY STRESSES

The stresses of modern executive life create some serious and very common family problems. In fact, these stresses are so severe that the relatively low divorce rate of executives is rather impressive evidence that they and their wives are generally very good at dealing with the problems of stress. But the wives receive the greatest stress, and they deserve most of the credit for keeping families together.

The wife is the one who is at home alone, taking care of the house and the children, when the executive is traveling. She suffers more than he does when they move. She usually feels more uncomfortable about dropping old friends as her husband moves up.

Many wives, of course, do not suffer in silence. They let their husbands know that they are unhappy and expect help from them. When they do, the husband is in a terrible position. He is torn between his career and his family. Both make powerful demands of him, and he cannot satisfy all the demands. He cannot work as hard, or travel as much as his career requires, and still spend as much time as he should with his family. He cannot comply both with his wife's demands that he stay in one place or that he keep their old friends, and with his company's demands that he relocate or that he so conduct himself that he has no time for friends at lower levels. These conflicts create serious problems and a great deal of anxiety. The greater a man's commitments to his family and his career, the more severe these problems and anxieties become. Several of these problems are so frequently encountered that they deserve to be analyzed in some detail.

Long hours. Executives put in more hours at the office than the men below them, and they bring more work home at night. The *Executive Life* survey found that one group (presidents, vice presidents, and high-potential middle managers) worked between 57 and 60 hours a week. They spent 45 to 48 hours a week in the office during the day, entertained once, and worked at night three times a week (once at the office and twice at home). And this was during normal times! When they had a trip, a convention, or an emergency, they might put in 70 or 80 hours.

Even when they are not working, executives' minds are usually still on business. They may be reading or only thinking about it, but their wives can recognize that "Do Not Disturb" sign.

Many wives grow very lonely, and they resent these long hours. They want more attention and companionship, but their husbands are too busy. Some wives keep asking their husbands—directly and indirectly—for more of their time and attention. Because the husbands know that their wives' demands are justified, they learn to dread that awful question: "Are you working again tonight?"

Some wives do suppress this feeling and make few demands on their husbands, but their loneliness, resentment, and jealousy of their husbands' careers are certain to create problems.

Company travel. Wives probably resent travel even more than long hours. A wife may resent long hours that keep her husband away during the day and evening, but at least she knows where he is and he can come home at night. When he is out of town she doesn't know where he is or what he is doing, and she doesn't even see him at breakfast. This problem is growing more serious as extensive company travel becomes more and more common. Many executives spend as much as one-third of their time away from home, and most successful executives are away at least two or three days a month.

Relocation. As noted earlier, executives may be transferred every few years. Because his job and career are his major sources of satisfaction, moving is not as hard on the executive as it is on his wife.

Her home, friends, and neighbors are usually very important to her, and she loses them when she moves. She has to go out and make new friends, find a house and make it livable, get the children started in school, and take care of the many other details. Some women enjoy these activities, and most executive wives have learned to live with them, but nearly all feel lonely and isolated at first. They therefore want more time, attention, and companionship from their husbands just when the husbands are busiest learning their new jobs. The first few weeks in a new town can be unpleasant for everyone in the family.

A few families, however, are sufficiently stable that this constant moving actually brings their members closer together. They have to rely more on each other, because everything else is constantly changing. They therefore spend more time together and develop closer and stronger relationships than they would have if they lived a more settled life.

Inadequacy feelings. Although executives' wives are an unusually talented and educated group, many feel unequal to the formidable demands that are made upon them. They must do all of the things that other wives and mothers do, frequently without much help from their husbands. Some executives' wives must also meet unrealistic standards of housekeeping, and many of them must change themselves to fit their husbands' changing status and position.

Although most executives are reasonable men who accept and even enjoy the confusion of a normal home, a few make impossible demands on their wives. They are pampered at work, and they expect to be pampered at home. Their secretaries and assistants obey their orders, and they expect the same from their wives and children. Their offices are neat, and they expect their homes to be just as neat. Office assistants handle routine tasks without argument or comment, and these executives expect home chores to be done in the same way.

They want dinner ready on time every night, the house neat and clean, the children quiet and obedient, and the chores out of the way. Most wives cannot provide that kind of home, and most children won't even try. Homes are rarely orderly, especially homes with children, and chores have a way of piling up. The grass doesn't get cut, the bills don't get paid, the rugs need cleaning—and so on.

Most executives accept this situation, but a few resent it and put pressure on their wives to improve their housekeeping, or spend their time in more compatible or predictable places. Some put in more and more hours at work; others take extra business trips; and a few spend most of their free time at their clubs, or in their studies, where they are isolated from the inevitable confusion of a normal home.

These men create real problems for their wives. Their wives usually want to provide a good home for them, and frequently try very hard. But the husbands' standards are impossible to satisfy, and failure is inevitable. Because providing a good home is such an important part of a wife's role, a wife who can't meet her husband's demands may feel very inadequate even if his demands are completely unreasonable.

Fortunately, for only a few wives is this problem so severe. Most executives don't expect their homes to be as orderly as their offices. But a great many wives feel inadequate about another set of demands. Their husbands have moved up several levels since they were married, and these wives feel that they can't keep up or fit in at his current level. A wife in this situation can have serious psychological problems.

At one time she may have known how to act with his associates and their wives. She felt comfortable with them and enjoyed going to parties and dinners. But now, everything about her is wrong— her clothes, habits, tastes, styles, grammar, accent—even her choice of friends. Her old friends are now several levels below, and she is not encouraged to associate with them any more.

So she has to drop her old friends and change herself to fit in. "Fitting in" is terribly important, especially in small, company-dominated towns. One wrong move at a cocktail party can ruin her husband's career, and she knows it.

Some wives enjoy moving up, and they gladly change themselves and drop old friends. Others do it out of loyalty to their husbands even though they prefer their old friends, habits, and tastes. But some wives can't or won't change, and they may have to endure terrible pressures. A woman's husband may criticize her, even call her disloyal. The wives of his associates and superiors may try to "straighten her out." She may even get a "friendly" tip that she is hurting her husband's career. These pressures obviously create a lot of anxiety and resentment, especially in a wife who tries but really can't change.

On the other hand, a wife who does change to fit her new situation may be no better off. She may get along better with her husband and his associates, but she may have even more serious psychological problems than the wife who can't adjust. She may change herself so much that she doesn't know who she is. We have repeatedly seen how much anxiety can be created by identity problems. This anxiety, with the natural resentment of her husband for causing it, can seriously damage their relationship.

The marital relationship. These pressures on wives can even harm their sexual relationship. For many women love, sex, tenderness, understanding, and companionship combine to make a marriage, and they can't enjoy sex without the other factors. They need to feel that their husbands love them more than anything else, even their careers; they want attention and consideration, flowers and perfume, and all the other little things they had before they were married, but now their husbands are usually too busy for all that.

These husbands are not deliberately selfish or inconsiderate. They just don't know what their wives need and want. They are too wrapped up in business and their careers to be the attentive, considerate lovers they once were. So their wives slowly lose interest; another bond between them weakens, and each is a little more alone.

Career-centeredness. All these factors can hurt an executive's marriage, but the real problem lies in the forces behind them—the husband's commitment to his career, and the general public attitude that his wife should repress her personality and independence to advance his career.

This commitment and attitude make wives feel lonely, neglected, and resentful, affect all the problems discussed here, and take much of the meaning out of their relationship with their husbands. They are also the primary cause of two of the worst aspects of modern executive life: the company's invasion of the family's privacy, and the unwritten rules for wives.

Thousands of companies look carefully at the wife before they hire or promote the husband. Most of them haven't used formal interviews with psychological tests for this purpose, but every wife knows that many social affairs are really screening interviews. A few companies employ psychologists who meet wives informally at cocktail parties and later make confidential reports on them. Some other companies even hire private detectives to investigate the wives and family lives of candidates for top jobs.

These overt invasions of privacy are very serious, but they do not occur very often. The unwritten rules, however, operate all the time. They constantly invade families' privacy by injecting company policy into personal problems and telling wives what to do in matters which are none of the company's business. Worst of all, these rules and the husband's acceptance of them clearly indicate that a wife is seen not as an important, independent person but as an extension of her husband's personality and an instrument for advancing his career.

The armed services openly express this attitude. They have published books—*The Army Wife* and *The Air Force Wife*, for example—which career officers' wives must read and obey. A few companies actually conduct programs for wives, but most companies don't bother to write out the rules. Knowing that the whole system is working for them, they let wives learn the rules by themselves. But whether they learn them in a classroom, from a book, or from experience, most wives know the rules and the penalties for violating them.

The company attitude is that a wife must move without complaint to wherever the corporation wants to send her husband, be cheerful and gracious when he brings home unexpected guests (even if she dislikes them), accept his long hours and company travel with a smile, run her home like a branch office, express the proper political and economic attitudes, drop her old friends as he moves up, and change her personality and habits, if necessary, to fit in with his job and associates. In other words, she is allowed to have no needs or personality of her own, because her husband's career is much more important than she is.

Surprisingly, many wives seem to accept these rules. They do what they are supposed to do and may even feel that the company has a right to make these demands. They become good corporate wives and lose their identities in the process. A particularly sad case was that of one group of executives' wives who talked about their experiences. With only a very few exceptions, they indicated that they had accepted the rules and repressed their independence and personality for their husbands' careers. They were more than willing to move to areas they disliked for the sake of a promotion; they would drop old friends, or avoid making the wrong friends, to help their husbands' careers; they would try to change their habits and personalities to fit in with their husbands' jobs. When asked why, many indicated that they felt these were legitimate demands, but several others suggested that they were afraid of their husbands' reaction to any real independence. One wife even said, jokingly, "If I didn't do it, he'd divorce me." They knew that their husbands would not tolerate any independent action on their part.

Incidentally, their husbands were very angry that these issues were raised; they wanted their wives to remain docile and dependent. They did not want their wives to think like adult, independent human beings.

Whether wives do accept them or not, these rules and the underlying attitude will certainly harm their relationships with their husbands. A wife cannot submerge her personality and repress her needs without feeling anxious and resentful. And the more successful she is at repressing herself, the more she follows these rules, the more empty and meaningless her marriage relationship becomes.

THE EXECUTIVE AND SOCIETY

A man needs to relate to his society, not only to the people closest to him. He has to relate to his society because he can't know who he is unless he knows where he is. He cannot have a clear sense of identity or belonging without understanding his own society and his role in it. He needs to understand his society's past, present, and future, the forces which made it and the forces which are changing it, and its people—all of the people, not just the businessmen.

This understanding is particularly important today because so many frightening things are happening. Our society, traditions, and basic attitudes seem to be disintegrating. Three of our leaders have been assassinated in recent years. We have several demonstrations every day, and riots almost as frequently. Our crime rate is soaring. Our sexual attitudes are changing, and so are our marriage and family patterns. Traditional beliefs about hard work and thrift are being discarded. Our underprivileged citizens are making frightening demands and using frightening methods to enforce them.

Traditionally conservative groups, such as schoolteachers and policemen, are striking illegally. We are in the longest war in our history and can't seem to get out of it. And over us all hangs the threat of instantaneous and massive destruction by unimaginably powerful weapons.

These events and possibilities frighten everyone, but they are most frightening to people who can't understand them or put them into perspective. To a man without perspective these problems are completely new, and he is completely helpless.

The most effective way to relieve these feelings has always been education—truly liberal education. A broad liberal education and a solid understanding of history, economics, literature, and sociology help a man to understand these things and put them in perspective. Every bond of understanding, every insight into the meaning and interrelationships of ourselves and our society, builds a stronger sense of identity and a stronger foundation for psychological security.

Unfortunately, American executives usually don't have this kind of education and understanding, nor are they interested in acquiring it. They are intensely practical men with practical educations and practical reading habits. Their education was vocational rather than liberal, and they have little understanding or interest in the humanities or liberal arts. They are interested in things, not people, and rarely have much insight into themselves or our society. They are doers, not thinkers, and their education and reading are focused on actions, not understanding.

They are, therefore, narrow men who understand little besides business and their own specialties. Whyte and Guzzardi, well-known writers about executive life in the corporate world, disagree on most issues, but they agree that many executives have little understanding of their societies, themselves, or their roles in society. And both authors feel that this situation is bad for business, society, and executives.

It is indeed an age of group action, of specialization, but this is all the more reason the organization man does not need the emphases of a training "geared for modern man." The pressures of organizational life will teach him that. But they will not teach him what the schools and colleges can—some kind of foundation, some sense of where we came from, so that he can judge where he is, and where he is going and why.[2]

Culturally, of course, these extracurricular habits make the young executive a narrow man. . . . The young executive has little interest in, and less understanding of, the liberal arts. In an academic sense, the young executive does not know what the humanities are. . . . He is a kind of technological illiterate.[3]

Because of this narrowness, most executives don't understand our society and feel isolated from it, with the result that they become insecure and anxious. They then turn their backs even more on society and concentrate even more on business, and become even more isolated.

There are, however, several encouraging signs. A growing number of American businessmen are becoming aware of social problems and trying to solve them. They are using their time and talent and their companies' money on our urban, racial, poverty, and unemployment problems.

In many of these areas they are far ahead of the liberal groups who generally condemn them for their "reactionary attitudes." For example, hundreds of companies are putting billions of dollars into the ghettos, but the unions and universities usually invest their money very conservatively. Each week several companies open plants in the inner city and provide jobs for the hard-core unemployed—Negroes, Puerto Ricans, Mexicans, even ex-convicts—and they often have to overcome union resistance to do so. Companies have also started, often at their own expense, training programs for the people whom the educational establishment has ignored. These and other developments indicate that some businessmen are becoming more aware of our society and more concerned with these problems. This awareness and concern will benefit both society and businessmen. Society needs their talent, and they need the relatedness and perspective that this work provides.

[2] William Whyte, *The Organization Man*, Simon and Schuster, New York, 1956, p. 78.
[3] Walter Guzzardi, *The Young Executives*, New American Library, New York, 1964, pp. 48 f.

Other encouraging signs are the increasing number of contacts between business and the universities and the growing number of broad-gauge executive programs. Thousands of companies encourage contacts, both formal and informal, between their executives and university professors, and these contacts broaden the perspective of both kinds of participants. Hundreds of executive programs (especially the ones on university campuses) go far beyond practical matters. In these programs executives leave their old habits and routines behind and spend weeks discussing foreign policy, race relations, domestic politics, and great literature. They read history, novels, and essays, meet executives from other countries, have dinner with professors, and hear lectures by civil rights activists. They may even attend sensitivity-training sessions and develop a new awareness of themselves and other people. Thus these executives are made more aware of who they are, what other people in our society are really like, and how they relate to the others. This awareness, in addition to its obvious benefits for business and society, strengthens their roots, identities, and psychological security. Unfortunately, these programs affect relatively few executives.

SATISFACTION AND CONTRIBUTION TO SOCIETY

Although their careers and attitudes can alienate them from their families, friends, associates, and even society, executives do have fairly strong ties to their work. Extensive research indicates that most executives enjoy their jobs and that their work builds their identities, security, and sense of relatedness. Certain pressures are, however, weakening these bonds for some executives. These executives may spend most of their waking hours working or thinking about their jobs but get relatively little intrinsic satisfaction or sense of contributing to society from their work. They acquire money, status, and power but may not attain much of the inner satisfaction and security which come from satisfying the "craftsman urge" and contributing to the betterment of society.

Of course, if we compare their working lives with the lives of the men below them, their jobs are very satisfying indeed. But some work at levels which give them little intrinsic satisfaction or sense of accomplishment. They are above the level in which they enjoyed their work and don't particularly like their present jobs. They had enjoyed being engineers, salesmen, scientists, or production men. They liked making a sale, or designing a machine, or meeting production schedules, but now they are administrators and spend most of their time pushing papers and talking to people. They don't like administration and don't get much sense of accomplishment from it, but they have to spend most of their time on it.

Although the proportion of people who are satisfied with their jobs increases with rank, a significant number prefer their previous jobs. When executive classes are asked: "How many of you enjoyed your previous jobs more than your current ones?" about 20 to 30 percent of the group usually raise their hands. As many people are embarrassed about publicly admitting that they don't like their jobs, 20 to 30 percent would seem to be a rather conservative estimate.

Because work is such an important part of their lives, it is rather surprising that men take jobs they don't like. They usually explain their actions in terms of "success" and "getting ahead." The company offered them more money and more prestige, and they couldn't turn it down just for satisfying work. A few say that they would have liked to turn down the promotion but were pressured into taking it or were afraid that to turn it down would ruin their future with the company.

Although administration can be very creative, some people don't regard it that way. They feel that they are not being creative and would rather design a bridge or build a car. Thwarting the creative desire can have some very unpleasant effects.

> In all types of creative work the worker and his object become one, man unites himself with the world in the process of creation. This, however, holds true only for productive work, for work in which I plan, produce, and see the results of my work. In the modern work process of a clerk or worker on the endless belt, little is left of this uniting quality of work. The worker becomes an appendix to the machine or to the bureaucratic organization.[4]

4 Fromm, *op. cit.*, p. 17.

Clerks and assembly line workers are not the only people who can't plan, produce, or see the results of their work, nor are they the only people who become appendixes to bureaucratic organizations. Many middle managers and a few higher-level executives have the same problem. They have more opportunities to create than workers do, but their organizations don't let them act independently or creatively, nor can these executives plan, execute, and evaluate an entire project, build an entire product, or see the entire picture. Their organizations are so large and bureaucratic that they can't get the satisfaction of solving a complete problem and can't see how their work contributes to the company as a whole.

Even if an executive can see how his work contributes to the company, he may still feel that he makes no real contribution to society. Our affluent society is flooded with goods; many of these goods are useless or superfluous; and a few are even harmful. Producing useless things doesn't bother some men, but many people feel that they should make a greater contribution to society. One of Guzzardi's young executives spoke for many men when he said: "The trouble is that I never feel I'm doing anything of intrinsic value . . . so I think from time to time that I am a failure." [5]

Although European executives may have similar feelings, this problem is particularly acute in America for three reasons. First, we are so fantastically rich and devote so many of our resources to making and selling superfluous products. We are inundated with hair creams, mouthwashes, guns, toys, breakfast foods, automobiles, and so on. We don't need the ones we have, but we keep producing more and spend billions of dollars trying to get people to buy things that they do not need.

Second, in America we believe that everyone should contribute to society, and the more able a man is, the more we expect of him. Even wealthy men are expected to do more than just manage the family fortune and live on its income. Many of our wealthiest men have devoted their lives to public service—the Kennedy brothers, Averell Harriman, Nelson and Winthrop Rockefeller, and H. L. Hunt, for example. In Europe these pressures are not nearly as strong, and wealthy people and executives can feel more comfortable about taking from society and giving nothing in return.

[5] Guzzardi, *op. cit.*, p. 65.

Third, and perhaps most painful, businessmen—who justifiably feel that they built this country's strength and affluence—find that they are rejected and despised by a large part of our society, including their own children. America has become so wealthy that it has forgotten who created its wealth. Professors whose income and institutions are supported by business berate the business community as sterile and unproductive. College students whose educations were paid for by business say that their lives are too important to waste on business. Government officials, who should understand economics, attack profits as socially irresponsible and morally indefensible.

In addition, nearly everyone ignores the past and present contributions of the business community. They forget that businessmen and profits built our society and ignore the very substantial contributions which businessmen are making today on some of our most serious problems—training the hard-core unemployed, creating jobs for them, and rebuilding our cities.

This situation has made many executives very defensive. They feel (justifiably) that people don't understand them. Unfortunately, their defensiveness has caused a further breakdown in communication. Instead of having a genuine dialogue with their critics—especially the college students—they have hired public relations men and put on high-powered campaigns to "sell business" and "improve its image."

For example, the chairman of one large corporation bought full-page advertisements in many college papers to report an exchange of letters with several students. It was painfully obvious that he was not listening to the students. He was trying to sell "business" as if it were a television set, and the students weren't buying. These hard-sell campaigns often do more harm than good: They increase public mistrust of businessmen as manipulators and make businessmen feel—correctly—that no one is listening to them.

This feeling of rejection and isolation, the belief that they are not really contributing to society, and the unsatisfactory nature of their work weaken the relationship between some executives and their work, increase their alienation from society and themselves, and increase their anxiety and insecurity.

THE EXECUTIVE AND HIS COMPANY

A few years ago most executives had roots in their companies. They expected to work for the same company for their entire careers and receive a pension from it when their careers were over. Their loyalty was to the company, and this loyalty and the company's stability and permanence gave them a sense of security and continuity. They might be transferred again and again, change from one specialty to another, or move up several levels, but the company remained constant. It didn't change, nor did their feelings about it.

Nowadays executives are developing more professional attitudes, and they are changing jobs more frequently. Management is becoming a profession, and executives are developing loyalty to that profession rather than to their companies. Many executives even regard company loyalty as passé and feel that their companies are temporary, rather than permanent, employers. They also have a professional attitude toward their work and judge it not only by what their superiors think of it but by comparison with professional standards. With this professional attitude comes a more cosmopolitan attitude toward their careers. Instead of comparing themselves and their jobs only with men in the same company, they compare themselves with people in other companies: If these comparisons are unfavorable, they are more than willing to move on.

This attitude is particularly common in the clearly defined professions—accounting, law, and engineering, to cite the obvious examples. These are professions which have associations that develop professional standards and work for their acceptance. The associations also make comparisons and job changes easier by publishing journals and information on salaries, hiring policies, and the like, and holding conventions at which a great deal of comparison and job switching occurs. Because of these associations, conventions, journals, and the long periods of training required to enter these professions, many identify with their professions and feel more loyal to them than they do to their companies. As general management becomes more professional, as its associations develop clearer and more consistent standards, as the requirements for entering management become more rigorous and consistent, executives will identify more with the profession of management and less with their companies. They will therefore change jobs more often than they do today.

This change in attitude has occurred despite very strenuous efforts by companies to build company loyalty and lock in their executives. Many companies work hard to keep their executives. They run development programs, provide lavish fringes, and pay excellent salaries. If the rewards don't succeed, they use deferred compensation, profit sharing, and pension plans to make it too expensive to leave. Even so, the professional attitude grows more popular, and more executives change jobs every year.

The companies, of course, are partially responsible for this development because most of them do not promote exclusively from within. When they want a man, they often look to the executive recruiters for help. Recruiting organizations have grown tremendously in the past few years, and they are both a symptom and a partial cause of the current situation. They can exist because so many executives change jobs, and many executives can change jobs because they exist.

Changing companies does not necessarily mean that a man has a professional attitude toward management. He may simply have been forced out. But the data clearly show that our most successful executives have usually worked for more than one company. Furthermore, the recruiters and the personnel executives generally agree that the really good men find it easier to move than the second-raters. *Fortune*'s 1952 survey of the 900 top executives in the country (average 1952 income for the group, $70,000) showed that two-thirds of them had worked for at least two companies and 44 percent had worked for three or more companies.[6] Ten years later, *Fortune* surveyed very successful younger executives and found that in their relatively brief careers they had changed companies almost as often as the older men had in 1952. Sixty-two percent had changed jobs at least once, and 32 percent had changed more than once.[7]

The growing professional attitude and the mobility it creates

[6] The editors of *Fortune, The Executive Life,* Doubleday, Garden City, New York, 1956, pp. 28–31.
[7] Guzzardi, *op. cit.,* p. 150.

have helped many executives to become more secure and comfortable. They increase the executives' independence and control over their own careers and provide a kind of roots that never existed before—identification with their profession. This identification can provide a sense of satisfaction and accomplishment by giving them independent and objective standards for judging their own work.

However, these same advantages—mobility and a professional attitude toward management—have another side: They obviously weaken or destroy the relationship which executives formerly had with their companies. As the pressures of executive life have isolated them and weakened most of their other roots, this relationship was a major foundation of their psychological security. The weakening or destruction of this relationship has helped some executives but made others more anxious and insecure.

5

Powerlessness
and Anxiety

POWERLESSNESS INEVITABLY LEADS TO ANXIETY. OUR DEEPEST, MOST basic desire is to survive, and a completely helpless man dies. If a man cannot act independently, if he does not have the power to get food, water, and shelter, he cannot exist. Power, the ability to act independently, to understand and control the environment, is therefore essential for survival.

Of course, under normal conditions no executive has to worry about survival; he has enough money to buy the necessities and many luxuries as well. But every executive, and every other human being, was once an entirely helpless infant, and no one ever completely forgets or escapes the anxiety that helplessness caused.

A newborn baby is the most helpless creature on earth. It cannot feed itself. It cannot get water. It cannot even breathe if something covers its nose and mouth. Babies are therefore completely helpless and completely dependent on other people. This helplessness and dependency are basic sources of their anxiety. Babies need a mother's care or they will die.

As every parent knows, babies panic if this need is not filled, if no one comes when they cry. We can all remember waking up slowly, rushing into the baby's room, and finding the baby in a state of utter terror. His clothes are drenched with perspiration; his whole body shakes; he sobs uncontrollably—yet nothing has happened. It took us a few minutes to wake up and get to him, but in these few minutes he felt the anxiety of total helplessness.

Nobody ever completely forgets that helplessness and anxiety; it remains with us for our entire lives. Usually it is buried pretty deeply, but occasionally something brings it back. Something makes us feel helpless for a moment—probably not altogether helpless, but helpless enough to bring back those memories and their anxiety. The anxiety we feel then is completely out of proportion to the current danger.

We may be bedridden with an illness and worry excessively about the possibility of fire and about our recovery. We may lose control over our car, with only slight danger because we were driving at low speed, but we sit there shaking and perspiring after the car has come to a safe stop. We may become very anxious when we can't solve a problem, even though the problem is not very important. Because our responses are much greater than the real dangers would cause, we can see how much anxiety the helplessness has created.

These same feelings of helplessness and anxiety can come from being restricted, either physically or psychologically. If we put a man in a straitjacket he will probably panic, even if we assure him that we will satisfy all his needs. He needs to be free to satisfy his own needs, and he feels anxious when he lacks the power and freedom to act independently. Physical things rarely restrict executives, but superiors, rules, committees, policies, procedures, psychological tests, unions, and the government are constantly restricting their freedom and taking away their power. These restrictions can arouse the same sort of anxiety as confinement in a straitjacket, and this anxiety is derived from the basic helplessness that we all felt as babies.

But power is not important just because it helps us survive and satisfy our other needs. It is also a basic human desire. We want to understand and master our environments; we need the satisfaction that can come only from independence and autonomy; we have to express ourselves; and to frustrate these needs can cause the same reaction as other frustrations—anger and anxiety.

Some very dramatic experiments illustrate how much anxiety

can be aroused by frustrating these needs. Psychologists have developed isolation chambers in which people receive almost no stimulation and can do virtually nothing. In the most extreme type of these chambers, people are immersed in lukewarm water and have translucent shades over their eyes and sound suppressors on their ears. They therefore cannot do, say, see, hear, or feel anything. Even though they have been repeatedly reassured that nothing will happen to them and they are in no objective danger, everyone who enters these chambers develops enormous anxiety, frequently within the first few minutes. And many people develop psychotic ("insane") symptoms—hallucinations, delusions, extreme depression or excitability—within a few hours.

Similar, but less extreme, anxiety occurs regularly in hospitals and prisons (where they even have a name for it—"stir crazy"). Men who do not have the power to act independently usually become anxious and behave abnormally.

These drives for power and independence are especially important among Americans because freedom and independence are such important parts of our culture. We are proud of our revolution and the men who made it. We idealize the pioneer and the small businessman, teach our children to be strong and independent, and criticize people who won't support themselves.

Executives generally accept these principles even more than other Americans and have even stronger power drives. They became executives because they are activists, energetic men who like to get things done. Some of them are literally unable to tolerate inactivity or dependency or helplessness. They have to be constantly exerting themselves, mastering their environments, and they feel restless and anxious if they aren't free.

Power is also important to them because it builds their egos and self-respect. They regard themselves as men who get results and need to prove themselves by accomplishing things. Since power is so important to them, it is fortunate that executives have more real power than most people in our society. But several modern developments have reduced almost everyone's power, and some of these developments have affected executives more than other people.

THE ERA OF HUGE ORGANIZATIONS

We live in an era of huge organizations. Our government, unions, and corporations are so big and powerful that our power as individuals is insignificant. These organizations tell us what to do, and then ignore or suppress our attempts to act independently or influence them. Each day they intrude a little further into our lives and restrict our freedom a little more.

They limit everyone's freedom, but some of their actions are aimed directly at executives. Governments tell us where our children will go to school and how much we must save for retirement, and they bury executives in a mountain of red tape and restrictions. Unions prevent us from taking a plane or a subway, keep our children out of school, and restrict us in hundreds of ways. Corporations determine what we eat, wear, and drive, censor our TV programs, and in some cases attempt to dominate and manipulate their executives. These giant organizations undermine everyone's independence and freedom. They restrict us in ways our forefathers could not have imagined and would not have tolerated. And they have had their major impact on executives.

Executives still have much more freedom, independence, and power than most other people; but, if we compare today's executives with their predecessors, we can see how much freedom they have lost. They are at the midpoint, the place where all three sets of pressures come together. Their companies squeeze them from above, the unions from below, and the government from all directions. Furthermore, the government often sides with the unions to increase the pressure from below. Since each of these pressures is very important, we shall examine them individually, beginning with the greatest threat to our traditional freedoms—big government.

GOVERNMENTS

Governments, especially the Federal Government, are clearly the greatest threat to our independence and freedom. Their rules touch every area of our lives, and we can't escape these rules or the penalties for disobeying them. The bureaucrats tie us up in red tape and spend one-fourth of our income, usually without our consent, often over our vehement protests. Governments today are so big, bureaucratic, and unresponsive to our wishes that they act more like our masters than our servants. And they grow larger and less responsive every day.

Executives are hemmed in by all the rules that restrict other people, but they also feel pressures that no other group suffers. They pay a higher rate of income tax than any other group in our society. Our income tax structure is biased in favor of people who own their own businesses, live on their investments, or don't make much money. Because executives' salaries are their primary source of income, they are allowed neither the deductions and exemptions of the property owners nor the low rates of the workers and the poor. In effect, they pay more than their share of the tax burden of our Federal Government. And, because most of them own their own homes and real estate taxes are the primary source of municipal tax revenue, they also pay more than their share of the local tax burden.

Their taxes frequently are applied to programs which harass and restrict executives. In addition to the restrictions everybody faces, executives and other businessmen must deal with countless government agencies—NLRB, FCC, FDA, FEPC, and many more. These agencies can completely hamper an executive and disrupt his operation. Their rules and procedures are so restrictive, complicated, and cumbersome that executives spend countless hours trying to comply with (or legally evade) them.

The agencies themselves are frequently able to violate the spirit and even the letter of the laws which created them. They become self-perpetuating and power-hungry, take actions which Congress never authorized and would never approve, hold hearings in which they are the judge, prosecutor, and jury, and deliberately work against business and executives.

Government interference with business is one of the most emotional issues in management today. Hundreds of articles, books, and speeches complain about the government's attacks on "management's right to manage," and usually calm executives can't discuss the topic without emotion.

Although their behavior clearly indicates how strongly they feel about this issue, most executives ignore the government's psychological impact on them and focus entirely on its impact on efficiency and profits. They can, of course, make a very persuasive case that many government acts and agencies are bad for everyone —business, labor, the consumer, and the economy. But these arguments should not confuse us. Executives do have rational reasons for objecting to government regulations and agencies—but the anger they display, their enthusiasm for writers and speakers who "give the government hell," and the inordinate and uneconomic amount of time they spend trying to "beat the government" clearly indicate that much of their behavior is emotional.

It is emotional because the government threatens one of our most basic values—freedom—and because it is so large, so domineering, and so autocratic that it arouses some of our deepest fears.

UNIONS

Unions have about the same impact as government on executives. They create the same kinds of stresses and the same kinds of emotional reactions. They undermine executives' authority and independence and stir up some of their strongest emotions.

Executives used to make most of the decisions about their units, but now union regulations and work rules drastically restrict their freedom of action. The union frequently tells them whom they can hire or promote; prevents them from firing or disciplining incompetents; determines when and whether they can schedule overtime; and dictates the way people will work in their organizations.

These restrictions on "prerogatives" and "the right to manage" create as much emotionalism as government interference. Despite executives' insistence that they are concerned only with profits and efficiency, we can tell how emotional they are by analyzing their behavior.

Some executives are literally unable to discuss unions and unionism rationally. They equate Walter Reuther with Joseph Stalin, say that unionism and communism are identical, and see the unions as an unmitigated evil. Others undergo costly strikes for principles and issues which have little economic importance but great emotional significance.

The contrast between executives' comments about efficiency and profits and their readiness to sacrifice both to defend their rights and prerogatives clearly indicates how emotional an issue this is to them. They feel penned in, restricted, frustrated, and powerless, and they occasionally strike out and try to exert their independence.

Men become heroes for standing up to the unions, and hundreds of men earn huge fees for repetitious speeches and articles attacking the unions. But speeches and heroic defenses of management prerogatives provide only temporary relief, and most executives know that the trend is against them.

Unions may not be expanding very rapidly in the economy as a whole, but in some companies and industries they grow more powerful every day. As they grow more powerful and get greater government support, they are likely to restrict executives even more and make them even less powerful and independent than they are today.

THE CORPORATIONS

The conservatives have repeatedly warned us of the dangers of big government and big unions and have tried to prevent the growth and abuses of both. But they have generally ignored the obvious fact that big corporations may also threaten individualism and independence. Many virtually dominate our economy today and are so powerful, centralized, and bureaucratic that they are in a position to dominate us as well.

They determine what we eat and wear and how much we pay. They decide our television entertainment with their advertising decisions. They can make or break a town by opening or relocating a plant. Their wages and salaries influence everyone's income and standard of living.

The left wing has, of course, repeatedly warned us about the power and dangers of big business, but the representatives of the left have always emphasized its effects on workers and consumers.

They have ignored its effects on executives because they prefer to divide the world into two classes (labor and management), emphasize the similarities within each class, and exaggerate the differences between classes. Workers are said to be the exploited, managers the exploiters.

This view is oversimplified and distorted. Because of unions and government protection, most workers are not exploited today. However, because of several developments which we will describe here, some executives would seem to be very much exploited. In the past few years we have seen the emergence of a new kind of exploitation, "an exploitation of the leaders rather than laborers," [1] of executives rather than workers.

Many executives have little real freedom. They do have a great deal of power over other people, but they have very little power over their own lives. Their organizations dominate them and move them about; company rules or customs tell them what to do, what to wear, and what to believe in; their constitutional rights are violated, their privacy is invaded, and their basic dignity is injured. All of these things are done without the executives' full understanding of what is happening to them.

Several factors have helped bring on this situation. Most executives have neither the capital nor the ability to start their own businesses. They are employees and will always be employees. They do not have unions or similar organizations to increase their bargaining power and must therefore bargain as individuals (which means that most of them have no bargaining power at all). Some executives themselves have even fallen into the same trap as the left-wingers. They want to believe that their interests and the corporation's are identical, that there are no real conflicts between them and their organizations; and they deliberately ignore the obvious fact that they are employees.

They do not want to regard themselves as employees; they identify with their superiors and set themselves apart from lower-level personnel. They want to believe that they are the controllers, not the controlled. These desires make it ridiculously easy for their organizations to dominate them. In fact, they are dominated so

[1] Vance Packard, *The Pyramid Climbers*, McGraw-Hill, 1962, p. 9.

subtly that many executives insist that they are not dominated at all.

Executives have generally ignored or misunderstood an old and popular saying: "Eternal vigilance is the price of liberty." They may even have used this saying to refer to the need to prevent government from dominating us all. But the term "eternal vigilance" means precisely what it says—constant awareness of *all* the threats to our freedom, not just those which come from our own or another government.

The first step in being free has always been to understand the forces that restrict people, but most executives have been reluctant to analyze or even discuss these forces. They have even gotten angry when someone has tried to point them out. They were angry with Whyte for writing *The Organization Man* and with Packard for writing *The Pyramid Climbers*. And many of them will certainly resent the next few pages. But once they get over their anger, they may realize that they have to understand these threats to their freedom if they want to remain free.

Size, power, and bureaucracy. Modern corporations are so large, complex, and bureaucratic that many people with executive titles really have very few opportunities to act independently. They must follow policies that they did not influence and may not even understand. They are so restricted by rules, procedures, customs, and committees that they can't take any really independent action. Even if they take independent action, it will have a negligible impact on the whole organization.

The real power in their organizations is so far above them, and so diffuse, that it is almost completely impersonal. They may have seen the president and the executive committee a few times, but these men are more of an abstraction than a group of real people, and orders from them are essentially anonymous.

Anonymous authority. Many of the restrictions on executive freedom of action are really anonymous. Every organization has procedures and customs which are as powerful and restrictive as law or authority, but no one knows who made them or why they exist. They are simply there, and they had better be obeyed. The executive who violates them, even unintentionally, is told very clearly: "We don't do things that way around here."

This authority, however anonymous it may be, takes away more real freedom and power than all the autocratic bosses put together. It dominates every aspect of executives' business and personal lives —the way they talk and dress, the hours they work, the people they associate with, the business decisions they make. And no appeal, much less revolt, is possible. A man can revolt against his boss or quit his job, but he can't do anything about anonymous authority. It is everywhere, there is no one to appeal to, and quitting would just mean finding the same kind of restrictions in another firm.

Management information systems. Recently, a new kind of restriction has begun to develop in sophisticated corporations, one which dramatically reduces executives' freedom and independence. Many corporations are using management information systems (usually, with computers), and these systems let top management exert very tight control over lower levels.

The systems let them look over their subordinates' shoulders and make decisions that they formerly delegated. As these systems are introduced in more firms, lower and middle managers' jobs will become more programmed and routine, and they will have less decision-making power.

The computer and the systems based on it restrict freedom in another, even more frustrating way: Some executives find they have to adjust their behavior and pace to the computer in almost exactly the same way that an automobile worker has to adjust himself to the assembly line. They do have more freedom than the assembly-line worker, but the principle is the same.

The system tells them what to do and when to do it. Reports must be in a certain form that the computer can handle and must be received by a certain date. To get these reports in the right form at the right time, the executives must reorganize the unit and its operations. In a very basic sense the computer runs their organization, and they have to adjust to it.

Because the computer is used more widely every day, more and more executives will have routine, programmed jobs and will be dominated by the computer and their superiors.

Lock-ins. Most companies have pension funds for their executives, and some have deferred-compensation, profit-sharing, and stock-option programs. These programs are often very generous, and a fairly well paid executive can accumulate a great deal of cash, not to mention pension rights. Because income taxes—plus spending habits—prevent executives from accumulating large estates, many of them have more in these programs than they have in personal savings and investments, and they depend on them for their basic security.

If they leave before retirement, however, they could lose all or most of their money and rights. This obviously gives the organization enormous power over them. Their organizations not only control their current salaries; they also control a large part of their assets. This situation dramatically reduces personal freedom and independence. Many executives literally cannot afford to quit. Furthermore, since independent action could get them fired, some executives are forced to follow orders passively.

Committees and group domination. Many modern corporations emphasize communications, committees, meetings, conferences, and "the team." These emphases also reduce independence and power. Many executives are dominated, not only by their superiors, but by their colleagues as well. They spend most of their time communicating with people and rarely have more than a few uninterrupted minutes to work alone.

They are, therefore, very different from the executive stereotype. Instead of rugged individualists, they are "organization men" and "team players." Instead of being free to make real decisions, they are hemmed in by rules, procedures, and committees. Instead of acting, they are selling.

Pseudo-democracy. Emphasis on committees is just one part of a general shift in numerous organizations from open autocracy to pseudo-democracy. The most progressive modern corporations are not as openly autocratic as their predecessors. They allow subordinates to speak up to their superiors, glorify the "open door" policy, and have many of the forms of democracy—committees, broad participation in decisions, and the like. Some top executives in these companies may sincerely want their subordinate executives and workers to have genuine freedom and upward influence, not only because they want these people to "grow," but because they need the cooperation of each member of the workforce. But often pseudo-democracy—the forms without the substance—increases their domination over their subordinates. They exert tighter control by giving their subordinates the forms of democracy and a feeling of participation while they retain all the real power.

This situation has its greatest impact on executives, not on workers. Most workers distrust management, and the unions deliberately emphasize conflict and resist the forms, and even the substance, of democracy. The unions' very existence depends on workers' distrust of management, and they do everything they can to emphasize the conflict between labor and management.

But executives, who neither have nor desire unions, generally like to feel that their interests and the corporation's are identical, that any conflicts are caused by "poor communication" and "misunderstandings." They are therefore, on the whole, fairly docile. They go to "problem solving" sessions and realize that "what's good for the organization is good for everybody." Their superiors make decisions and then let them reach the same decisions "democratically." And some superiors have even learned how to use another powerful technique—nondirective counseling.

Psychologists have found that just letting people talk about their problems makes them feel better, even if the conditions which cause the problem have not changed! Some executives have learned this technique, although they have not adopted its underlying philosophy, and use it extensively. The trouble is that they may use it to make their subordinates feel better without doing anything about their complaints.

The net effect of pseudo-democracy is to prevent individuals from realizing when they are being dominated and managed. Without this awareness, they don't know where to make a stand or when to exert their own independence. William Whyte has written on this point:

> It is not so much that The Organization is going to push the individual around more than it used to. It is that it is becoming increasingly hard for the individual to figure out when he is being pushed around.[2]

---

[2] William Whyte, *The Organization Man*, Simon and Schuster, New York, 1956, p. 166.

The same author has observed: "For it is not the evils of organization life that puzzle him, *but its very beneficence.* He is imprisoned in brotherhood." [3]

Whether a man is imprisoned in brotherhood or is openly dominated by his superiors and his organization, he knows—perhaps clearly, perhaps only vaguely—that he is not free. He knows that he does not control his own life, that he is dependent on forces that he cannot control; and this knowledge creates anxiety.

Discrimination and basic rights. In addition to exerting tighter though less direct control over their executives' work, some modern corporations dominate activities that the old-style autocracies left alone. They dictate what men's morals and habits shall be, investigate their wives and home lives, and probe the deepest recesses of their personalities.

Directly or indirectly, too many organizations punish their members for having the wrong political, economic, or religious beliefs, for speaking out on these issues or working for the wrong party. The universities, for example, are famed for allowing freedom of speech, but many discriminate against political conservatives and a few discriminate against political liberals. Numerous organizations violate a man's rights in this way, but very few do so as consistently as some modern corporations.

Many organizations have unwritten but rigidly enforced rules that no Negro, Jew, Democrat, or liberal can become a senior executive. Some insist that their executives contribute to political parties or become involved in community affairs. And a great many corporations will not tolerate any sort of controversial political, social, or economic beliefs or statements.

Corporations may also invade the privacy of executives and their families. As described in Chapter 4, some large companies interview wives; a few get psychologists' and detectives' reports on them, and many may even tell them how to dress and behave. Likewise, they may tell their executives what they should wear, when and how much they should drink, and what kinds of homes and cars they should buy.

All these matters, of course, are unrelated to performance and

[3] *Ibid.,* p. 12.

profits, but these corporations try to control them anyway. Certain executives, therefore, have less personal freedom than many other members of our society.

Psychological tests and interviews. Psychological tests and interviews constitute perhaps the most hotly argued interference with executives' freedom. They contain questions which are none of a company's business; they take the decision making completely out of the hands of the individual executive and perhaps even out of his superiors' hands. If the decision about his career is based on almost any other criteria, an executive can do something to influence that decision. He may not be able to do much, but he can work harder, or study at night, or make friends with the right people. But he is virtually helpless as far as the tests and interviews are concerned. He can't change his test scores, the psychologist's report, or the action based on it.

He may not even be allowed to read the psychologist's report—and may not even know that it exists if he was interviewed surreptitiously (a rare but growing practice). Even if he does read the report, he probably will not know how it will affect his career. Every person has assets and liabilities, and he doesn't know which his superiors will emphasize in making their decisions. Many executives are now working for companies in which, because of unfavorable psychological reports, they have almost no chance for future promotion. These reports, which they have probably never seen, may prevent them from being considered fairly no matter how hard they work or how well they perform.

Of course, an executive can try to exert some control by faking tests or covering up in the interview, but he will probably not succeed. Most psychologists can tell when a man is trying to avoid a topic and will either probe this topic or (worse yet) conclude that something is wrong there. It is even harder to fake the tests. Psychologists have given them to millions of people and have learned how to prevent faking. "Lie scores," "social desirability scores," "forced-choice items," and "projective tests" make it very hard for an inexperienced person to present the image he wants.

William Whyte violently objected to personality tests and tried to show executives how to beat them. He published a set of rules for

95

faking them, and these rules have been widely discussed. His rules look reasonable, and many executives have probably tried them, but they don't work.

By having some people take a personality test twice, one psychologist proved that Whyte's rules are ineffective. The first time, he told them to be completely honest. The second time, he instructed them to follow Whyte's rules and had each person keep a copy of the rules on his desk while taking the tests. The psychologist found no significant differences between the scores on the first and second test. In other words, these rules didn't help people fake the tests, even when they had them right at hand and tried to follow them.

Some firms use instruments which reduce executives' power even more than psychological tests—weighted biographical forms. These forms assign points for different kinds of background information, some of which is absolutely unrelated to executives' behavior, ability, personality, or performance. Many of them, for example, include questions about parents' education and occupation. Obviously, if a man is not going to get a job or promotion because his mother didn't go to college or his father was a barber, he is completely helpless; there is nothing he can do about it.

Despite their generally low validity, these tests, interviews, and biographical forms have an enormous influence on many decisions. They *look* objective and scientific. People are rarely sure about who should be hired or promoted, because there are so many factors and no candidate is best on all of them. But test scores are numbers, and numbers have a magic all their own—even if they are wrong! A "5" is better than a "4." The 80th percentile is higher than the 60th. The tests may therefore have more impact than other information even if the other information is very significant and the test scores are complete nonsense.

Some companies even subject wives to psychological testing, and many more have psychologists interview the wives, sometimes without the wives' realizing it. A wife may meet someone at a cocktail party, chat with him, and never realize that he is the one who will write a report that can make or break her husband's career.

Even if only the husband is investigated, the tests and interviews invade his privacy by covering topics which are completely unrelated to the company or his performance. Every day executives are asked questions about their religious, political, and economic beliefs, their attitudes toward parents, wife, and children, even their sexual behavior. Obviously, if a man's answers to these questions can be used against him, his privacy has been violated and his freedom and independence have been undermined.

These are not rare or scattered instances. Thousands of companies use psychological tests and interviews, and hundreds more start using them every year. In an age that worships science, the appeal of anything that looks scientific is very powerful.

Furthermore, the field of industrial psychological testing is plagued by incompetents, salesmen, and promoters, and many tests are sold and promoted in very dishonest ways. There are some completely ethical and competent psychological testers, and the American Psychological Association has a code of ethical practices; but they have relatively little impact on industrial testing. The ethical psychologists refuse to make exaggerated claims or use dishonest sales techniques, but many testers do both. They overstate the validity of their tests and use a plausible but completely dishonest sales pitch.

They tell a prospect: "Look, we don't want you to buy this test unless you are absolutely convinced that it works. So take the test yourself. We will score it and give you a personality analysis. If you aren't amazed at its accuracy, we will forget everything." If a man falls for that (and it does sound reasonable) they've got him. He will be amazed at the accuracy of their report, even if the report is complete nonsense!

Several professors have shown how easy it is to write "amazingly accurate" psychological analyses. Their method was to give personality tests to a group of students. A few days later they gave each student a personality analysis and asked him to read it and rate its accuracy. The students usually rated these analyses as very accurate. Then they were told that *they all had the same analysis.*

This demonstration has been repeated dozens of times with similar results. It works for the same reason that palm reading and astrology "work." There are so many things which are true for everyone that anyone can write "amazingly accurate" personality analyses. We can say: "Although you are calm on the outside, inside you are often very emotional. You have some doubts about yourself.

97

You sometimes feel depressed for no reason at all. You have made some serious mistakes by acting too quickly. You've missed some good opportunities by not acting quickly enough." And so on and on.

This sort of nonsense sells many tests, and exaggerated claims sell many more. Since no ethical psychologist would use such tactics, the field is rapidly becoming dominated by unethical, unknowledgeable promoters. And, surprisingly, the businessmen, not the ethical psychologists, are at fault! Psychologists have published dozens of books and articles on the limitations of testing. In fact, Martin Gross (whose book *The Brainwatchers* became a best seller) based most of his criticisms on them. But many businessmen don't bother to read the critics. They look for fast, perfect answers, and no one has them.

If a businessman asks an ethical psychologist to suggest tests for analyzing his executives, the psychologist won't just sell the tests to him. He will want the businessman to understand that psychological tests are not very good for predicting executives' success; he will warn management that all scores need to be interpreted very cautiously; he will state emphatically that no decision should be based solely or primarily on tests; he will comment on his responsibility to the people taking the tests and insist that he be allowed to fulfill this responsibility.

By this time the businessman has probably had enough. He wants to have his problems solved, not to hear a lecture on limitations, validity, and ethics. So he finds a man who gives him the reassurance and promises he wants. Of course, anyone who does this is ignoring his ethical and professional responsibilities toward both the businessman and his executives, and he is probably not very competent; but the executive doesn't realize that. He knows only that the man promises to solve his problems, usually with a special test that he can't buy anywhere else. And tests which are not publicly available are almost invariably worthless.

Career decisions. Even without the effects of psychological tests, most executives have very little control over decisions about their careers. They do their jobs and hope that their careers will grow in the right directions, but the decisions are usually made by their superiors.

All powerlessness has undesirable effects, but inability to control

98

one's career is especially unfortunate. It can create enormous anxiety, because an executive's career is so important to him and the conflicts between individual and organization are so great in this area. The executive wants more money, but the company needs lower costs. He wants to live in a certain area, but the company may need him in places he dislikes. He wants variety and interesting work, but the company needs standardization and routine. He wants to act in his own interests, but the company demands loyalty. These and other conflicts are inevitable, and every executive knows it. But three factors keep most executives from acting independently and controlling their careers.

1. *They don't have the power to influence the decisions.* Their superiors make the decisions; they may not know how or why these decisions are made; and they can do very little to influence their decisions. They can work hard, do superb jobs, even develop the right friends, but they still don't make the decisions, and very few executives have the bargaining power to control the decisions their superiors make. And, as every other kind of negotiation clearly indicates, power determines who gets what.

2. *They don't know how to control their careers.* Even if they have the power, most executives don't know how to use it. No business school offers courses on bargaining with the boss, job interview techniques, company politics, or any of the other skills a man needs to control his own career.

The schools, in fact, seem to be working for the corporations, not their students. They turn out what the corporations appear to want and ignore the ambitions and desires of the students. For example, professors often refer to the "market" (the corporations) for their "product" (students) and plan their curriculum to meet the needs of that market. Furthermore, they may object strenuously to any efforts to determine what the students want or to help them select jobs, learn bargaining techniques, or develop the skills that might help them to act independently.

Nor are there any really good books which help an executive control his career. A few books on these topics have appeared recently—among them *The Executive Job Market,* by Auren Uris, *Executive Jobs Unlimited,* by Carl Boll, and *Realizing Your Executive Potential,* by Allen Rood. These books have invariably been written by laymen. Some of them are useful, but they are all rather superficial. They don't have the solid foundation that only research can provide, because social scientists have generally preferred helping organizations dominate individuals to helping individuals act independently.

3. *Even if a man had the power and knew how to use it, he might be reluctant to take advantage of his situation.* There is a generally held—and strong—belief that a man should do his job and leave the decisions about his career to his superiors. Most people feel that a man should produce and contribute to his organization rather than work for his own interests. They feel that it is unethical and antisocial for a man to concentrate on what he can get out of his career rather than what he can contribute to his organization.

We can see the evidence of this thinking everywhere: in satirical plays and books such as *How to Succeed in Business Without Really Trying,* in ugly remarks about "company politicians," in the adjectives used to describe executive recruiters ("pirates," "body-snatchers"), in the business schools' failure to teach their students how to control their careers, and in the social scientists' refusal to focus any attention on the problems of individualism and independence.

This sort of thinking is so popular and influential because we Americans have not outgrown the poverty of our past. In earlier times we had to glorify production as well as organizations which produced because we needed goods. We needed food, clothing, shelter, and transportation for our people, weapons for our defense, and a solid capital base for our future economic and social development.

But we have all these things now. We have more goods than we can use, more productive capacity than we can keep busy, and the equivalent of thousands of pounds of TNT for every member of the human race. Our most pressing need is not for more goods but for more freedom, but we let our obsession with goods crush freedom and ignore the problems of individualism.

Since independence and individualism are absolutely essential for psychological health and are very hard to obtain today, much of Chapter 13 focuses on methods for increasing your level of independence.

SOME ENCOURAGING SIGNS

As previously shown, many executives have relatively little real power and autonomy today, and it is rather obvious that they will have even less power tomorrow. Corporations, unions, and the government are growing larger and more powerful; procedures and controls are becoming more restrictive; bosses are becoming more adept at domination; psychological tests are becoming more popular. Still, even though overshadowed by these trends, there are a few encouraging developments.

Although more companies preach participation than practice it, a few companies and executives are sincerely trying to give their executives and even their workers more freedom and autonomy. Some of it, of course, is pseudo-democracy, but management by objectives, T-groups, job enlargement, project management, and similar developments have given many executives a chance to operate independently.

The growth of conglomerates—in which the top management does not know very much about the day-to-day operations of its subsidiaries—has given many executives a chance to make real decisions. Unfortunately, some conglomerates are very sophisticated at using the computer to look over executives' shoulders.

A less publicized but perhaps equally important development is the growing practice of vesting pension rights; vesting makes it less expensive for an executive to quit his job and dramatically increases his real power.

But the most important changes have not been initiated benevolently by companies' boards of directors; they have been developed by the executives themselves and by outsiders. The growing popularity of the professional attitude toward management, plus increased knowledge about how to change jobs and the help of executive recruiters and counselors, has made it possible for executives to leave —or bargain with—their organizations instead of passively accepting the role they are given and doing what they are told.

Unfortunately, only a few executives may benefit directly from these trends. Most may end up with less power and autonomy tomorrow than they did today. But at least some executives will have more power, and others will know how to get it.

6

Not Everyone
Can Be a Success

EVEN THOUGH THE WORLD REGARDS THEM AS SUCCESSFUL, MANY EX-
ecutives must ultimately feel that they have failed, and this
feeling can create almost unbearable anxiety. Even the executives
who don't fail may feel anxious about the possibility of failing. These
feelings are not caused by any objective or economic failure; most
executives are paid well and can point to many solid accomplishments. Feelings of failure are caused by the conflict between the
realities of organizational life and their personal definitions of "success" and "failure."

Dr. Eugene Jennings, who has conducted extensive research on
executive mobility, states that many modern executives define
success and failure in terms of mobility. ("Success" is moving up,
and "failure" is being passed over or fired.) Because there are very
few places at the top, it is not in the power of many executives
to attain them; in this sense most executives must ultimately "fail."
And because they do not know who will reach the top, nearly all
executives are occasionally afraid that they may fail.

In an earlier era, success and failure were defined differently.
The emphasis was on today, not tomorrow, on performance rather
than mobility. Executives obtained most of their satisfaction and
feeling of accomplishment from doing their jobs well, not from being

mobile. "Success" meant that a man was doing a good job; "failure," that he was doing a poor one. They were interested in mobility but as a means to an end, not an end in itself. Mobility provided opportunities for bigger and more satisfying achievements, new worlds to conquer, new problems to solve, new challenges to meet. Jennings, in *The Mobile Manager*, has commented on this earlier attitude toward mobility:

> To them, mobility was a means for maintaining a high degree of achievement satisfaction. The manager was equally bored by repetition and routine and sought mobility largely, if not entirely, because mobility brought new and more challenging tasks. There was relatively little fun in movement itself; the fun was found in performance.[1]

Today's executives are certainly interested in achievements and good performance; they want interesting challenges and difficult problems. But many of them feel very differently about mobility; to them it is not a means but an end, a goal in and of itself. Their primary satisfaction and sense of accomplishment come not from their current performance but from their mobility, their promotions, especially the ones they haven't received yet. "Success" does not mean merely performing well; it means being promoted. "Failure" means being passed over, or—the ultimate nightmare—being fired. Today executives value their current jobs more for the opportunities they offer for future mobility than for their current opportunities for accomplishment. They want interesting and challenging jobs, but most of all they want jobs which are springboards to "bigger and better things." Jennings has also commented on this change in aspiration.

> Success is mobility. It is not so much position, title, salary, or exceptional performance as it is success in moving and movement.[2]

The new generation is still motivated to achieve, but achieve-

[1] Eugene E. Jennings, *The Mobile Manager*, University of Michigan Press, Ann Arbor, 1967, p. 96.
[2] *Ibid.*, pp. 24 f.

ment is not performing the task and hoping for the opportunity of performing in the higher level of challenge. The highest form of achievement is to become and stay mobile. Performance is a means, not an end.[3]

Because executives define success and failure in terms of mobility, no lasting satisfaction is gained through their promotions. At first they enjoy their new pay, responsibilities, and status. But soon they begin eying the next rung on the ladder, their goal now is to reach that rung, and to attain that goal becomes as important to them as reaching their current level used to be. A vice president can be just as hungry for the presidency as his subordinates are for his job and their subordinates are for their jobs. They all want to move up, and they all can feel like failures if they don't make it to the next level.

When he was younger a vice president might have hungered for his department head's job. That was his goal, and he thought that reaching it would satisfy him. Now that he has gone much higher, however, he is still dissatisfied. He wants to become president as keenly as he formerly wanted to become department head. His past accomplishments and promotions don't matter any more; the next promotion is what counts. "Failing" now can be as devastating as "failing" then would have been. A passed-over vice president and a passed-over assistant sales manager may have the same psychological problem, and the differences in their incomes, status, and past accomplishments may not affect the way they feel. They can both have the same doubts about their abilities, the same problems with their associates and families, the same confusion about their identity.

The current system guarantees that many executives will ultimately feel that they have failed. Most executives are extremely concerned with success; some are even obsessed by it; and "success" is, of course, defined as moving up. But most of them can't move up indefinitely; there is simply not enough room at the top. All organizations are shaped like pyramids with fewer jobs at each succeeding level and very little room at the top.

A company may have 10,000 men in management, but it has

[3] *Ibid.*, p. 96.

only one chief executive and a handful of vice presidents—and getting a vice presidency does not necessarily solve the executive's psychological problem. Therefore, only a tiny percentage of executives can make it to the top, and most end their careers many levels below it. Sooner or later, nearly every executive must be passed over.

For some executives, being passed over will be relatively unimportant; it will not be a failure because promotion was not their primary goal. For a few, it would be a relief; they don't really want the promotion and are afraid they would have to take it if it were offered. But for many executives, being passed over will be a disaster, a personal failure which will destroy their self-confidence, create an identity crisis, take the fun out of their jobs, and ruin their relationships with their superiors, associates, and families.

Superiors' Actions the Clue to "Success"

A mobility-centered executive has another problem: His basic beliefs about himself are primarily controlled by his superiors' actions, not by his own. We all need approval, and we are all affected by what other people think of us, but the need for approval and dependence on other people's opinions are central parts of this executive's personality. He defines success not in terms of his own performance but in terms of his superiors' decisions and opinions. He does the work, but they evaluate it, and they make the promotion decisions. If they promote him, he feels successful—at least temporarily. If they pass him over, he feels that he has failed—even though his performance is exactly the same in both cases.

Promotion decisions even dominate the way the mobility-centered executive feels about his current performance. He really doesn't know how to evaluate his own work; so he depends on his superiors' evaluation. If they promote him, they say he has done a good job; and he probably believes them. If they pass him over, he thinks they don't like his work; and he may not like it either. Even if they try to show their approval by giving him high performance ratings and a raise in pay, he may still feel they don't like his work. Their promotion decision speaks louder than anything else they can say or do. Again and again executives find that their own promotion decisions are misinterpreted; their subordinates ask: "If I am doing such a good job, why didn't I get promoted?" Very few can think of a good answer.

The achievement-centered executive had much more control over his own self-image. His satisfaction and feeling of success depended more on his performance than on promotions, and he controlled and evaluated his own work. His superiors' opinions certainly influenced how he felt about himself and his work, but he made most of his own decisions, looked at his own work, and judged it by his own standards. Even if he was not promoted, he could feel successful if he met most of his own standards.

The shifts in emphasis from achievement to mobility and from independent to superior-dominated self-evaluations are part of much larger trends in American society. Americans are becoming less "inner-directed" and more "other-directed," less individualistic and more concerned with other people's opinions.

Many executives have read Whyte's description of these trends in *Fortune* magazine or *The Organization Man,* but Whyte's work was based on David Riesman's *The Lonely Crowd.* Riesman, a distinguished social scientist, went much deeper into the causes and effects of these trends.

He noted that most Americans used to be inner-directed: They had an internalized set of goals, a "psychological gyroscope" which kept them moving toward these goals, and independent standards which they used to control and evaluate their own behavior. They developed these goals and standards at an early age and kept them for their entire lives. An inner-directed person cared about what other people thought of him, but he cared much more about what he thought of himself. His self-image was primarily determined not by their opinions but by whether he progressed toward his own goals and lived according to his own standards.

In recent years, however, the other-directed personality has become common, especially in the upper middle class, and this type is becoming more common every day. The other-directed person is essentially a conformist. He is guided not by inner goals and standards but by what other people think and expect. He is very aware of other people's standards and expectations and tries to meet them, because he has no fixed standards of his own. Instead of gaining his satisfaction and psychological security from his own efforts, he obtains them from approval and acceptance.

> His need for approval and direction from others . . . goes beyond the reasons that led most people in any era to care very much about what other people think of them. While all people want and need to be liked by some of the people some of the time, it is only the modern other-directed types who make this their chief source of direction and their chief area of sensitivity. It is perhaps the insatiable force of this psychological need for approval that differentiates the people of the metropolitan American upper-middle class whom we regard as other-directed.[4]

This insatiable need for approval is, seemingly, the primary reason that so many executives are mobility-centered today. The mobility-centered executive needs the approval which only promotion can provide. A promotion shows that his superiors approve of him, raises him in the eyes of his associates, and increases his own self-respect. It proves to him that he is a good man. Because he doesn't have much faith in himself or in his ability to judge his own worth, he needs that proof again and again. As promotion and approval are so crucially important to him, anxiety is a basic fact of life for nearly every mobility-centered executive. His psychological security depends upon his superiors' opinions and decisions, and these can change at any time. The man who is approved by his superiors today may be phased out tomorrow and may not even know why it happened.

And the signs are so hard to read! A chat in the elevator, an ignored memo, a social invitation, a special assignment, or any of a thousand other actions can mean that a man is mobile or on the shelf, secure in his job or being phased out, on the way to the top or on the way out. Executives therefore spend a great deal of time in trying to read the signs but are never completely sure that they have read them correctly. Being actually passed over or fired can crush a man, but these things don't happen very often. Anticipating them happens every day.

[4] David Riesman (with R. Denney and N. Glazer), *The Lonely Crowd,* Yale University Press, New Haven, Connecticut, 1950.

THE ANXIETY OF ANTICIPATION

When Henry Ford fired a man, that man knew it. He might find his furniture in the street, with a sign saying "You're fired" on the hatrack, or he might be fired more politely, but he always knew he was out. Ford and similar men of his era were rough on men's egos, but the men knew where they stood, at least for the moment.

Today's top executives are not nearly as severe on their subordinates' egos, but they still create serious psychological problems for them. People, especially other-directed people, need to know where they stand, but in many companies no one ever tells them. No one tells them how well they are doing or what sort of plans exist for their future. Even firings—the most extreme of all personnel actions —can be so subtle and indirect that "many executives are fired without being aware of it." [5]

Instead of openly firing a man, many top executives merely create conditions which slowly force him out. Then, since some of these conditions look normal, he frequently doesn't know what is happening or what people think of him. Exactly the same action can mean that he has a bright future or no future at all. A few of the more subtle firing techniques are described in *The Executive Life* by the editors of *Fortune*.[6]

> *"The situation just deteriorates."* In this, the most common and passive technique, nothing happens: no new assignments are made, a man has little or nothing to do, and he slowly gets disgusted and leaves.

> *"The 'unavailable' treatment."* He can't get appointments with his boss, or he gets in only when the boss is too busy to listen to him. If he insists on seeing the boss, he gets brushed off firmly and perhaps impolitely.

> *"The gradual freeze-out."* His authority is slowly reduced, his suggestions ridiculed, or he gets a new title but no responsibility.

> *"The by-pass."* "The variations of this treatment range from omit-

[5] The editors of *Fortune*, *The Executive Life*, Doubleday, Garden City, New York, 1956, p. 187.
[6] *Ibid.*, pp. 185 ff.

108

ting an executive's name from important memos and excluding him from conferences, to taking assignments away from him . . . to withholding essential facts from him and then publicly embarrassing him because he doesn't have them."

"Unwanted assignments." He is assigned tasks he dislikes, or given ambiguous responsibilities and directions, and is criticized for not doing the right thing.

"Continual transfers." He is moved from plant to plant to wear down his patience (and his wife's tolerance).

When these tactics are used, an executive can't be sure of what is happening, at least not for the first few days or weeks. Perhaps his boss is giving him the "unavailable treatment," but the boss may just be very busy. Perhaps the latest assignment or transfer is an attempt to push him out, but it may be a tough job which they think is just right for him. When these techniques are used, most executives are likely to be confused. But there are even more subtle techniques; some are so subtle that they can confuse even the most sensitive and politically attuned executive.

"Some by-pass techniques may be twisted around so they appear to be 'opportunities.'" He can be given a challenging job in hope that he will be unable to fill it. Or the job may be so demanding and the standards so high that no one can perform satisfactorily, and this "poor performance" can be the basis for a later firing.

"Managements have also used promotions as a lever to hoist a man up and out." These aren't always the obvious "kick him upstairs" promotions. Sometimes they look like genuine opportunities.

"In one tool company, the president sometimes would promote an executive, give him a fat raise, and send him out to be a plant manager in the field. After six months or so the man would be recalled to headquarters and assigned some special project, such as a merchandising study. From there he went nowhere. . . . Some top executives have developed a technique of promoting undesired assistants to their personal staffs and then applying the freeze-out technique." [7]

Being fired is not the only or most common type of failure. Only a few executives are fired, but most are put on the shelf sooner or later. It is much harder to know whether it has happened. Firings, no matter how smoothly or subtly they are handled, are still definite acts which take place in fairly brief periods; but a man can spend years wondering whether he will ever be promoted again.

He wonders because his superiors never give him a definite answer about his chances for promotion; they may not even tell him what they think of his work. Most companies have some kind of periodic performance review, but it is usually more ritualistic than informative. Furthermore, the information provided by the performance review refers to the present job, not to future promotions.

If a man wants more information about his future and directly asks his bosses for it, he may actually harm his chances for promotion. Executives are expected to concentrate on their jobs and leave the promotion decisions to their bosses.

> The organization communicates to the manager that he is not expected to take responsibility for his own career at the same time it is trying to teach him how to take responsibility for important decisions! [8]

To ask direct questions about promotions is bad manners and may mark a man as being "interested in the wrong things." Even if a man does ask that question, he probably won't get a direct answer or a specific commitment (unless he is very highly valued, has an offer from another company, and knows how to put pressure on his superiors). The superior will probably just make some vague references to "the good things we have planned for you" or "the opportunities in a growing company like ours for a man like yourself."

Companies have good reasons for not making specific commitments. They do not want to tie their hands or to lose their men. If

---

[7] *Ibid.*, p. 196.
[8] Edgar H. Schein, "Management Development as a Process of Influence," *Industrial Management Review*, May 1961, pp. 59–77.

they make a specific commitment, it makes it hard to change their plans if conditions change. One large manufacturer has an unusually comprehensive manpower-planning program with specific replacements chosen for every one of the top 500 jobs, but it goes to great lengths to insure that none of the replacements learns that he has been selected. Management does not make specific commitments to individuals, because the replacements depend on each other and the situation; and management can't be sure who will have to be replaced first or how it will feel when the openings occur.

Management certainly does not want to tell men who are already on the shelf that they will never be promoted. For one thing, it can't be sure. The man who sits on the shelf now may suddenly become promotable if he gets a new boss or a different set of responsibilities. But the primary reason for not telling such men is rather obvious; for, in a mobility-conscious society such as ours, to tell a man that he is not promotable can cause him to leave the company, or at least to start looking for another job. And many men who will never go higher do very fine work at their present jobs.

In this kind of situation, anxiety is inevitable. The need to know where we stand is as basic as the need for food and drink. To frustrate this need will almost always cause anxiety, particularly in other-directed people. This anxiety is the primary cause for much of the behavior that is found in every organization. People keep trying to read the signs, and the signs are ambiguous and contradictory. People worry about the boss's expression and the way he says "hello." They wonder about the implications of social invitations, job assignments, memos, and reactions to their comments at meetings. They spread rumors, even wildly improbable rumors, about new opportunities or personnel cutbacks. They spend a vast amount of time trying to learn what will happen to them, trying to relieve their anxieties, but usually it doesn't help because the information is ambiguous and contradictory. Some executives therefore spend hours weighing the signs and trying to make sense of them: "The boss did like that suggestion, but he hasn't been very friendly lately. . . . This is a good assignment; but Fred had one like it, and look what happened to him. . . . The boss wrote 'nice job' on that memo, but he hasn't discussed it with me." And so on.

111

Because their need for information is so strong and the situations are so ambiguous, people frequently read more into them than is really there. There is so much ambiguous information that they can find whatever they are looking for. If a man expects a promotion or new assignment, he can find evidence that he will get it. If he is afraid of being fired, he can find evidence for that too.

Superiors, especially those who play it "close to the vest," cause a great deal of this ambiguity and projection. Nearly every boss is very important to his subordinates, who usually read more meaning into his statements, actions, and expressions than is really there. Most of these misconceptions remain secret, but a few become public and can be corrected. For example, every boss has been reminded of a promise that he made and has replied that he didn't remember giving it, only to be told: "Don't you remember? You said, 'Go ahead,' when we were leaving the meeting." Or, "When we were coming back from lunch, you said it was a good idea and should be followed up." Or, "You said you thought I would be an excellent controller, when we were reviewing my performance." The boss doesn't remember saying it, and probably didn't mean what his subordinate interpreted it to mean anyway!

In a few cases this tendency to find certain meanings in a situation is a sign that the executive is very anxious and upset. He has a fixed and probably frightening idea in his mind, and finds plenty of evidence to support it. One man started several consecutive sessions with a counselor by reporting the week's "evidence" that he was going to be fired: "The boss didn't say 'good morning' on Tuesday." "He looked dissatisfied with my report on Thursday." "He sent Bill on that assignment on Friday." This sort of problem can't be helped by facts, logic, or reassurance, but it can be helped by using the counseling techniques described in Appendix A of this book.

But there are worse things than the anxiety caused by ambiguity and anticipation. Wondering whether he will fail can make an executive very anxious, but actually failing is usually much worse. Sometimes being passed over or fired is a relief; sometimes it is just a minor annoyance; but frequently it is a disaster which causes overwhelming anxiety and very abnormal behavior.

112

THE PLIGHT OF BEING PASSED OVER

If a particular promotion was very important to a man, or if he feels that being passed over now means that he is permanently on the shelf, he may have a serious attack of failure anxiety. Medical research indicates how serious and common a problem this is. This research shows that, contrary to popular opinion, ulcers and other psychosomatic diseases are much more common among middle than top managers, and that being passed over can have very serious effects on the body.

> The incidence of psychosomatic diseases is significantly higher among members of the passed-over generation, as well as the premature death rate due to heart attacks and suicides. For many, stress without success has become unbearable during this period of high mobility.[9]

> The most likely candidate for a coronary is not the senior executive. It is the junior executive, probably striving for the top, or the white collar worker surrounded by frustration.[10]

It appears that this problem is going to become more, not less serious. More and more executives will be put on the shelf, and it will have more serious effects on them than it does now. If Riesman and other sociologists are correct, Americans are becoming more other-directed every day. An other-directed person desperately needs other people's approval to maintain his self-confidence and self-image. As more people become other-directed and mobility-centered, more will regard being passed over as a serious personal failure. And as people become more other-directed, this "failure" will become more devastating.

Unfortunately, this is going to happen to more people. More executives are on the shelf now than were there ten years ago; and more people, especially young people, will be put there in the future. There are many reasons for this development, but four major trends in our society and corporations are particularly important.

[9] Jennings, *op. cit.*, p. 3.
[10] Adapted from Paul D. White, specialist in diseases of the heart, as quoted by Vance Packard in *The Pyramid Climbers*, McGraw-Hill, New York, 1962, p. 259.

1. We live in an era of rapid change and rapid obsolescence. Our cars, planes, boats, and machines are usually obsolete long before they are worn out. But skills and people can become as obsolete as machines. "Executive obsolescence" is not just a phrase; it is a bitter reality for tens of thousands of men now and for hundreds of thousands more in the near future. Executive jobs are changing; some new skills are becoming necessary, some old ones useless. Some executives have the right skills and backgrounds; others can acquire them; but many will simply become obsolete and be put on the shelf or phased out.

2. A second important development is that the number of people entering the lower levels of management is growing much faster than the number of top jobs. Our colleges are currently overcrowded with students who were born in the postwar "baby boom." Some of them have already graduated and begun competing for jobs and promotions. Their high starting salaries (about $12,000 for a man with a master's degree in business administration but no experience) and the general pattern of recruiting create completely unrealistic expectations. They are paid so much, and recruited so eagerly, that they expect to be vice presidents within a few years. But there isn't a vice presidency for everybody, and many other people are ahead in the line. When they realize this, many will become bitter and disillusioned. There is some evidence, in fact, which suggests that they become disillusioned within one year after graduation.

3. The recentralization of many large corporations is a third important factor. Corporations decentralized and created many satisfying and relatively autonomous executive positions during the 1940's and 1950's. They decentralized because they were so large that the top executives could not get the information they needed to make their decisions and exert direct control. Now, however, the computers and modern information systems give them that information quickly and in great detail. Equipped with this information, they can make decisions that they formerly delegated and can keep much tighter control over lower levels. Many jobs which required independent decision-making executives can therefore be eliminated or handled in a routine way. As routine jobs do not provide much intrinsic satisfaction or sense of achievement, these

114

developments increase people's desires to move up at the same time that they reduce the chances for doing so!

4. Mergers are almost unbelievably popular today. Executive obsolescence, increased competition for executive jobs, and corporate recentralization will frustrate many executives, but mergers will have even greater effect. Mergers create a few executive jobs in the acquiring company but usually eliminate several times as many in the acquired company. We all know executives who have lost their jobs or chances for promotion because of a merger. And it is not just the small firms which are being gobbled up. Men in Wilson, Jones and Laughlin, and Westinghouse Air Brake formerly thought, "It can't happen to us," but now they know better.

The executive recruiters are probably the best index of the impact of mergers. They live on their ability to move people. Just as soon as a merger is rumored or announced, they are on the phone. They know that they can get people because some executives will be pushed out, others passed over, and still others will be anxious about their futures.

The net result of these and other factors has been an enormous increase in the number of shelf-sitters in the past few years, and this trend will probably be even stronger in the future. From his research on executive mobility, Professor Jennings has concluded:

> The number of executives and managers who were once very mobile but who now sit on shelves is fantastically large. Estimates . . . suggest that the number of shelf-sitters in the large industrial corporations is three to five times as great as it was in the early fifties.[11]

We have, then, many people on the shelf, and some are in their thirties or forties. What happens to them? Some don't mind at all. They enjoy their jobs and their lives and feel little or no anxiety. Others feel anxious at first, but adjust to the situations and lead satisfying lives. Still others can't accept their situations or adjust to them; they may take extreme actions of some kind or become chronically anxious and dissatisfied.

Being passed over is, therefore, a trifle to some men but a disas-

[11] Jennings, *op. cit.*, p. 16.

ter to others; their feelings depend more on their personalities and attitudes than on their positions and previous records. A brilliant vice president who has been passed over for the presidency may feel that he is a failure, although a mediocre man may not mind not becoming head of his department.

If we focus only on the men who feel that they have failed, we find that their problems fall into four main groups: physical reactions, feelings about the job, feelings about themselves, and feelings about other people. The extreme nature of these reactions indicates clearly how serious a problem this is for them.

Physical reactions. Men can have anxiety attacks when they hear that they have been passed over or can be gradually worn down by the constant frustration of not moving up. In Chapter 11 we shall see that anxiety affects many disorders which most people think are purely physical. These disorders range from minor nuisances such as colds, warts, and allergies to killers such as cancer and heart disease.

Feelings about the job. A few men work harder, but others conclude that hard work doesn't pay. Because they don't want to believe that their performance is poor, they may decide that company politics is more important than performance; so they engage in politics, leave in disgust, or become apathetic and "play for retirement." Blaming politics saves face, but it certainly doesn't improve performance.

Feelings about themselves. If a promotion was very important to him, or if someone he looks down on (especially a younger man) gets the promotion, an executive may lose his self-confidence and go through a serious identity crisis. He may become unsure of who he is and wonder whether he is as good a man as he once believed. He may even criticize himself very harshly and decide that he didn't deserve the promotion, that his superiors saw through him and knew he wasn't good enough.

Some superiors try to prevent this situation by praising or giving raises to the man they passed over; but if he is deeply troubled because of his lost promotion, he probably won't believe them. If they really thought he was so good, why didn't they promote him? They obviously think the other man is better, or they wouldn't have given him the job.

Although a serious identity crisis is relatively rare, only a very secure and self-confident executive can go through this experience without having some doubts about himself. His superiors have rejected him; they have said that someone else is a better man. How can he be sure that they aren't right?

Feelings about other people. Many executives feel angry—at least momentarily—with their superiors and the man who got the job. They are hurt, and they may lash back. They are humiliated, and their first impulse is to save their pride. They may think that their superiors are stupid and biased or that the winner got the job by playing politics. If a man continues to feel this way—and some do—cooperation may be impossible, especially if the winner is his new boss.

This experience can also affect his feelings about his wife, his children, and his associates. He may feel that time spent with his family cost him the promotion, or blame his wife for not helping his career by mixing with the right people. He may distrust his associates and feel that some of them "knifed him in the back" or are "out to get him."

Even if he doesn't blame his family or associates, his changed feelings about himself and his job can hurt his relations with them. They are accustomed to a confident man who enjoys his work, and they don't know what to do when he changes.

They may try to cheer him up, or reason with him, or tell him to "snap out of it," or point to past successes and future opportunities; but facts, logic, and suggestions don't solve emotional problems. He feels rejected, isolated, and unsure of himself. He needs understanding, not lectures, but everyone keeps trying to "straighten him out." The more they try, the lonelier he feels.

THE ULTIMATE REJECTION: BEING FIRED

To be passed over is a disaster for many executives, but to be fired is much worse—for everyone. It is the worst failure in an executive career. It has all the personal implications and effects of being passed over, but they are much more severe. His rejection is complete. His bosses have told him in absolutely unmistakable terms that they don't want him. His self-confidence may collapse, and it may be years before he completely regains it.

Of course, very few executives are fired. They are usually allowed to resign. We have already seen how subtly and smoothly they can be pushed out. But firings do occur more often than most people believe. In *The Executive Life* the authors estimate that "the vast majority of resignations—perhaps four out of five—are forced; that is, they are in fact firings." [12] Estimates of the total number of executives fired each year are as high as 250,000.

Some of these executives are "lucky"—even though they don't think so: They are given time to find another job before they have to resign. Being fired is still a failure and a humiliating rejection, but at least their lives are not changed very much. The unlucky ones are forced out, with no place to go, and their entire lives are disrupted. Their income stops, and their savings dwindle. They have nothing to do and nowhere to go. Tension builds between them and their families. They suffer the public stigma of being unemployed. They have to look for a job, a depressing task which is alien and humiliating to them. Each of these factors creates anxiety, and together they can create very serious psychological problems.

1. *Loss of income and financial security.* Executives are paid quite well, but usually they don't save much money. Their incomes have risen steadily; their corporations provide insurance, retirement, and profit sharing; and they are expected to live well. They therefore spend most of their incomes and have relatively small bank accounts. *The Young Executives* reports that more than 45 per cent of a very successful group studied had less than $15,000 in liquid assets even though their incomes ranged from $20,000 to $75,000 per year.[13]

A man with expensive habits and a small bank account is in trouble, perhaps serious trouble, when his income and company fringes stop. He is certainly not a candidate for the welfare rolls; but as the bills come in and the bank account drops, his morale drops with it. He worries more and more about financial security, and because he is under so much pressure from other sources, he may not be able to bear the strain.

[12] The editors of *Fortune, op. cit.,* p. 187.
[13] Walter Guzzardi, *The Young Executives,* New American Library, New York, pp. 157 f.

This problem has been so severe for some executives that it has been recommended that they accept undesirable and even low-paying jobs just so they have an income. An income, even an insufficient one, takes some of the pressure off and gives them the confidence and time they need to obtain the right position.

2. *Changes in habits.* Being unemployed disrupts a man's entire routine. He is accustomed to going to work, thinking about problems, meeting challenges—all the actions of an executive life. Now he has nothing to do and nowhere to go. It doesn't make any difference whether he gets up in the morning. He can linger over breakfast. He doesn't have to catch the train or worry about being at the plant. He is simply idle, most of the time. He will have a few interviews each week, but most of his time is free. Energetic men grow restless when they have too much time on their hands.

To deal with this problem there are two standard recommendations for nearly all executives. First, they should take every interview they can get, even if the jobs don't interest them. Something may develop from any interview, or they may get a referral; they will certainly sharpen their interview technique. Even if there are no concrete benefits, having interviews gives them something to do and somewhere to go.

The second recommendation is that they should treat job hunting like any other job. They should get up at the usual time, shave, dress neatly, leave the house, and go where the jobs are. This routine increases their chances of getting a job and keeps up their morale.

3. *Family tensions.* To treat job hunting as if it were a regular job, including the routine of leaving the house, may also keep the family tensions down. Two tense people in constant contact are bound to irritate each other, and a wife can become very dissatisfied and critical if she thinks her husband is not trying hard enough to find a job.

No matter what he does, however, tension with his family can be severe. Both he and his wife will be tense, and tense people irritate each other. He may feel that he is not fulfilling his role as head of the family, and she may secretly agree. He will probably become very sensitive to criticism, and she may become more critical and less understanding because of her own anxieties.

Perhaps the most explosive combination is a status- and

achievement-centered husband and a security-centered wife. She doesn't understand what his work means to him and will press him to take any job, even one with lower pay, responsibility, or status. He will probably resent her pressing and insist on waiting for the right job. She in turn will resent what she thinks is his stubbornness. If he stays unemployed very long, an explosion is almost inevitable. When it comes, both may say and do things which will permanently damage their relationship.

4. *Masculinity crisis.* All of these factors can create a masculinity crisis. The man is just not fulfilling the male role. He is not supporting his family, or working, or contributing to society. He is not busy, important, confident, or successful. Both he and his wife may therefore have real doubts about how good a man he is.

In such a situation sexual problems are quite common. Sexual problems usually indicate that a husband and wife have other problems, and we have already seen how serious these other problems can be. These sexual problems have not been thoroughly investigated, but it does appear that they are fairly common and are sometimes quite severe. When they do occur, they are another blow to a man's already weakened ego, and they greatly increase his anxiety.

5. *The public humiliation.* To be unemployed is a humiliating failure, and a public failure at that. The unemployed executive's friends, relatives, and neighbors will probably learn that he has lost his job, and most of them will regard it as a personal failure. Because he knows this, he may be ashamed or afraid to face them, even though he wants and needs their companionship. If they do get together, his situation may make everyone feel awkward and behave unnaturally, and his sensitivity may make him misinterpret their behavior or motives. His feelings of isolation are therefore intensified just when he most needs understanding, friendship, and psychological support.

6. *Job hunting.* Looking for a job is an extremely unpleasant experience, especially for unemployed executives. The whole process can be demoralizing and humiliating for anyone, but it is especially difficult for a man who feels he has failed. He doesn't want to tell people why he left his last job or explain why he is still unemployed. He is very sensitive to rejection, but he is rejected again and again.

120

This is so disagreeable that almost every unemployed executive does not work as hard at job hunting as he did at his regular job, even though he knows how important it is to be diligent in the search.

Job hunting would not be so unpleasant if executives knew how to do it, but most of them do not. They have spent their lives working at their jobs, not looking for them, and they are "as stupid at selling themselves as a youngster trying for his first job." [14] Job hunting is a skill, and a fairly simple skill at that, but one which has to be learned and practiced.

Because they have neither the skill nor the practice, it takes unemployed executives much longer to get a job than it should. They make mistakes, prolong the process, and become discouraged and demoralized. Many executives become so anxious and upset after a few unsuccessful days or weeks that they will pay huge fees to "executive counselors." Some of these counselors are ethical, but many others charge huge fees—as much as $3,000—and do very little in return for their client's money. The New York City Department of Licenses has begun an investigation into these schools, and the acting license commissioner has stated that some of them are "nothing more than charm schools for executives." Even the more prestigious firms use very dubious methods. Some, for example, give psychological tests and then mail out "unbiased psychological reports" which no employer takes seriously. Nearly all of the information these firms provide is published in books which can be purchased at any good bookstore.

The fact that executives will pay huge fees for such questionable services clearly indicates their degree of anxiety. Hardheaded, results-oriented executives pay thousands of dollars for services which have little or no value, and because they are so desperately anxious they are ready to believe promises which are obvious nonsense.

14 The editors of *Fortune, op. cit.,* p. 45.

PART THREE

The Effects of Anxiety

7

General Effects
on the Individual

THERE ARE TWO PURPOSES IN THE DISCUSSIONS IN THIS CHAPTER AND the four following: first, to show how reactions to anxiety can be either constructive or destructive. The focus will be on what happens after anxiety has been aroused and on the ways that people react to it. Most of these reactions are defensive: anxiety is so painful that we usually try to get away from its pain as quickly as possible and ignore the longer-term consequences of our actions. We run away from the pain but don't solve the underlying problems, and the anxiety returns. It may even become stronger because the defenses have caused other problems. However, anxiety also has some distinctly positive benefits which we cannot afford to ignore.

We shall also try to prove that anxiety is an extremely serious problem. The preceding chapters dealt essentially with logic and theory. We pointed out how certain conditions could make people feel powerless, lonely, uncertain, anxious, and so on. Now we shall present direct evidence of this anxiety. Our arguments about the causes of anxiety can be easily disregarded, but it is very hard to argue with the evidence that one out of every 20 executives is an alcoholic; that a mental patient sleeps in every other hospital bed; that anxiety causes heart attacks, ulcers, ulcerative colitis, and a

125

host of other diseases; and, most important of all, that on the average men live five years less than women. In other words, we want to indicate how important a problem this is by talking about the most basic issues in the world—life, health, and happiness.

Although many other factors are involved, anxiety causes men to die sooner than women in two ways: Most women are not subjected to the same pressures as men, and they can express their feelings more easily. Their world has changed much less than men's, and they are better equipped to live in it than men are in theirs. When they compete in the business world, they face some very severe pressures, but thousands of years of evolution and civilization have prepared them for raising children and taking care of a home, the basic role of most women. Men's role is ambiguous, and the conditions they face are changing very rapidly.

This difference probably makes men more anxious than women, and their basic nature and culture prevent them from dealing with their anxieties as well as women do. Women can cry, or openly express fear, or lean on a man, but men can't. They are supposed to be brave and strong and unemotional even though they are all sometimes afraid and want to cry or lean a little. They therefore keep their feelings inside of themselves to preserve their masculine images, but they pay a high price for these images—heart attacks, ulcers, and years of their lives.

No one can change the fact that men experience more pressures than women, nor can men use women's methods to deal with anxiety. We are what we are, and we can't change our basic natures or situations. But we can realize the price we are paying for our defenses and can find better ways of handling our anxieties. The next few chapters show how present methods fail to solve the problem. Part Four offers better solutions.

ANXIETY, MOTIVATION, AND PRODUCTION

Anxiety motivates people in the same way as hunger and thirst. Anxiety, hunger, and thirst are painful and act as drives; they make people act. Usually these actions are goal-directed and help to reduce the drive: We drink when we are thirsty and eat when we are hungry. But drives can also cause random acts that don't solve the problem or reduce the drive; they simply express the tension we feel. We may pace the floor when we are worried, or swear when we are angry, or toss and turn when we can't sleep. Both random and goal-directed acts can affect a man's efficiency and production.

Motivation and performance. Although some people assume that increased motivation will increase performance, the relationship is much more complicated. Increasing motivation will generally improve performance up to a point, but increasing it past that point can actually cause poorer performance. A simple diagram illustrates this principle.

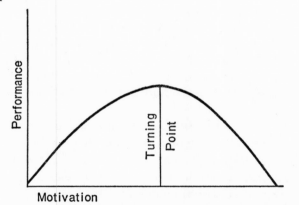

At very low levels of motivation, a small increase in motivation greatly improves performance; but, as we approach the turning point, the curve flattens out and we need a much larger increase in motivation to get the same improvement in production; after the turning point, increasing motivation lowers performance. A few concrete examples may make this principle clearer.

If we place a bone just outside a U-shaped fence and a dog inside it, the dog's performance will depend on his degree of

127

motivation. If the dog is not hungry, he won't even try to get the food. If he is mildly hungry, he will scratch at the fence but will soon realize that he has to go away from the food to get outside the fence. If he is starved, he may scratch and whine indefinitely, and it will almost certainly take longer for him to solve the problem.

This example shows that extreme motivation can make the animal lose perspective and narrow his vision. The dog can't realize that he must run away from the food in order to reach it. The same thing can happen with men, but extreme motivation can even reduce performance on a very simple task. For example: If you were offered ten dollars to walk ten feet along a board 12 inches wide lying on the ground, you could do it quickly and easily. If you had to walk along the same board when it was your only escape from the fifteenth floor of a burning building to an adjacent building, you would probably have more difficulty in doing it. You would be so highly motivated that you might not be able to do it at all, and you almost certainly would do it slowly and rather clumsily. You might even crawl, or sit down and try to slide across the board one foot at a time.

The effect of the task. In this case an extreme amount of motivation reduced performance on a very simple task, but it would have had an even greater impact on a complicated one. If you had to undo a complicated latch or untie a huge knot to escape from the same fire, your performance would be even poorer, relative to your performance on the same task under more normal conditions. The extreme motivation would narrow your vision and ruin your judgment in the same way that starving affected the dog. You would be too direct and would not have the detachment you needed to analyze the problem.

We can easily relate this principle about tasks to the motivation curve. The complexity of the task affects the turning point and the general shape of the curve; more complex tasks have lower turning points; the same amount of motivation can therefore improve performance on a simple task but reduce it on a complicated one.

Let us get away from theoretical examples and apply this principle to industrial problems: If one of your subordinates has a simple job to do, you can generally improve his performance by putting pressure on him; but if the task is complex and requires judgment and creative thinking, pressure can have exactly the opposite effect. He may not be able to think clearly, or may try to solve the problem too quickly in order to get rid of it, or overlook some important aspects of the problem, but the net result can be poor performance. You must therefore vary your approach to subordinates and apply less pressure when men are working on complicated tasks.

Mild anxiety. You must also consider how much stress other people are putting on a man. If a person is not anxious or under stress, creating mild anxiety—by criticizing him, for example—can increase his motivation, raise his aspirations, and stimulate him to find new solutions to an old problem. The simpler the task, the more anxiety you can create before causing a problem or harming his performance.

Severe anxiety. If the man is already under stress, the same action that ordinarily would create only mild anxiety can have very different effects. His anxiety becomes so painful that he can't think straight and wants only to get away from it. Increasing anxiety in this case, therefore, will generally make matters worse. For example, if a person is already under heavy pressure from his boss and associates, to insist that he finish a job sooner or criticize his progress will often lower his performance, especially if his job requires judgment and independent thinking. He may work harder, but his anxiety and other tensions will affect his judgment and lower his overall performance.

Personality and stress. Not all anxiety comes from external stress. Some people are basically more anxious than others or are less resistant to stresses. Putting pressure on them can have the same undesirable effects as criticizing a man who is under pressure from his boss: It affects his judgment and lowers his performance. On the other hand, if a man is basically relaxed and unmotivated, putting some pressure on can increase both motivation and performance.

A series of experiments illustrates this principle. First a group was divided into people with low and high anxiety scores. Then each person performed a series of tasks under threatening and non-threatening conditions. Under the threatening condition the low-anxiety group performed better than the high-anxiety group, but the pattern was reversed for the nonthreatening condition. This experiment indicates that threatening naturally anxious people lowers performance, but threatening comfortable people improves performance. An executive can therefore improve his subordinates' performance by: (1) learning which subordinates are basically anxious and which are naturally relaxed; (2) recognizing the signs of temporary anxiety and stress; (3) varying his approach to fit the individual and the situation. He can improve his own performance by recognizing the amount of pressure that brings out the best in him and avoiding situations and jobs which either bore or overwhelm him.

DEFENSES

The natural desire to get away from the pain of anxiety is the basic cause of defensiveness. Anxiety is so painful that everyone has some defenses; no one could live without them entirely. They ease our pain and make us less aware of our anxiety and psychological problems. We may compensate for inadequacy feelings by boasting, feel anger rather than anxiety when someone threatens us, or take a drink when we feel tense, but all these actions have the same general effect: They make us more comfortable and less aware of our anxiety and the problems that cause it.

The fact that anxiety can cause actions as varied as boasting, drinking, and working harder illustrates another important truth: Everyone has some anxiety and some defenses, but certain defenses are much more acceptable and constructive than others. The world approves and rewards men who sacrifice to get ahead but disapproves of drinking and boasting and rejects these as unacceptable behavior. The braggart and the hard-charger may have the same psychological problems (feelings of inadequacy) but very different objective problems: The braggart alienates people, harms his career, and feels even more inadequate, whereas the hard-charger gains respect, advances his career, and may feel more adequate.

The amount of anxiety a man feels may therefore be less important than the way he handles it. Defenses are a part of everyone's "psychic economy." They control anxiety and keep this economy functioning. Sometimes they are too costly and don't provide very good protection against anxiety; they may create other problems or fail to preserve comfort. We can therefore improve our comfort and effectiveness in three ways: (1) by reducing our total amount of anxiety; (2) by learning better ways of handling the anxiety we already have; (3) by doing both. Part Three of this book will describe several ineffective ways of handling anxiety; Part Four will contain suggestions for reducing anxiety and handling it more effectively.

Learning. The actual defenses each person uses are learned, not inherited or instinctive. They are learned in the same way that we learn to ease pains such as hunger or thirst. Nearly all this learning is based on a very simple principle; psychologists call it "the law of effect," but everyone who has ever trained a dog or reared a child knows it: People tend to repeat actions that result in rewards. A dog that is given a biscuit for rolling over learns the trick; the child who gets attention when he cries at night learns to cry almost every night.

Anxiety causes the same kind of learning. Since it is very painful, reducing it is a reward. Any behavior which reduces or eliminates anxiety—even temporarily—is rewarded, and the person is likely to repeat it. If this behavior is rewarded enough times, he learns a habit, a habitual way of dealing with anxiety; and the more effectively this habit reduces anxiety, the stronger it becomes.

Alcohol works for some people, so they drink. Other people use tranquilizers because they find them more effective or acceptable. One person may find that being aggressive reduces his anxiety about personal relationships, but another may be shy and withdrawn, and a third may be overfriendly and eager to please; and all three act as they do for the same reason. The behaviors are very different, but they all serve the same purpose and they all have been learned in the same way: People found that they reduced anxiety.

These habits will persist as long as they are effective, as long as they make the person more comfortable—even if this comfort is very temporary, even if these defenses cause severe long-term problems. Extensive research on learning proves that a very small reward or punishment immediately after an action has much more effect than a larger but delayed reward or punishment. For example, most people who want to lose weight "cheat" on their diets occasionally because the immediate satisfaction of eating has more impact on them than the great but delayed benefit of losing weight.

Thus it is hard to change or drop our defenses even if they are very destructive. They provide immediate relief, and this relief has much more impact on us than the longer-term costs. An alcoholic's drinking is probably the best illustration of this principle, but it applies to all other defenses and most human behavior. An alcoholic knows that alcohol is ruining his health, career, and family life, but the immediate relief he gets from drinking means more to him than these delayed but greater costs.

The classical conception of human rationality is thus directly contradicted. A classically rational man evaluates the long-term costs and benefits of each action and selects the most advantageous one. But here are men taking actions which provide very limited and temporary benefits at very severe long-term costs. Because there is absolutely no doubt that men do take that kind of action, we have no choice but to modify the classical conception. *Men do try to maximize rewards and minimize punishments, but immediate rewards and punishments have much more impact on them than larger but delayed rewards and punishments.*

This principle applies to everyone, even executives, although it may not be as powerful for them as it is for other people. Executives and the middle class in general have been taught to control their desires and defer gratification. They generally plan for the future, spend money on their own and their children's education, and so on. However, although they can analyze long-term costs and benefits in many other areas, their own anxiety is so powerful and so misunderstood that they yield to it and sacrifice long-term gains for temporary relief.

Anyone who attempts to change or get rid of a man's defenses must therefore first reduce the amount of his anxiety and pain so that the defenses are less necessary. No one will drop his defenses as long as he is under pressure. Therapists, counselors, and clergymen who are attempting to help a man will therefore try to reduce his anxiety so that he will have the courage to drop his defenses temporarily and look for new ways of handling his problems. Appendix A spells out the differences among various methods, but they all agree on one point: A man will not drop his defenses as long as he needs them, and the counselor's job is to make them less necessary.

Expression. In addition to warding off anxiety, defenses often help us to express it and related feelings while avoiding the guilt and shame we would feel if we expressed them directly. By expressing these feelings very indirectly and symbolically, they let us drain off tension without recognizing our own feelings and problems. A man can express his feelings of inadequacy by being physically inadequate, by developing physical symptoms which justify his failure and express his feelings about himself. He can't succeed, because he is sick, not because he is weak or psychologically disturbed. These symptoms can also express his dependency needs without his having to recognize them; other people have to take care of him—not because he wants them to but because he is sick. Another man may be ashamed of hating his father and displace his aggression onto the police and other authority figures. A mother can express her resentment toward her children by smothering them with "love." She does everything for them but prevents them from growing up or becoming independent. If someone points out that she is harming the children, she can preserve her self-image and insist that she is merely protecting them.

Defenses, therefore, contribute to the psychic economy by letting people express their feelings in less costly ways. Expression drains off tension; but if we express some feelings directly, we will recognize what they really are and feel guilty and ashamed. Our defenses let us drain off some tension by expressing our feelings, but they disguise the feelings so that we don't recognize them and feel ashamed of them. The net result can be less tension and greater comfort.

Recognizing defenses. Because they express feelings, we can recognize some defenses—if we understand the language they use. This language is very symbolic, and it takes years to understand it fully; but, as the following chapters will show, some messages are fairly easy to read.

Even if they don't express feelings, most defenses have characteristics that help us to recognize them. They are usually rigid and repetitious and have undesirable results that the person ignores—even if they are obvious to everyone else. Many defenses are also rather extreme: Some people can never take advice, or are always calm, or work extremely hard. In addition to being repetitious, ineffective, and extreme, defenses are usually "sore spots." People are sensitive about them and become angry or upset if someone questions them. They are sensitive because they know that they are vulnerable and that exposing these defenses would make them anxious and uncomfortable.

A hypochondriac, for example, will insist that he is really sick and grow very angry when doctors tell him that his problem is psychological. Alcoholics have a few standard replies when they receive criticisms of their drinking: "I know my limit." "I can quit any time I want to." Or they may simply say, "Leave me alone."

Although people try to deceive us about their defenses, to recognize them is extremely important. We have to know when people are defensive, because the usual rules for communicating with them don't apply at those times. If a person is not emotional or defensive, he will listen to facts and logic. When he is defensive, facts and logic will have little effect. He is protecting himself from pain and cannot agree to facts that will weaken his defenses and increase his pain. We can only influence him by making him less defensive, less afraid of our facts and logic. We must therefore avoid challenging his defenses and create an atmosphere that will let him relax and act reasonably. Chapters 12 and 13 and Appendix A contain several suggestions on how this may be done.

It is even more important to recognize our own defenses, and we can recognize them in the same way that we recognize other people's. Our own defenses are as rigid, repetitious, and ineffective as other people's, and they cause other problems that we try to ignore. Unfortunately, because we depend on our defenses it is usually very hard to recognize and understand them without help. They are solving our problems, and we can't let go and look objectively at them as long as we need them. The comfort they provide also takes away our motivation to solve our underlying problems. Our defenses, however, are as costly as those of other people: They create other problems, drain our energy, and—most important of all—keep us from knowing who we are or what we want. If we don't know that,

134

we can't control our lives or be truly free and independent. A lasting solution to the problem of anxiety therefore requires that we become less dependent on our defenses and more aware of ourselves. These chapters will help you understand the principles of defenses, and Chapter 13 and Appendix A contain several suggestions for dealing with your defenses or getting help in doing so.

Solutions to the problem. Because they ease the pain and awareness of anxiety and let us indirectly express feelings we are ashamed of, defenses are *solutions* to the problem of anxiety. They may cause some serious problems, but we should not overlook their very substantial benefits.

First, by distracting our attention from anxiety and psychological problems, they can help us to solve other problems. If we were aware of all our psychological problems and anxieties, we probably could not accomplish anything. We would be incapacitated and would spend our time worrying rather than doing our jobs, raising our children, or performing our other functions. For example, a man who felt inadequate sexually might be unable to work if his defenses didn't keep these feelings buried. Failing at his job would only make him feel more inadequate as a man.

Certain defenses can also help a man achieve economic and other kinds of success and help him relate to other men. Many men have become successful executives because they were compensating for feelings of inadequacy, and one of the reasons that executives feel comfortable with each other is that they share the same attitudes and defenses.

These same attitudes and defenses have also led to enormous social and economic contributions. An obsession with profits or personal success can help a man to control his anxiety, but it can also help build a gigantic corporation, provide thousands of jobs, and produce vitally important goods. The executive culture may be partially defensive, but it is one of the major reasons for America's strength and affluence.

But the solution is inadequate. Even though everyone has them, even though they provide some substantial benefits, defenses are usually temporary and inadequate solutions to the problems of anxiety. They reduce anxiety briefly, but it returns because the underlying problem has not been solved. And the long-term effect

135

of defensive behavior is often even greater anxiety. Defenses, therefore, are generally self-defeating.

Defenses reduce pain, but pain is useful. Pain lets us know that we have a problem which has to be solved. Physical pain tells us that something is wrong with our bodies. If we didn't feel it, we probably could not survive. We would not know when we had a serious infection, a ruptured appendix, or an ulcer. We wouldn't have our teeth fixed or our broken bones set. And our bodies would be ruined.

Anxiety serves the same purpose as physical pain: It tells us that we have a problem and that we had better start solving it. But the problem is psychological rather than physical, and we don't want to get the message. We don't want to know that we have a problem, and we don't like the pain of anxiety; so we use our defenses to escape from ourselves and our problems. We get temporary relief, but the problem continues and may get worse.

Defenses can also make the underlying problem more serious or create other problems. They can make a serious situation much worse by causing the wrong decision or by making people dislike or lose confidence in a person. An executive who feels anxious when he has to make difficult decisions may relieve his anxiety by making hurried decisions, but such decisions can have disastrous consequences. Drinking to relieve an executive's anxieties about his job may cost him his boss's confidence and the job. An executive can relieve his anxieties about being in complete control of his unit by being domineering but lose key subordinates, or cause a revolt, or be subtly undercut by his men. Unfortunately, as the problem grows more severe, each executive is likely to become more anxious and defensive. The first might make his decisions even more impetuously; the second might drink more heavily; and the third could become even more domineering.

Defenses are also self-defeating because they can work only if a person deceives himself, and self-deception becomes more difficult and exhausting as time goes on. Defenses relieve anxiety by preventing us from becoming aware of a problem, but our attempts to relieve this anxiety may appear irrational to us. Because doubts about our own rationality create intense anxiety, we have to deceive ourselves about both the underlying problem and the defensive behavior it has caused. We become defensive about our defensiveness. We have to rationalize and justify our defensive behavior, and this becomes very exhausting.

Perhaps the best example of the extreme demands of this kind of self-deception is the Don Juan. Nearly every great lover has very serious doubts about his masculinity and may even be trying to overcome latent homosexual desires. If he became aware of these doubts and feelings he would feel very anxious. He therefore has to prove himself by seducing one woman after another. Then, since his behavior is so unusual, he has to justify it or avoid thinking about it. He has to deceive himself about his desires and the behavior they cause. This deception is very difficult and exhausting (and may cause even more frantic attempts to prove himself).

Defenses are, therefore, very costly. They prevent us from solving the problems which cause anxiety, may make these problems more severe or create other ones, and may make us spend increasing amounts of energy in self-deception. These effects combine to create a vicious circle: As the problem worsens and other problems arise, anxiety increases, causing more defensiveness—which may then aggravate the problems and make us spend still more energy deceiving ourselves.

8

Defense Mechanisms:
Protectors and Destroyers

DEFENSE MECHANISMS ARE THE MOST COMMON REACTION TO ANXI-
ety. We all use them, and they are very valuable. They protect
us from the pain of anxiety and other emotions and help us to live
comfortable and productive lives. But some defenses are destructive,
and any defense can be self-defeating and destructive if it is used
excessively.

TYPES OF DEFENSE MECHANISMS

Repression. Repression is our most basic defense mechanism,
our first barrier against anxiety. It keeps unpleasant memories, feelings, and desires out of our consciousness and protects us from the
anxiety they would cause if we became aware of them. We forget
our dental appointments. Women forget the terrible pain of child-

138

birth. We remember the good things from our school years and early romances and usually don't think about the loneliness and doubts we felt then.

Repression, however, is not the same as ordinary forgetting. Both involve a lost awareness of certain things, but the resemblance ends there. We forget things because they are unimportant, but we repress things because they are unpleasant. We misplace our glasses or forget to buy gasoline or a loaf of bread, but we repress our hatred for people we are supposed to love, our feelings of inadequacy, our antisocial desires, and our unpleasant memories. Forgetting is therefore accidental and random, but repression is motivated and selective. We don't repress everything, only the things that would hurt us.

But that does not mean that repression is deliberate or conscious. On the contrary, it is an unconscious process. We do not realize that we are repressing something; we just do it automatically. But how can it be unconscious? How can we repress things that are unpleasant, if we are not aware of them?

Freud answered that question by using an analogy. If we view our conscious mind as a house, repression occurs in the vestibule. Unpleasant memories, thoughts, and feelings try to enter the house but are stopped at the vestibule. They are recognized as threatening and are repressed before we can become completely aware of them.

A final difference between repression and forgetting is that repression is much more complete and permanent. If we forget something, we can easily be reminded of it. A service station, a radio commercial, or an oil truck can remind us to buy gasoline. Thinking about dinner or our children can remind us to buy a quart of milk. When something is repressed, reminders usually don't work. We resist being reminded of our repressed feelings or memories even if they are obvious to other people.

This resistance is most easily observed in mental patients, but the same sort of thing happens in all of us. A man who has amnesia may not recognize his wife or children or remember events, even if they are described to him in great detail. Many murderers do not remember their crimes even though the evidence is overwhelmingly against them. They do not remember because remembering would be very painful.

It is harder to recognize repression in normal people, but we all use it. We have thoughts or feelings that we don't accept, or we have done things that we are ashamed of, but we are not aware of them. For example, if we broke down almost anyone's repression with hypnosis or "truth serum," he would admit that he has sometimes wished that his parents, wife, or children would die and leave him alone. But he was probably unaware of these desires before we broke down his repression, and he will probably be unaware of them after he has returned to normal. He doesn't want to be aware of them, because that would make him feel guilty, anxious, and ashamed.

Repressing this kind of feeling helps us to live with ourselves, but sometimes repression is not strong enough to protect us completely. Repression involves some of our strongest feelings, and it cannot always prevent us from expressing them indirectly and symbolically. We repress our hatred for our loved ones but express it by criticizing or frustrating them. We repress our basic aggressions and cruelty but enjoy boxing matches or hunting. We repress our desires to lean and depend on other people but express them by getting sick and letting the doctors dominate us.

These actions threaten to undo the work of repression and create the anxiety we are avoiding. They can make us realize what we really feel, and this knowledge would make us anxious and ashamed. To prevent this from happening we support repression with other defense mechanisms. We deny that our criticisms hurt our children, or rationalize that boxing and hunting are good healthy sports, or insist that our health is so bad that we have to let doctors make our decisions. That is, we use these other defenses to finish the job that repression started, to keep us from becoming aware of our own feelings.

Suppression. Suppression is also an attempt to keep from thinking about unpleasant things, but it is a conscious rather than an unconscious process. We suppress something when we deliberately avoid thinking or talking about it. We respond to questions about a missed deal or an argument with the boss by saying, "I don't feel like talking about it." Or we deliberately throw ourselves into our work to take our minds off unpleasant problems and memories.

Reaction formation. If repressed material threatens to become conscious, we may try to keep it repressed by overreacting and acting exactly the opposite to the way we feel. The puritan in Chapter 1 acted as a censor and critic of everyone's behavior to keep from recognizing his own unacceptable desires. Nearly all anti-vice crusaders are doing the same thing, and we can see reaction formation in many other places.

Some executives are extremely tough and independent because they don't want to recognize their own need to depend on other people. Others are so afraid of their own hostility that they are extremely nice to people and can't express honest anger. A few are so ashamed of their desires to dominate people that they are unable to accept the responsibility of giving orders. Because everyone desires to lean on people, gets angry, and would like to dominate people, we can easily recognize reaction formation. A person who is *always* independent or submissive or calm is probably using reaction format:on to deceive and control himself.

Projection. We can also keep from recognizing repressed feelings by projecting them onto other people. ("We don't feel that way about them; they feel that way about us.") We keep from realizing what we are really like by projecting our undesirable characteristics onto other people and overlooking them in ourselves. We say that people are basically selfish and hostile, but we can't see our own selfishness and hostility.

We can project any kind of feeling or trait onto other people, but we usually project the ones which justify our own unacceptable thoughts or actions. If we want to hurt someone, we believe that he is "out to get us." We therefore have to get him first. If we use unethical practices against a competitor, we believe that he would do the same thing to us if he had a chance. If we act inhumanly in wartime, we believe that the enemy is so inhuman and evil that our actions are justified. Projection therefore justifies our acts, lets us preserve our self-image as decent, rational men, and keeps us from realizing what we are really like.

Rationalization. Rationalization accomplishes the same thing in a slightly different way. Instead of projecting our feelings onto other people we give rational justifications for our actions and ignore their real causes. These justifications preserve our self-images and protect us from the anxiety we would feel if we knew why we did things.

141

We saw many examples of rationalization in Chapter 1. All of our anxious executives gave reasonable—but incorrect—justifications for their behavior. The tough guy was domineering, not because he felt anxious about people but "to get production." The conformist followed all the rules, not to avoid decisions and uncertainty but "to prevent chaos." The gypsy changed jobs "to get ahead." Even the drinker said that drinking made him "think better." And, as will be described in Chapter 9, rationalizations are a basic part of many executives' attitudes.

Isolation. We all have attitudes which are inconsistent with each other or do things that conflict with our own values. Because to recognize these conflicts and inconsistencies would make us anxious, we keep them isolated from each other. We keep each idea or action in its own compartment and remain unaware of any conflict between them.

The attitudes of many people toward traffic laws, income taxes, and student demonstrators provide an unusually clear example of isolation. Many people have declared that we should crack down on student demonstrators and preserve law and order. But the same people, in the same conversations, have admitted—or even boasted —that they cheat on their income tax (a felony), regularly drive too fast (a misdemeanor which kills thousands of people every year), or "fix" traffic tickets (a felony). These people were completely unaware of any contradiction between their concern for law and order and their own behavior. Although this particular contradiction is very common and obvious, we all have similar contradictions between our attitudes and behaviors, and we all try not to recognize them.

Flight. We may also try to run away from anxiety. The gypsy does this regularly, and most of us do it occasionally. We take long walks or long drives to relax, go on business trips and vacations when pressures are too heavy, or change jobs when we don't enjoy our work.

If the threatening situation really is a cause of our problems, running away can be very realistic and useful. If our problems are within us, as they frequently are, running away won't solve anything. It will only distract our attention and temporarily relieve our anxiety.

142

Fantasy. We can also escape from unpleasant realities, threats, and anxieties by psychological flight—daydreaming, identifying with people on television, reading novels, and so on. Almost everyone does these things, even though some people can't remember dreaming at night (because they repress their dreams).

In small amounts, fantasy is very useful. It relaxes us, lets us try out different kinds of roles, and indirectly satisfies our frustrated desires. We may be frustrated and unsuccessful in real life, but in our dreams we can satisfy all our desires: We can be the boss, have our own business, rule the United States, be a great lover, or inherit a million dollars.

Unfortunately, some people find that their fantasies are more satisfying than reality and become very dependent on them. A few retreat entirely into their fantasy worlds and shut out reality; they think they are Napoleon, or George Washington, or a secret agent, and are literally unable to cope with reality.

These are just the most extreme and obvious cases of excessive use of fantasy, and many superficially normal people depend very heavily on their fantasies. They know who they are, and they can do their jobs; but they derive most of their satisfaction from their daydreams, detective stories, sports, television shows, and similar pleasures. They may read several mystery stories a week, or watch television five hours a day, or daydream a great deal, or become extremely concerned about the local football team. Their preoccupation with these activities suggests that they are not satisfied with their lives and want to avoid reality.

Compensation. Compensation is one of the healthiest defense mechanisms. It doesn't merely help us avoid anxiety; it also rechannels our efforts into more profitable activities and can cause some very significant accomplishments. We compensate when we offset failure or inferiority in some areas with success in other areas. This success can make us less aware of our own inadequacies and build a firmer sense of our own value.

Many very successful executives—for example—have reached the top because they had to overcome feelings of personal and social inadequacy by being successful in business. Some of them felt inferior and anxious because they were short, or poor athletes, or unpopular. They made up for these "weaknesses" by working

143

hard. Their hard work and business success have made them more comfortable and have also contributed to our society.

Like all defense mechanisms, however, compensation can be harmful if it is overdone. Some excessively ambitious executives are trying to compensate for their feelings of inadequacy but alienate people and ruin their careers by being too ambitious and ruthless. All braggarts are compensating for their own feelings of inferiority, and their boasting causes more problems than it solves. Other executives are so concerned with building their egos that they do only those things they can do very well, and they live narrow, impoverished lives.

A few people feel so inferior that no amount of success can satisfy them. Many of the great conquerors have been in this category. Napoleon and Stalin were very short men, and both were very sensitive about it; in fact, Stalin always stood on a box when he reviewed parades, so that he would look taller than the men next to him. Julius Caesar was epileptic; Hitler was said to be impotent and epileptic. Although no corporation executive demonstrates as great a need for power and success as these dictators, many "little Hitlers" in industry compensate for their own sense of inferiority.

Identification. We can also make up for our feelings of inadequacy, weakness, aloneness, and uncertainty by identifying ourselves with certain people, groups, and institutions. America's accomplishments and strength make us feel proud and strong; our corporation's strength and prestige build our own confidence and prestige; our bosses and colleagues provide a model for our behavior and help us to know what to do.

Our identifications provide some security, but this security can be rather costly. They can help us escape from the anxiety of aloneness, weakness, and uncertainty, but they add to our burden of anonymous authority and take away some of our freedom and uniqueness. Because we identify with groups which have incompatible standards, our identifications can also create some very uncomfortable conflicts.

We can't satisfy both sets of standards; so anything we do is wrong. We may have to choose between our companies and our countries, or between our professional and religious ethics. These choices can be very painful, generate a great deal of anxiety, and make us rely on still other defense mechanisms. We may rationalize that what is good for the company is ultimately good for the country and ignore short-term conflicts, or isolate our business and religious ethics and follow one set of ethics during the week and the other on Sunday.

Sublimation. Sometimes we express our unacceptable feelings and desires in indirect and socially acceptable ways. This lets us drain off some of the tension produced by these frustrated desires but does not cause the guilt and anxiety that we would feel if we expressed them more directly. We would feel guilty if we yielded to our hostile impulses and hurt someone seriously, but we don't feel guilty about playing football and watching boxing matches and violent television shows.

But the term "sublimation" usually refers to sexual desires. Reading or talking about sex, writing poetry, and going to sexy movies are rather obvious examples of sublimation. They let us express our sexual desires without causing the guilt we would feel if we had extramarital affairs.

Displaced aggression. Displaced aggression is a very common defense mechanism that is rather similar to sublimation. We displace aggression when we are openly hostile but attack people who haven't hurt us. The boss shouts at us; we shout at our wives; and they shout at the children. We choose safe or convenient targets for our feelings because expressing them to the real targets may lead to punishment, either from the person we attack or from our own conscience.

Racial prejudice is the most obvious example of displaced aggression. Germany had a long tradition of anti-Semitism, but the excesses of the Nazi era were partially caused by the frustrations and restrictions of the Nazi regime. Because people were frustrated and angry but were afraid to attack the Nazis, they attacked the Jews. Furthermore, racial prejudice is generally strongest among the poorest and most frustrated members of any society, and it rises during stressful periods. One classic study even found that when cotton prices fell and economic conditions worsened, Southern whites took out their frustrations by lynching more Negroes.

We don't have to look at social trends or race prejudice to recognize displaced aggression. It is all around us. When the boss puts pressure on us, we may be hard on our subordinates or shout at our children. The unions, government, Democrats, foreign aid, and the Supreme Court are very common targets for displaced aggression, and we grow more angry with them when other things are bothering us. For certain people (union leaders, students, some racial minorities), big business, executive salaries, and "excessive" profits are convenient targets for their own aggressions.

Displaced aggression can be very useful because it lets us drain off some of our tensions, but it can create more tensions than it relieves. The targets for displaced aggression strike back or displace their own aggressions, and the tension level can rise very rapidly.

Our riot-torn cities are painful examples of this escalation. Negroes have been the targets of our aggressions for centuries, and now they are openly attacking the police—partly because of real police abuses, partly because the police are convenient targets and symbols of white society. These attacks frighten us, and we in turn attack the government and courts for not being tough enough, and many people are even expressing greater racial prejudice. As the tensions increase, gun sales zoom, lines of communication break down, and our society is in grave danger of breaking apart.

Costs and Benefits

Although their costs far exceed their benefits, defense mechanisms do serve a very useful purpose. They temporarily reduce our anxiety and tensions, make us feel more comfortable, and help us to work on our other problems. Without them we would feel the full impact of all our anxieties and would be incapacitated part of the time. Our anxieties about family, sex, or personal problems would interfere with our work and might even cost us our jobs, and losing our jobs would certainly not solve our personal, family, or sexual problems. But our defenses help us to ride out the storms and hold down our jobs.

We do pay a high price for this stability. As shown in Chapter 7, our defenses are essentially self-defeating; they give us temporary relief but aggravate our problems and may ultimately make us feel even more anxious. Defensiveness therefore feeds on itself. Un-

146

derlying problems are not solved; new problems develop; the person becomes more dependent on his defenses; and more and more of his energy is devoted to self-deception and defenses against anxiety. In a few cases, a man's defenses seriously interfere with his life, family, and career. These men are called "neurotics"—an unfortunate and misused term but one which we should clearly understand.

NEUROSES

The word "neurotic" has been overused and misused in our psychologically oriented age. Some people use it in an abusive sense to describe people whom they don't like, and most people don't really understand what the word means.

Most neurotics are not easily recognized as such; they are not crazy, disorganized, confused, paranoid, or violent. They are similar to normal people, use the same sorts of defense mechanisms, and differ only in the *amount* that they use them and the *effects* their defenses have on themselves. They rely more heavily on their defenses, and their defenses have a greater impact on them. They are somewhat more anxious than other people, more dependent on their defenses, and less able to enjoy life. Some neuroses interfere with men's careers, but others actually help men to become successful executives.

Obsessive-compulsive neurotics. The man who cares only about getting ahead, who is willing to sacrifice everything for success, is a compulsive neurotic. His neurosis may make him and his family unhappy, but it can certainly help his career.

Compulsions and obsessions can occur independently of each other, but they often go together. An obsession is a thought that keeps coming into the mind and can't be forgotten or ignored. We have all had some mild obsessions—silly songs that lodge obstinately in our minds, for example, or excessive and repeated worry about not having turned off the gas before we left home to go on vacation. The obsessive neurotic, however, has much more disturbing thoughts, and they are with him most of the time. He may worry all the time about automobile accidents, nuclear war, falling profits, or the

147

possible infidelity of his wife; these thoughts make him very uncomfortable and interfere with his work and family.

Many obsessive people also behave compulsively. They repeatedly do strange or illogical things which have little or no value. Some people are very careful not to step on cracks in the sidewalk, wash their hands frequently, put their clothes on in exactly the same order every morning, or make sure that the papers on their desks and the furniture in their offices are in exactly the right places.

Both obsessions and compulsions are partial—but expensive—solutions to the problem of anxiety. They distract a person's attention from his real problems and anxiety and give him something else to worry about. His irrelevant thoughts keep him from thinking about his real problems, and he is so busy avoiding cracks in the sidewalk, keeping his desk and office neat, or making money that he doesn't have the time or energy to think about himself or his problems. But neither does he have the time or energy to enjoy life.

Obsessions and compulsions are clear illustrations of the difference between normal and neurotic defensiveness. All of us occasionally use obsessions and compulsions to distract our attention from our problems, but neurotics use them so much that they don't have enough energy left over to enjoy life. Their defenses become the centers of their lives and consume most of their time and energy.

Phobias. Phobias—irrational fears—are another example of the price of the neuroses. We all have some fears that are out of proportion to the real dangers we face, but we can live with these fears. We may be afraid of spiders, perhaps, or dislike air travel; but we don't inspect every room for spiders, and we will take a plane trip if we must.

But some people let their irrational fears dominate their lives. A few executives hurt their careers by absolutely refusing to travel by air, even though flying is much safer than driving a car. Others become extremely uncomfortable and may even panic when they are in a small room or a high place.

These phobias serve approximately the same purpose as obsessions and compulsions and are another solution to the problem of anxiety. They distract a person from his real problems and anxieties and let him displace all his fears onto a few objects. Instead of being anxious about many things that he can't escape (his impulses, ca-

148

reer, and abilities), he can be afraid of one or two things (airplanes or small rooms) that he can avoid. In this way, a man's phobias can actually help him live with himself. However, if he has to come in contact with these things regularly, if he must travel by air or work in a small office or ride in elevators, his phobias can be very costly.

Hysteria, hypochondria, and chronic exhaustion. In these neuroses, psychological problems cause physical symptoms. Hypochondriacs are extremely concerned with their health and go from doctor to doctor describing their symptoms. A person with hysteria has actual physical symptoms—blindness, paralysis, or deafness—for which there is no organic basis. Chronically exhausted persons are always tired and may suffer from vague pains or a ringing in the ears. All three neuroses serve the same general purpose as obsessions, compulsions, and phobias: to distract a person's attention from what is really bothering him. And, as will be described in Chapter 11, they may also express his feelings and get him some sympathy and attention.

Anxiety neurosis. Some neurotics don't focus their anxieties. Instead of developing phobias, compulsions, or physical symptoms, they feel the full impact of their own anxieties. Some research suggests that this type of neurosis may be more common among executives than in the general public, and we have all met executives who had anxiety neuroses. Some feel anxious ("nervous") all the time, and others experience occasional but severe anxiety attacks. Both types feel very uncomfortable, and their anxieties are so strong that they interfere with their lives and work.

PSYCHOSES

As previously stated, neurotics are not easily recognized, and their differences from normal people exist only in the degree to which they use their defenses and in the effects their defenses have on themselves. They are more anxious and depend more on their defenses; and their defenses interfere more with their lives. Psychotics ("insane people"), on the other hand, can usually be recognized quite easily, and their defenses completely dominate their lives.

Normal people and neurotics are usually aware of themselves, realize that some of their behavior is abnormal, and can usually take care of themselves. Psychotics generally do not realize that their behavior is abnormal, no matter how bizarre it may be, and usually cannot take care of themselves.

Many psychotics have hallucinations (see visions or hear voices) or delusions (believe that they are Napoleon or that people are persecuting them). Some are so depressed that they don't even move and have to be fed intravenously. Others are so excitable and restless that they sing for hours, run around wildly, and make erratic and uncontrolled gestures. Because psychotic symptoms are so easy to identify and are extremely rare among executives, they will not be further discussed here. They are also solutions to the problem of anxiety but rare and extraordinarily expensive ones.

9

How Defensive Attitudes
Contribute to Anxiety

M OST PEOPLE IGNORE THE CAUSES OF ATTITUDES AND ACCEPT THE
attitudes themselves as the simple result of man's past experience, his learned way of looking at the world. Attitudes are
certainly learned, but the learning process is much more complicated
than most people believe, and anxiety often plays a role in them.
Douglas McGregor's famous but oversimplified analysis of attitudes toward leadership illustrates the complexity of this process.

McGregor's description of Theory X and Theory Y is probably
the most widely read passage in the literature of industrial psychology, and hundreds of articles have referred to it. He claimed that
many supervisory practices are based on implicit assumptions about
men: that they are lazy, want nothing but money, shirk responsibility, and have to be controlled. He then assumed that he could
change these attitudes by citing scientific evidence about human
nature and showing that these attitudes cause some severe management problems. However, although many people have read his books
and articles, relatively few of them have changed their attitudes.
And, as countless observers have deplored, most executives still
accept Theory X even thought they may pay lip service to Theory Y.

McGregor's work has not had much impact because he did not
understand the causal relationship between attitudes and evidence

and he did not realize that unaided facts and logic will not change attitudes. He assumed that Theory X was simply a mistake—that executives had tried to understand human nature but had misunderstood it. He also assumed that this misunderstanding caused them to use certain supervisory methods. The relationship is not so simple. Attitudes can be learned in a variety of ways, and they can cause behavior. Behavior can also cause attitudes, and the cause and effect relationship is usually circular.

One man may be domineering because he believes that people have to be controlled; but another can believe that they have to be controlled because he is domineering. He may build his ego by dominating them, or he may simply enjoy exerting power; but his behavior is not *caused* by his beliefs. His beliefs are rationalizations which keep him from recognizing his own motives; he thinks he dominates people because he has to, not because he wants to. His attitude may also keep him from feeling guilty about treating people badly: He is not frustrating their needs to achieve and to relate to other people, because they don't have these needs; they just want money. That is, he treats people in an inhuman way, but feels more comfortable because he believes that they are subhuman.

This process can be observed more clearly in racial prejudice. People don't dislike Negroes and discriminate against them because they think Negroes are inferior. They rationalize that Negroes are inferior simply because they dislike and discriminate against Negroes. They feel and act first and think afterward. Their beliefs justify their feelings and actions and are caused by them, not by the facts. The facts certainly don't justify their actions and feelings, but bigots ignore most facts and select the ones that fit their prejudice. They overlook Negro achievements, deny or distort scientific research, and love to cite statistics on crime and illegitimacy rates. They can't accept evidence against their belief because their beliefs justify their irrational and immoral feelings and actions.

Theory X serves the same purpose for some executives: It justifies their actions and helps them preserve their images of rationality, morality, and efficiency. Attempts to change their beliefs by citing evidence have usually been unsuccessful and will continue to fail as long as some executives want to deceive themselves about their own motives.

In other words, some attitudes develop and persist because they satisfy people's needs, and one important need is to reduce anxiety. Attitudes can do this by justifying irrational and immoral actions, distracting our attention from ourselves and our problems, avoiding uncomfortable situations, eliminating uncertainty, and so on. Like other defenses, they persist as long as they reduce anxiety, and they are not greatly affected by facts, logic, or persuasion. However, defensive attitudes have the same faults as other defenses: They give temporary relief but don't solve the problem, and they can even cause greater anxiety. This process is encountered several times in the present book; many of the problems listed in Chapters 3, 4, 5, and 6 were caused or aggravated by defensive attitudes.

Although the defensive nature of some attitudes cannot be ignored, it would be equally incorrect to assume that all attitudes are defensive or partially defensive. Attitudes are learned for a wide variety of reasons and satisfy many needs besides the need of reducing anxiety. They can be learned by simple social reward: People are rewarded for having a particular attitude—toward hard work, for example. They may be learned by association with pleasant and unpleasant experiences: Positive attitudes toward motherhood, for example, develop partly because mothers are associated with feeding and comfort. Attitudes express important underlying values: attitudes toward the flag, for example, are related to basic feelings about the country and patriotism. People can therefore have the same attitude but for very different reasons. One man may discriminate against Negroes because his associates insist on it; another, because they are convenient scapegoats for his aggressions; a third, because of unpleasant experiences with them; a fourth, because he fears any changes in the status quo; and a fifth, because he needs to have someone beneath him in the pecking order. We therefore cannot assume that a man's attitude is a defense for him just because it is a defense for other people.

The process is complicated still further because very few human feelings or actions are caused by only one motive. Most attitudes satisfy more than one need and are learned from many experiences over long periods of time. Autocratic attitudes toward supervision can therefore be a rationalization, *and* a response to organizational pressures, *and* an attempt to build status, *and* a sincere belief based on past experiences.

Because the purpose here is a limited one, we shall devote most of our attention to anxiety and spend relatively little time on the other factors even though they may be much more important than anxiety. We shall also simplify our analysis by focusing on just a few attitudes (toward personal success, profits and production, feelings, order, power, and personal relations). These attitudes are very important, and most of them form the core of the executive culture and are consistent with all of its norms and values. A man has little chance of becoming an executive if he does not share these attitudes.

With one exception (personal relations) these attitudes are also part of the value system of the entire American middle class. Executives generally feel more strongly than others about them, but most middle-class Americans share them.

This sharing reinforces the attitudes. We regard them as proper and reward other people for having them. The attitudes also reinforce each other. Belief in ambition and personal success is consistent with the emphasis on rationality and supports the desire for profits and productivity. This combination of social and mutual reinforcements makes these attitudes very hard to change. A person can't change any one of them without creating doubts about the others, and his associates even punish attempts to question these attitudes.

This interrelationship and social reinforcement also increase their effectiveness as defenses. Because his attitudes agree with each other and those of other people, a man doesn't have to doubt his reason for having them, and they can do a better job of protecting him from anxiety.

One important question remains unanswered: Do they have these attitudes because they are executives, or do they become executives because they have these attitudes? Research indicates that both processes are important: People with certain attitudes are more likely to become executives, and executive life reinforces these attitudes. College students who plan to enter the business world have similar though weaker attitudes than executives; this similarity

154

increases, and their attitudes become stronger, after they have worked for a while. Now that we have explored some of the basic issues, let us discuss some of the attitudes and see how they are related to anxiety.

PERSONAL SUCCESS

Executives are generally very concerned with personal success and define it in terms of income and position. They may also want to contribute to society, to express themselves, and to have warm personal relations, but these other goals are generally less important to them than money and status. These attitudes are a basic part of our free enterprise system and an important contributor to it. We pride ourselves on our personal and economic freedom and teach our children to want success, money, and status.

Most Americans share these attitudes, but executives feel more strongly about them. They value money and status more, and other goals less, than the general population. We are, of course, fortunate that so many executives have these attitudes which keep them working and our economy moving. Although these attitudes further their careers, some executives feel too strongly; they are obsessed with money and status, and this obsession is partially a defense. All obsessions are defenses, and an obsessive desire for success relieves anxiety by distracting a person's attention from his psychological problems and compensating for his feelings of inadequacy. The man who is obsessed with success, who devotes most of his energy to getting ahead, who makes extreme sacrifices to advance his career, is probably running away from his own feelings and trying to prove that he is a good man—because he doesn't believe it himself.

Other kinds of success might build his ego, but there is something concrete and reassuring about money and status. A man can't be certain about how people feel about him or how much he is contributing to society, but he knows how much money he is paid and where he stands in the corporate pyramid. Unquestionably, $30,000 a year is more than $25,000; unquestionably, a vice president is higher than his assistants.

Although we can see the defensive nature of an attitude most clearly when it is an obsession, less extreme attitudes toward success may also be partially caused by anxiety: A man may want money and status because they are pleasant things to have, but also because they distract his attention from his problems, define who he is, and prove that he is a good man. Since people are usually touchy about their defenses, we can tell approximately how defensive a particular executive's attitude is toward success by noting how he feels about status symbols. The man who cares a great deal about the size of his desk or the number of pens in his desk set is generally—but not always—more defensive than the person who doesn't care very much about these symbols. He is less sure of himself and needs constant reminders that he is a good man.

Whether the executive attitude toward money and status is defensive or not, it has some desirable and some undesirable consequences. Even if it is a defense, this attitude causes men to work harder and therefore contributes to our organizations and economic system. In fact, the national economy probably would not be so healthy if most executives did not have this attitude. They would not be willing to work so hard or to stand the pressure after they had earned enough money to live comfortably.

Although the attitude is very good for the economy, it can be very hard on the executive even if it is not a defense. A great deal of the pressure discussed in earlier chapters comes from the system, but at least as much originates in the executive himself, in his own attitudes and drives. And the drive that exerts the most pressure, the one that affects most of the problems we have analyzed, is this drive for success, this insatiable hunger for money and status.

PROFITS AND PRODUCTION

Attitudes toward profits and production are closely related to this drive for success, and they are also part of the American economic system and values. We respect people with money and position, but we expect men to earn their way, to produce something. We do respect people with inherited wealth, but they have relatively less status here than they have in most other countries; in fact, many of them work to increase their status. Attitudes toward profits and productivity are therefore learned as part of a regular middle-class education; most Americans share them; and they are important contributors to our system. But executives clearly care more about them than other groups do. Their primary job is to preserve and increase profits, and they could not do their jobs without these attitudes. However, even though they are shared by most Americans and are necessary for their jobs, these attitudes also act as defenses for some executives.

These attitudes divert attention from the executives themselves and their relations with other people, because they refer to extrinsics —to what men do or make, not what they are or what they feel about each other. They replace feelings about our own or other people's worth with an external measure: A man is worth the amount he produces, the profits he makes for the firm, and the money he is paid. This attitude, therefore, keeps people from confronting each other on a human level and helps them avoid difficult problems about who they are and how they value each other.

Because questions of identity and personal value can create a great deal of anxiety, these attitudes are an important part of some executives' defense systems. We can often tell how defensive a man's attitude is by seeing how rigidly he adheres to it. If he usually values profits and production but can also see the value of other goals, his attitude is probably a rational response to the demands of his job.

If, on the other hand, he feels that "profits" and "production" are sacred words, that they are the only goals for which a business or a businessman should strive, that men's satisfaction and dignity should always be sacrificed for them, his attitudes have probably helped reduce his anxiety. They are, in effect, an obsession, and—as previously noted—all obsessions are defensive.

This attitude is, of course, a crucial one for our society; we need it to keep our economy going, whether it is a defense or not. Our system is based on profits and production, and we will be in serious trouble if executives ever lose interest in them. Again we see that executives pay a high price for the general welfare. They work for profits, but they may sometimes wonder if this is what they really want, whether they are working for their own goals or for the goals someone else has imposed on them. Because they have so much responsibility for profits and production, they find themselves in some unpleasant conflicts. They want to be friendly with people but may have to keep the pressure on to maintain production, or they may have to sacrifice a friendship or a moral principle for profits. Like the drive for success, this attitude toward profits and production can cause a great deal of anxiety, whether it is a defense or not.

DENIAL OF FEELINGS

Most Americans try to control their emotions, but executives generally work harder at it. Their entire culture emphasizes rationality and denies or suppresses feelings. They are not supposed to act emotionally or discuss their feelings, and an executive who violates these rules will almost always be criticized or prevented from doing it again by his associates, unless he happens to be the boss.

In one company, in fact, Chris Argyris found that executives simply refused to permit emotions to be considered, even when they were obviously present and active. If a deep disagreement or emotional outburst occurred in a meeting, they would stop the meeting, or insist that the people discuss the facts, or use other methods to transform emotions into seemingly rational, intellectual problems.*

This tendency can contribute to organizational efficiency by keeping discussion focused on the facts and preventing emotions from getting out of hand. However, as so many researchers have pointed out, it frequently has exactly the opposite effect: Emotions are denied and suppressed, but they don't go away; and they can cause poor cooperation, disagreement over "facts," overlong meetings, inadequate communication, and ineffective decisions. These researchers have therefore suggested that the undesirable effects of emotions can be managed most effectively by discussing them openly.

Because many executives have read the analyses and suggestions of these researchers but have not changed their own attitudes or the unwritten rules of their organizations, we may conclude that these attitudes and rules do not exist solely to maximize efficiency,

* Chris Argyris, *Interpersonal Competence and Organizational Effectiveness*, Irwin, Homewood, Illinois, 1962.

158

production, and profits. They serve other needs, and one of these needs is to reduce anxiety. Denying feelings can be an individual defense mechanism, and the rules against expressing or discussing feelings are sometimes a group or cultural defense mechanism, an unwritten agreement to bury frightening thoughts and feelings.

This interpretation is supported by a very common occurrence in executive groups, especially groups led by psychologists to increase openness toward feelings (T-groups): Negative feelings are almost invariably discussed before positive ones. People are much more willing to say what and whom they dislike or resent than they are to express affection or emotional support.

Although a rational analysis would suggest that positive feelings are more useful to the group than negative ones, they are not expressed very often or very directly, and to express them even indirectly can make everyone embarrassed and uncomfortable. Their discomfort and reluctance to express positive feelings suggest how isolated, vulnerable, and defensive executives are about their own feelings and their relations with each other. They are afraid to express affection because they are not sure how it will be received, and they don't want to risk rejection. If affection is expressed, the person who receives it is often embarrassed and does not know how to respond (but everyone knows how to respond to hostility). Executives therefore try to avoid all show of feelings or express only the negative ones.

The causal relationship here is completely circular: They don't express feelings because they are afraid of them, and they are afraid of their feelings because they are not used to dealing with them. They have been taught from childhood that men should be rational and unemotional, and the executive culture reinforces these attitudes and prevents men from exploring or understanding their own feelings or openly dealing with the feelings they have about each other. They therefore do not know how to deal with their feelings; they distrust them, see the unemotional facades of their associates, conclude that they themselves are more emotional than their associates, and reject their own emotions as undesirable. The distrust, rejection, and inability to handle feelings increase the pressures to deny them and continue the cycle.

Although this attitude toward feelings has some undesirable

effects, we should not minimize its value to individuals, organizations, and our economy. We psychologists often assume that everyone wants the same things we want, and that open expression of feelings would benefit everyone. These assumptions are correct in some situations, but many individuals and organizations prefer to avoid feelings, and this preference may be a very reasonable one. Denying feelings may lead to more cooperation, superficial personal relations, alienation, and indirect expression of conflicts; but it can also lead to rapid, intelligent decision making, efficient operations, unity of command, and comfortable (though distant) personal relations. Thus, even if this attitude is a defense, it is not necessarily a destructive one and may sometimes be quite valuable. However, as with all defenses, excessive use ultimately leads to anxiety and other problems; and this attitude toward feelings is clearly carried too far in many executive groups.

POWER

Executives generally have strong power drives; they place a high value on power and want a good deal of it for themselves. This attitude is, of course, one of the reasons they become executives and want to move up in the pyramid. Executives have a great deal of power over resources and other people, and the higher they go, the more they have. High positions also provide more money and status, but some executives have been willing to sacrifice one or both for greater power. Robert McNamara, Sol Linowitz, Charles Percy, and many other successful executives have given up six-figure incomes and stock options to serve in the government, but they were compensated with both status and power. Many other executives have taken cuts in salary in return for very powerful positions, but sometimes they have actually lost status. They were formerly big men in their firm and community, but have since become relatively anonymous—though powerful—officials in Washington, New York, and other major cities.

The extent and nature of executives' attitudes toward power have been clarified by a very common research finding. Executives at all levels think that their supervisors should give them more independence and let them exert more influence upward, but believe that their subordinates have too much independence and power over them. That is, they want more power over themselves, their subordinates, and their superiors.

This attitude is, of course, a central part of the executive role. An executive without power is useless, and the quest for power is partially caused by the desire for performance, production, profits, and personal success. An executive needs many kinds of power to do his job: control of resources, expertise, authority, friends in the right places, and so on. Without these things he can't reach any of his goals, but he can fulfill his responsibilities and advance his career if he has enough power.

However, although power helps men reach these goals, power seeking can also conflict with other individual and organizational goals. Many organizations and careers have been ruined by political conflicts; unprofitable mergers have been made because some executives were more interested in their power and empires than profits; individual units and empires often grow at the expense of overall organizational effectiveness. We can see this process most clearly in government bodies such as the Department of Agriculture, which has grown steadily as the number of farmers has declined; but it occurs in most organizations. Men build their organizations because they want more power, even if this power cuts down profits or overall organizational effectiveness.

We may say, then, that executives need power to do their jobs and advance their careers but may also want it for other reasons, which include the psychological satisfaction of having it and its value as a defense against anxiety. In cases where it serves as a defense, it provides the same sort of distraction and compensation as money and status and can also increase security against real attacks or feelings of helplessness. It can give a man something to think about and work for, build up his ego, and make him feel more secure.

However, objective power may not be a very effective defense against anxiety because it may not provide adequate protection against attacks or anticipations of attacks. We can see this weakness at several levels: In international relations the leaders and citizens of the great powers spend billions for weapons but don't feel nearly as secure against attack as people in Switzerland or Sweden, countries which are essentially defenseless. In corporations a vice president has more power than a department head, but he may also be a better target. And, if the real problem is inside a man, if he needs power to counter his own feelings of insecurity and inadequacy, he may be much more aware of his vulnerability and attractiveness as a target than he is of his real power. He may therefore become more defensive as his power increases.

Again, the political realm offers the best examples of defensiveness. Stalin, for instance, destroyed his army and almost lost World War II because he was so afraid of plots against him.

Executives' attitudes toward power cannot have such dramatic effects, but as Sewell Avery so clearly demonstrated, these attitudes can force out good men and retard the growth of an organization. They can also harm an organization or a career in many ways—by causing strikes and other union-management problems, alienating superiors, or irritating and threatening colleagues. If a man's attitude toward power is a defense, it may not be an effective one and may even trap him in a vicious cycle.

ORDERLINESS AND THE EXECUTIVE

The attitudes previously discussed are found in nearly all executives and are a basic part of the executive culture. Many executives, especially those who have backgrounds in engineering, accounting, and law, feel very strongly about order, but these attitudes are not quite as common as the other four.

Order is an important part of the executive role. Executives must create and maintain order and are constantly fighting uncertainty and unpredictability. They have to hold the organization together, keep it moving in the right direction, and must constantly resist the pressures which will destroy it or divert it from its goals. They therefore devote a great deal of their time to developing policies and procedures which will create and preserve order.

This problem is particularly acute in our rapidly changing society. Executives cannot afford to fall behind their competition, but they must still preserve order and continuity. Most executives are therefore more willing to make changes in technology and products than in policies and procedures, and nearly all executives resist very rapid or extreme changes in any area.

Although this attitude helps them fulfill their responsibilities, it

162

is not restricted to jobs. Many executives like order in everything, resist most changes, and feel uncomfortable with uncertainties and deviations from orderly principles.

They are generally political and economic conservatives who like our society the way it is and resist changes in it. They also dislike the people who are trying to change it, and they have no respect at all for anyone who violates its rules. Radicals, do-gooders, and social critics irritate them, and they cannot tolerate demonstrators. Part of their reaction to demonstrators is caused by their resistance to social change; but, as their comments make very clear, they are very disturbed by the fact that some demonstrators wear beards, don't bathe regularly, and generally violate our laws and rules.

Their interest in preserving order is closely related to other executive attitudes. Power can be used to preserve order, control, and predictability; and disorder threatens profits, production, and efficiency. One reason for denying and suppressing feelings is that they are so ambiguous and cause so much confusion and unpredictability.

Although their attitude toward order helps our organizations and society to function and survive, it also serves as a defense for some executives. These people want order so that they can do their jobs well, but they care so much and become so emotional about even minor disorders that we can see the defensive nature of their attitudes. A few executives are literally obsessed with order and cannot tolerate disorders in any form, however trivial. They want their homes orderly, their children restrained, their meals served on time, their desks neat, their subordinates deferential, their mail opened, their meetings orderly. Any deviation from the rules, even an insignificant one, can make them very angry and upset.

Although their visible reaction is usually anger, these executives are really afraid of disorder. They control their feelings by controlling their behavior and the world around them, and any deviation in established order—whether it be a late memo, a teachers' strike, or a noisy child—reminds them of how weak their control really is, how little control they have over the world, and how easily their anxiety can break through their defenses.

This defense, even its extreme forms, actually helps some executives' careers and their organizations. They work on certain kinds of accounting, engineering, or legal problems where details are very important and an extreme concern for order is a decided asset. But other executives harm their careers and organizations by stifling dissent, resisting necessary changes, or simply annoying other people with their fussiness.

The fact that the same attitudes can be an asset or a liability underscores the importance of a man's understanding of his own defenses. Defenses are very hard to change, and it is much more reasonable to choose a career that matches one's defenses and personality than it is to try to change defenses and personality to fit a particular career. This issue will be discussed at some length in the final chapter of this book.

PERSONAL RELATIONS

On all the other issues, the rules in the executive culture are rather explicit and consistent: Profits are good; disorder is bad; people should be ambitious; and so on. But the rules on personal relations are unclear and contradictory; there is much greater disagreement between executives; and many executives are unsure of their own attitudes. There is, however, a general trend.

Executives tend to regard personal relations as less important than profits, production, efficiency, and success. They are generally expected to put their organizations and careers ahead of friendship and avoid being too close to subordinates, and most of them follow these rules. If a conflict arises between friendship and job, they will usually favor the job. But this norm is much less consistent and is violated more often than the norms for profits, production, feelings, or order. Some executives drop their friends as they move up, or are willing to discipline friends for poor performance, or will associate with people whom they dislike to help their careers; but others won't, and nearly all executives are a bit unsure of the morality of this attitude.

This ambiguity is partly caused by a clash between the executive and general middle-class cultures. On the other issues there was very little conflict between the two cultures. Most middle-class Americans value profits, production, efficiency, rationality, and order —although not quite as much as executives do. However, the middle class generally values friendship and personal relations and looks down on manipulation, exploitation, politics, and insincerity, but most organizations expect their executives to put their jobs and careers ahead of their friendships. Furthermore, this conflict is increased by executives' basic human needs. All human beings need warm personal relations, but executives face powerful organizational pressures to force them to place their careers ahead of their friendships—in some cases, even ahead of their marriages.

Executives therefore find themselves in some painful conflicts and have problems in developing a consistent and comfortable attitude toward personal relations. Some executives try to avoid this conflict by being impersonal, others by obtaining their satisfaction from their friends and families and minimizing the demands of their organizations and careers; but most executives try to compromise, and they feel uncomfortable when compromises become impossible. They like a man but have to fire him; or they enjoy their friends but are offered promotion in another city; or they must mix with people they dislike if they are to do their jobs or advance their careers.

In these situations, they can't compromise. They have to take some action, and most executives favor their careers. They may be reluctant to do so; they may feel guilty about yielding to the organization; but when the chips are down, these executives usually show that they value their careers more than their friendships, perhaps even more than their marriages.

Although this attitude is a rather reasonable response to the severe pressures that they receive from their organizations, it can also be both an effect and a cause of anxiety. An attitude of impersonality and a belief that job and career are more important than warm personal relationships help executives to avoid becoming involved with each other. If they are not involved, they are not vulnerable; they can't be hurt or rejected, because they have so little invested in each other.

Although this attitude advances their careers and protects executives from anxiety and rejection, it sometimes costs more than it is worth. They may pay too high a price for successful careers or gain less security than they bargained for. The net result is often loneliness, rootlessness, insecurity, and even greater anxiety.

10

Drinking
and the Executive

EVERYONE KNOWS THAT DRINKING RELIEVES ANXIETY. IT NUMBS PART of our brains and relaxes our bodies. It lowers our inhibitions and lets us drain off tension by doing and saying things that we usually keep inside ourselves. It gratifies our oral needs and gives us the same kind of relief as a baby's thumb sucking and an adult's smoking or nail biting.

Alcohol also acts as a "social lubricant" and helps us to overcome our anxieties about relating to each other. It lets us relax with each other and helps create the appearance of friendliness and sociability. And, if a person doesn't want to drink, the anxiety of other people can cause some very severe pressures. The others insist that he take a drink "to be sociable," or call him a "bad sport," or regard him as a sissy.

The popularity of drinking is one of the clearest illustrations of a point that we have made many times: Men are not rational in the classical sense of the word. A classically rational man evaluates the long-term costs and benefits of his actions and chooses the ones that are most beneficial. But drinking is very popular, although it provides very temporary relief at rather severe long-term costs. It provides physical relaxation, oral gratification, and social acceptance, but—among its several disadvantages—it adds pounds that we don't want and causes some people to cut down on more necessary foods to save calories. It makes us say and do things that we later regret. It gives us hangovers. Chronic heavy drinking ruins health, family life, and careers for some people. We all know these things, and many of us have said that we would cut down or stop drinking, but we don't do it. We want or need its satisfaction and relief and are willing to pay for it.

EXECUTIVE DRINKING

Many factors besides anxiety are related to drinking: Men drink more than women; some nationalities drink more than others; some children learn temperance from their parents; others learn moderation; and a few learn drunkenness.

Because of these other factors, we must be very cautious in drawing conclusions about people's anxiety from their drinking behavior. We can't say that a particular man is more anxious than his wife because he drinks more than she does, or compare the effects of drinking on an Italian as opposed to an Englishman. But, if we discount these unmeasurable other factors, drinking can tell us a great deal about how anxious people are and what they feel anxious about. Generally, the more anxious a person is the more he drinks, and people drink most heavily in uncomfortable situations. The questions are, then: (1) How much do executives drink? (2) When do they drink?

How much? The answer to this question is very clear: As a group, executives are among the heaviest drinkers in our society. Very few Americans drink at lunch, but many executives regularly do so. Most of their business affairs feature drinking. Conferences and conventions almost always have "hospitality rooms" and "happy hours," and cocktail parties are a basic part of the executive culture. Furthermore, although many executives accuse the lower classes of heavy drinking, several surveys have found that drinking and excessive drinking increase as income, education, and occupational status rise.

These facts suggest that many executives feel quite anxious and

167

that their anxieties have very heavy effects on them. But, as we have observed many times, executives prefer to ignore this evidence and insist that they do not feel anxious and act only for rational reasons. This denial and distortion was especially clear in one nine-week executive program. The men had happy hours every afternoon and heavy drinking parties almost every night; they boasted about the amount of alcohol they went through; but many of them complained about a lecture on anxiety because it didn't apply to them!

When? Most drinking occurs in social situations. People at all levels in our society drink more at parties and other affairs than they do when they are alone. In fact, drinking alone usually indicates more severe anxiety and personal problems than social drinking. Still, the fact that executives rarely get together without drinking suggests that they need social lubricants because they don't feel very comfortable with each other.

This interpretation is consistent with many points made earlier in this book. Executives don't know each other very well because they move around so much. They are very competitive and can't relax with each other. They don't develop real intimacy because of their attitudes toward themselves and other people. They therefore need social lubricants to get comfortable with each other.

ALCOHOLISM AMONG EXECUTIVES

The hidden problem. Very few executives will admit that alcoholism among executives is a serious problem, even though they may complain about alcoholic workers. However, after reviewing several studies, *Fortune* reached this conclusion: "Alcoholism has been found to be more of a problem in the executive suite than on skid row." [1] And The National Council on Alcoholism estimates that one out of every 20 top executives is an alcoholic.

Alcoholism is therefore another hidden problem of executive life, and it is kept hidden in spite of its fantastic cost. The National Council on Alcoholism estimates that alcoholism among executives and workers costs American businesses $4 billion per year, $16 mil-

[1] H. Maurer, "The Beginning of Wisdom About Alcoholism," *Fortune*, May 1968.

168

lion per working day. More than three million workers and executives are alcoholics, making alcoholism America's fourth largest health problem (following heart disease, mental illness, and cancer). And many industrial psychiatrists regard it as their most common problem. Despite the overwhelming evidence of the magnitude and cost of the problem, very few companies have any sort of program for dealing with alcoholism, and most companies won't even admit that it is a problem.

In fact, many executives deliberately cover up their subordinates' drinking, and some companies follow a policy—an unwritten policy, however—of paying an economic premium for the concealment of alcoholism. "This premium comes in the form of keeping an alcoholic on the job, promoting him, and paying him fringe benefits. When he can no longer conceal his condition, the company ordinarily fires him." [2] In addition to the help that they receive from their bosses in this respect, most executives can easily cover up their own drinking: They have private offices, are not supervised closely, can leave the office "on business," and have secretaries and assistants to cover up their absences, drunkenness, and mistakes.

But why has such a costly and extensive problem been kept hidden? Executives are usually hardheaded and cost-conscious. Why have they ignored alcoholism, especially among their associates? The answer seems quite clear: They have ignored it because they are afraid of it. It threatens their basic beliefs about themselves and executives in general. They prefer to preserve the myth of executive rationality even if it costs their companies millions of dollars (and one bad decision by an alcoholic executive can cost them that much). In other words, ignoring alcoholic executives is essentially a group defense mechanism, a costly attempt to preserve a false image.

Definition. Although many people still regard alcoholism in moralistic terms and feel that alcoholics simply lack character and will power, doctors generally believe that it is a disease. Alcoholism is a disease that is similar to an obsessive compulsive neurosis. The alcoholic cannot control his drinking. It is not under his voluntary

[2] L. F. Presnal, "Alcoholism—an Employee Health Problem," address at the Ninth Annual Pacific Northwest Occupational Health Conference, Portland, Oregon, September 10, 1962.

control because he has an insatiable need for alcohol and is extremely dependent on it.

Although all alcoholics have insatiable needs for alcohol, not all alcoholics are frequent drinkers. Frequent drinking and alcoholism usually go together (especially in the later stages of alcoholism), but many heavy drinkers are not alcoholics, and some real or potential alcoholics drink infrequently. The distinction between alcoholics and nonalcoholics is not how often or even how much they drink, but whether they can control their drinking once they begin. A heavy drinker who is a nonalcoholic can control his drinking; he may have several drinks almost every day, but he can get along with only one or two. On the other hand, some alcoholics drink only on weekends or even less frequently; but when they start drinking, they lose control and continue until they are completely intoxicated. In other words, the first drink triggers their need for alcohol and makes them lose control of themselves. Alcoholics can therefore stop drinking, but they can never drink moderately. Their symptoms can be cured; they can stop drinking, but the cure is not permanent. A "cured" alcoholic is still an alcoholic. He can go for years without a drink, but one drink can start the whole process over again.

Alcoholics Anonymous therefore declares that people should never insist that a man have a drink. He may be an alcoholic, and that one drink can ruin years of restraint.

Are you an alcoholic? From time to time, most drinkers wonder whether they are alcoholic or in danger of becoming so. Usually, it is just a passing thought; they read something about alcoholism, recognize a similarity between themselves and alcoholics, and wonder about themselves. Sometimes it is a more pressing and frightening feeling; they know that they drink more than they should, see similarities between themselves and known alcoholics, and are afraid that their drinking is getting out of hand.

Unfortunately, there is no completely accurate test for alcoholism. Nonetheless, several organizations have developed questionnaires which can help identify real and potential alcoholics. These questionnaires have been widely distributed, and thousands of people have used them; but they may do more harm than good. They may help a few alcoholics recognize their problem, but they can easily exaggerate unjustified fears of many nonalcoholics. They

170

frighten people unnecessarily because they ask questions about very common behaviors and identify these behaviors as alcoholic.

Many of these questionnaires ask, for example, if a person ever drinks alone, or if he drinks because he feels shy with people, or if he drinks when he feels worried or nervous, or if he ever wishes he didn't drink. As anyone from a hardened alcoholic to a man who drinks only two beers in a month can answer "yes" to these questions, they frighten many people unnecessarily.

A far better test for alcoholism has been suggested by the executive director of The National Council on Alcoholism, Mrs. Mann. Because alcoholism is essentially an inability to control drinking, and because alcoholics cannot drink moderately, she suggests that people who are afraid of becoming alcoholics have from one to three drinks every day for six months. If a person normally doesn't drink every day, he should have one to three drinks on the days he normally drinks. No exceptions are allowed. If a person exceeds the limit even once, he has failed the test. And this failure suggests that he cannot control his drinking, that he is an alcoholic or in danger of becoming one.

The Causes of Alcoholism

Although doctors agree that alcoholism is a disease, most other people don't regard it as one; nor do they try to understand its causes. They think about it in moralistic terms ("alcoholics lack will power and character") or feel that it is just a very bad habit. As long as they feel this way about alcoholism, they will not be able to understand or help alcoholics.

The moralistic arguments are essentially irrelevant. "Will power," "character," and other moralistic terms refer only to voluntary acts. A man can exert will power and demonstrate character only if he is free to choose. But the core of alcoholism, its very definition, is that alcoholics cannot control their drinking. It is not a voluntary act; no amount of character or will power can help them, once they have that first drink.

Nor is their drinking just a bad habit. It looks like a habit; they do drink repetitiously; but repetition alone will not cause alcoholism.

171

Some men drink heavily for years but don't become alcoholics, whereas others drink less frequently but develop alcoholism. The key issue is not repetition but motivation. Alcoholism "comes only when there is a *motive* for repeating."[3] "The alcoholic is not sick because he drinks, but drinks because he is sick, and then becomes doubly sick."[4] This irresistible motive is the core of the disease.

We can therefore best understand the disease if we drop moralistic terms and superficial approaches and ask the question: *Why* do alcoholics drink? The basic answer is very simple: They drink because drinking solves their problems, especially the problem of anxiety.

> One will not fully understand alcoholism as a problem until one sees it as a solution. For the alcoholic, alcohol is a magic, but tragic, solution to his personality problems. . . . The alcoholic's inner conflicts and anxiety cause intense pain. Alcohol is a cheap, easily obtainable pain-killer.[5]

But this is just the beginning of an answer. Alcoholism is a solution to their problem, but why do they select this particular solution rather than some other defense? These are not easy questions, and alcoholism is not a simple disease. It is a complex disease which is caused by three sets of factors—cultural, physical, and psychological.

Generally, a person will not become an alcoholic unless (1) he has certain personality characteristics, especially an inability to handle his anxieties and frustrations; (2) he obtains great physical and psychological relief from drinking; (3) his associates regard drinking—perhaps even excessive drinking—as an acceptable way of dealing with psychological problems. The scope of this book does not permit a lengthy discussion of these problems, but let us briefly discuss the cultural and physical aspects of alcoholism before we examine the role of anxiety and other psychological problems.

Cultural factors. Certain cultures severely condemn excessive drinking, and as a result very few alcoholics are found in these cultural groups. Jews, for example, have the highest percentage of

---

[3] Jellinek, as cited by H. J. Clinebell, *Understanding and Counseling the Alcoholic,* Abingdon Press, Nashville, Tennessee, 1968, p. 58.

[4] Carroll Wise, as cited by Clinebell, *op. cit.,* p. 59.

[5] Clinebell, *op. cit.,* p. 57.

drinkers in our society. Only 10 percent of the Jews totally abstain from drinking, compared with 37 percent for Protestants. But there are almost no alcoholic Jews because the Jewish culture condemns excessive drinking unequivocally. Drunkenness is simply not tolerated, and relatively few Jews are ever intoxicated. On the other hand, drunkenness among the Irish is not only tolerated but even joked about, and their alcoholism rate is extremely high. Still other groups influence attitudes toward drinking and drunkenness. These attitudes vary in different parts of the country and among social classes, companies, and other social groups. Regardless of their nature, groups that tolerate excessive drinking generally have a much higher alcoholism rate than those that condemn it.

Physical factors. Some people obtain much more relief from alcohol than others. Because anxiety is both physical and psychological, cultural factors affect this relief, but some people's bodies simply react more favorably to alcohol. Furthermore, alcoholism is essentially an addiction, and some people's constitutions are more easily addicted to alcohol. Alcohol changes the chemistry of their bodies and "gives them a sensitivity or 'allergy' to alcohol so that one drink sets off a chronic reaction leading inevitably to a drunk." [6]

Psychological factors. The hard-driving perfectionist executive who drinks even moderately may well be on his way to becoming an alcoholic. Research has found great similarities between alcoholic and executive personalities. A large number of alcoholics worship success, feel anxious about personal relationships, and are authoritarian, moralistic, and perfectionist. The very qualities that make a man successful can therefore make him an alcoholic.

> The man susceptible to alcoholism very often seems to be the man who is a little better at his job, and a little more intelligent than his fellows. . . . He is more sensitive than nonalcoholics, more imaginative, more aware, and he hates routine. The qualities that make an executive also characterize alcoholics.[7]

It is easy to see why these characteristics can make a man drink too much. A sensitive, imaginative man with very high standards

[6] *Ibid.*, p. 68.
[7] "The Alcoholic Executive," *Fortune*, January 1960.

will know when his performance does not match his standards, when his success does not equal his ambition. He may also feel that his creativity is being worn down by bureaucracy, that he has no choice but to devote his life to the routine work he despises. He therefore drinks to relieve his anxieties and frustrations. Alcohol relieves him and makes him less aware of himself and his situation. The tragedy is that his solution to the problem destroys him.

The Stages of Alcoholism

Because alcoholism is a progressive disease, it destroys its victim slowly. Alcoholism usually develops over several years and can be stopped fairly easily if it is identified in the early stages. Each alcoholic develops his symptoms in a slightly different order, and not all alcoholics have the same symptoms; but the disease usually develops in four major phases.

Preparatory phase (length indefinite). In this phase a man is not yet an alcoholic and can exert some control over his drinking. He may not drink frequently, but when he does drink, he drinks a great deal. (Some people in this phase get drunk each time they begin drinking; others simply get tight, or high.) If he is to meet friends for a drink, he arrives early and gets a "head start." He drinks very rapidly and may sneak drinks when no one is looking. (A few people in this stage have occasional blackouts after drinking.)

Basic phase (averages ten years' duration). The alcoholic is beginning to lose control over himself. He promises to cut down on his drinking but gets drunk very frequently and lies about his drinking. He realizes that his drinking is getting out of control but tries to deceive himself and other people about his need for alcohol. ("I know my limit." "I can quit any time I want to.") He has to have a drink at certain times and can't work or relax without one. Eating habits may become irregular. He drinks very rapidly and exhibits various forms of erratic behavior after a few drinks—treats his friends, makes numerous phone calls, humiliates his family, drives while drunk, or becomes argumentative. Blackouts occur fairly frequently; other people may not notice them, but he blacks out and can't remember anything after a certain number of drinks.

174

Middle phase (*two to five years*). The alcoholic has now lost control over himself. For a while he lies about his drinking but ultimately grows tired of the subject and refuses to discuss it. He needs more liquor to get the same effect, and so he changes his drinking pattern: He drinks in the morning, when he is alone, before and after meals, on weekend benders, at any time. At home he always makes everyone else's drink, makes his very strong, and often sneaks an extra drink. He eats very irregularly, often feels tired, nervous, and depressed, and must drink to relax and feel comfortable. He becomes antisocial and aggressive even when he is not drinking; he may do poor work, lose his job, neglect his family, drop his friends, get into fights, or have trouble with the police. Occasionally, he is frightened by his drinking and may even seek help from physicians or Alcoholics Anonymous. But he probably won't see them, because he wants to prove that he can control himself by "taking the pledge." Unfortunately, he can't control himself and soon starts the whole pattern all over again.

Late phase (*continues until death, insanity, or recovery*). All vestiges of self-control are gone. The alcoholic is a "hopeless drunk" who "drinks to live and lives to drink." Drinking is the core of his life, and he builds his entire pattern of living around it. He hides bottles and carries a flask so that he can always get a drink, needs a drink in the morning, rarely "goes on the wagon," and may even steal liquor or drink dangerous alcoholic substances such as hair tonic or rubbing alcohol. Drinking is so important to him that he has lost interest in everything else—sex, food, work, family, and friends. He feels isolated and disgusted with himself and loses hope of ever leading a normal life. His body and mind crumble from years of alcoholic abuse. He feels nauseated and dizzy; his hands shake, and his legs won't hold him; he sees lights and hears voices. He is thoroughly miserable, and he may even commit suicide.

IDENTIFYING THE ALCOHOLIC

Although alcoholism is a progressive and horrible disease, alcoholics can be helped. However, the longer they continue as alcoholics, the greater the damage to their health, family life, and work, and the lower their chances for recovery. It is therefore crucially im-

175

portant that they be identified and treated while they are still in the early stages. Unfortunately, most alcoholics are not identified then, partly because their associates and superiors don't want to recognize the problem, partly because the common beliefs about their behavior are inaccurate. Recent research has shown that alcoholics in the early stages do behave in certain ways which readily identify them, and some companies have been very successful at identifying and helping them.[8]

Absenteeism. Alcoholics are absent from work much more frequently than other people. They miss an average of a full month of work each year. Some of these absences are directly caused by drinking and hangovers, some by diseases which they develop because of their drinking. Partial absenteeism is also very common: They come to work in the morning but take long lunches and may not return in the afternoon. "On-the-job absenteeism" is an even more common and serious problem: They may be physically present but essentially useless or waiting restlessly for five o'clock so they can start drinking. However, despite the prevailing notion about their behavior they usually are not late for work, and absences are spread throughout the week instead of occurring primarily on Monday and Friday.

Their absences are even more noticeable because they make unlikely excuses and rationalizations for them. "Here, then, we have a cluster of tell-tale signs associated with alcoholism—a sharp overall increase in the rate, combined with recurrent 'partial absences,' and unlikely excuses for being away from the job."

Drinking behavior. Alcoholics also drink differently from other people: They want "to keep on drinking after their companions have finished and make a point of insisting that the others keep them company." They also "drink noticeably faster than others and keep urging their companions to 'drink up.'" They might have an extra drink between rounds, arrive early at the bar, or even leave their companions to drink faster alone. They also "spend substantially more money on alcohol than their colleagues." Their drinking and spending behavior often gives them a great deal of emotional satis-

---

[8] The material in this section on identifying the alcoholic, including all quotations, is taken from Harrison Trice, "Identifying the Problem Drinker on the Job," *Personnel,* May 1957.

faction. They may enjoy the prestige of being able to outdrink their companions or like having the reputation of being a big spender.

Rejection of associates. However, as his drinking behavior becomes more abnormal, the alcoholic and his associates feel uncomfortable and avoid each other. They don't approve of his behavior, and he likes people who drink the way he does.

Physical signs. Certain physical signs can be noted if people want to notice them. Hangover signs are quite visible, and many alcoholics have hand tremors and smell of alcohol or mints and other breath cover-ups. However, the popular impression that alcoholics are untidy is extremely inaccurate. In fact, most early alcoholics "take unusual pains to appear spic and span on the job." The early alcoholic "is in the 'denial' stage . . . hoping to show by these outer symbols that there is nothing wrong with him."

Work pace. Their work pace is often very erratic. An alcoholic may "work in spurts to catch up, but after hurrying for an hour or so a nagging fatigue sets in and reduces him to a slump." However, the common belief that alcoholics make a great number of mistakes is inaccurate in the early stages. Their work pace lowers the amount of work done but does not increase the number of mistakes. The early alcoholic "is extremely cautious about errors and accidents—he is trying to avoid calling attention to himself." Of course, in the later stages errors and accidents become quite common.

Personality. Alcoholics are unusually moody; their moods often change from one extreme to another after a few drinks—from happy to sad, or from depressed to excited. They are also easily angered, especially by criticism of their drinking. "This sensitivity about drinking extends to other areas as well." They dislike criticism and behave suspiciously and sarcastically. They frequently distrust people and feel that their associates are "out to get them."

"Despite these negative personality features, [they do] not change jobs frequently. Instead of leaving at the slightest provocation, they stay with the job. This finding . . . indicates that the problem drinker cannot be spotted by his turnover rate—he is a 'stable' employee."

Off-the-job signs. "A problem drinker gets himself into a rash of domestic, financial, and community problems." He borrows money and usually has family problems. At first his wife probably covers up for him, but most grow disgusted and complain about their husbands. Some alcoholics—usually in the more advanced stages—even have trouble with neighbors and the police.

The cover-up. With all these obvious signs, how can a company fail to realize that a man—especially an executive—has a drinking problem? The answer to this question brings us right back to our original position. They don't realize it because they don't want to face the truth: "His associates who are in a position to observe the signs tend to cover up for him rather than bring him to the attention of personnel or medical workers. Even his boss may do so. In fact . . . the two persons who are mainly responsible for the cover-up are the alcoholic himself and his immediate boss."

But this cover-up is obviously costly for both the man and the company. It lowers the chances for his recovery, harms his health, and can cause a disaster for both him and the company. It is therefore imperative that problem drinkers be referred to personnel and medical departments as soon as possible.

This referral, however, will do no good unless the company has an adequate program for dealing with alcoholics. Most companies do not have such programs, but they are becoming more common.

HELPING THE ALCOHOLIC

The common-sense methods for helping alcoholics are oversimplified, moralistic, and ineffective, but they are completely consistent with the popular conception of alcoholism. People who believe that alcoholism is just a bad habit or an evidence of poor character will punish or criticize alcoholics or exhort them to stop drinking. But exhortations, punishments, and criticisms actually prevent or hinder recovery because they make alcoholics feel even more anxious and defensive. They are already defensive about their drinking, and criticism only makes things worse. Until they face the truth and really want help, nothing can be done for them.

The defensiveness problem is intimately related to the motivation problem. The alcoholic has very conflicting motives: He is con-

178

cerned about his drinking but doesn't want to believe that he can't control it. He wants to be helped but doesn't want to admit that he needs help. He wants to be cured but does not want to give up alcohol. Alcohol is destroying him, but it also solves his problem, and "it is very difficult for him even to visualize any other solution. . . . Becoming abstinent is, in effect, giving up the core around which he has organized his life." [9] Very few of us will reorganize our lives or give up our defenses, no matter how destructive they are.

Therefore, if one of your subordinates or associates has a drinking problem, you are not helping him if you either ignore it or criticize him for it. Nor do you have the competence to treat his disease. Amateur psychiatrists are as useful as amateur brain surgeons, but there are many more of them. An astonishing number of people feel that they can treat difficult psychological problems. You can't, and you may as well admit it. The *only* thing you can do to help him is to give him the courage, motivation, and opportunity to see a competent specialist. The basic techniques described in Chapter 12 and Appendix A can help you to relieve his anxieties and make him less defensive, but you *must* refer him to AA or a competent psychiatrist. Fortunately, several companies have developed these referral programs, and there are organizations which can help you to develop a program or deal with individual drinking problems. Information can be obtained from local offices of Alcoholics Anonymous or from The National Council on Alcoholism, 2 East 103 Street, New York, N.Y. 10029.

[9] H. J. Clinebell, *op. cit.*, p. 69.

11

Effects of Anxiety
on the Body

NXIETY IS NOT MERELY A VERY COMMON HEALTH PROBLEM; IT IS
also an extremely serious one. It kills thousands of people and
ruins the health of millions of others. One physician has even stated:

> Anxiety is the most universal and disturbing symptom that con-
> fronts the practicing doctor of medicine. It is conservatively esti-
> mated that at least 75 percent of the daily patient load is afflicted
> to some degree with anxiety.*

Anxiety kills directly by causing heart attacks, cerebral hemorrhages, ulcers, and ulcerative colitis. It aggravates diabetes, cancer,
and tuberculosis. It makes some people ruin their health by losing
sleep or eating, drinking, and smoking too much. It is a factor in a
wide variety of less serious health problems (asthma, diarrhea, constipation, arthritis, migraine headaches, hay fever, and eczema, for
example), and causes many physical symptoms which do not damage the body itself (impotence, frigidity, backaches, headaches, and
some forms of blindness, deafness, and paralysis).

* Nathan K. Rickles, *Management of Anxiety for the General Practitioner*, Charles
C Thomas, Springfield, Illinois, 1963, p. viii.

180

WHY DISCUSS THIS TOPIC?

But why should a book for executives discuss health problems? There are three good reasons. First, it may help you to realize how high a price you are paying for your "success" or your current habits. And, if the price is too high, you may want to reconsider your priorities and habits. Are you really willing to sacrifice your health, even your life, for that promotion? Would you rather get an ulcer than learn how to delegate authority?

Second, knowledge of health problems can help you preserve or recover your health by dealing with causes rather than symptoms. Most "health aids" are useless, and some are even dangerous; but people spend billions of dollars on them. They poison themselves with vitamin pills, try crazy diets, eat margarine as if it were medicine, and take millions of headache and stomach remedies. These "cures" do more harm than good.

Some actually hurt the body, but they all divert attention from causes to symptoms; and treating symptoms is wasteful and dangerous. If anxiety is raising your blood pressure and cholesterol levels, margarine with corn oil is not going to lower them. If anxiety causes your chronic indigestion, alkalizers are a waste of money. If you are overweight because you eat or drink too much in order to relieve your anxieties, *no* diet is going to help—and diet pills are absolutely dangerous, both physically and psychologically. Until you face reality and start dealing with the causes of your health problems, your health will continue to deteriorate.

Third, understanding anxiety's effect on the body can help you to understand yourself and other people. Most people won't discuss or even face their psychological problems. But their physical symptoms are out in the open, and they will accept them and even discuss them with other people. Therefore, if you understand how anxiety causes symptoms, you can learn a great deal about yourself and other people.

The body has a language all its own. If you understand that language, you will obtain insights that you couldn't get in any other way. Symptoms tell us things that people won't talk about—what really upsets them, what kind of people they really are. You may even learn something about yourself.

181

If you suffer from hay fever, ulcers, ulcerative colitis, asthma, eczema, migraine headaches, high blood pressure, or many other ailments, your symptoms will generally be more severe when you are anxious—even if your anxiety has been repressed, even if you are completely unaware of it. If your attacks usually occur when you do certain things or are with certain people, the message is rather obvious, and you ignore it at your own risk.

The language of the body can also help you understand what kind of person is "behind the executive mask." Some diseases usually occur in certain kinds of people. If you understand a man's symptoms—and they are right in front of you—you can get below the surface to his basic personality. A man with an ulcer—for example—may look aggressive and independent, but he probably wants to lean on people and let them make decisions for him. An outwardly calm man with high blood pressure and migraine headaches probably is very angry at times, though he may not even realize it.

But two warnings are in order. First, you can never be sure that a particular symptom means that a man is a certain kind of person. The relationship between symptoms of diseases and types of personality is far from perfect. Second, *don't try to help your associates by diagnosing their problems.* If you think you understand why someone has a health problem, don't give him the doubtful benefit of your insight and diagnosis. Even if you are right, it won't do any good, and he won't appreciate your help. If his health problem is really caused by anxiety, you *may* be able to help him by relieving his anxiety. And you *may* be able to do this by listening to him and accepting him, anxieties and all. You *may* also help by avoiding situations or actions which make him feel more anxious. But if you try to solve his problem directly by diagnosing it, you will not help him and will probably hurt him. He probably does not want to know what is causing his problem, and telling him can increase his anxiety and aggravate his problem.

How Anxiety Affects the Body

Anxiety's effects on the body depend on many different factors, and these factors can operate individually or in combination with each other. Furthermore, anxiety is not the only emotion which causes health problems, though it is the most important one.

Bad habits. Anxiety lowers resistance and wears out our bodies by ruining our sleep. Some people always have difficulty in sleeping, and most of us don't sleep well when we are under a great deal of pressure.

Anxiety can also make people eat, drink, or smoke too much. These bad habits ruin the health of millions of people. Drinking and smoking have been linked to many serious diseases, and obesity is our most visible health problem. Countless Americans are trying to give up smoking or cut down on their eating and drinking, but very few of them succeed in the effort. Eating, drinking, and smoking reward them by reducing their anxieties, and the appeal of this immediate reward is much more powerful than the long-term benefits of better health.

Smoking, eating, and drinking are very rewarding because they are intimately related to our first and most important satisfaction —being fed as babies. To a baby, being hungry is an overwhelmingly painful and frightening experience. He hurts all over and has no idea of when the pain will stop. When he is fed, his pain and anxiety are relieved. Because he is usually fed by a loving and reassuring mother, eating and the entire feeding process become associated with being loved, happy, and secure. We can see this association by observing any baby. When a baby is anxious or uncomfortable, he sucks his thumb or pacifier. Sucking relieves him because it is associated with feeding, love, and security.

The same general process can be seen in adults. They don't suck their thumbs, but they do suck on cigarettes, and eat or drink too much, especially when they feel anxious. Using their mouths relieves the anxiety because the mouth is associated with being fed, loved, and secure.

Direct strain on the body. When we are frightened or anxious, our glands secrete adrenalin and many other chemicals which increase our strength and energy. We breathe more deeply and more rapidly, thus increasing our intake of oxygen. Our blood pressure and sugar levels rise and our hearts beat faster, carrying more oxygen and energy to the muscles. Blood vessels in the digestive system contract and those in the arms and legs expand, slowing digestion and transferring blood and energy to the arms and legs. These and other changes are very useful in physically dangerous situations: They make our bodies ready to fight or run away.

But these same changes usually hurt us today. We are not savages who must fight or run. We are civilized and rarely do either. Our bodies are therefore ready for responses that we don't make. If this happens too often or lasts too long, our bodies become exhausted. Some people suffer from general exhaustion (called by the Germans *Manager-Krankheit,* "the manager's disease"); others develop problems in only one part of the body.

Physical weakness. One part of the body rather than another may become diseased because it is constitutionally weaker or has been injured before. Anxiety may damage one man's heart because it is constitutionally weak; and it may attack another's lungs because he has hurt them by smoking too much.

Emotional expression. Anxiety can harm different parts of individuals' bodies because each individual can symbolically express his emotions better with one organ than another. We can see this process most clearly with purely psychological symptoms. One man expresses his feeling of being overworked by developing backaches. Another expresses his rejection of his wife and the adult male role by becoming impotent. But heart attacks, tuberculosis, asthma, and other serious physical diseases can also express a man's emotions even though the symbols are much harder to understand.

Secondary gain. When we are sick, we obtain all sorts of secondary gains. We get sympathy and attention; people take care of us; we don't have to work; and so on. Since these gains are rewarding, we can learn to contract certain kinds of diseases in the same way we learn other habits. We repeat actions which are rewarded and drop those which are not. If a child gets attention and "mothering" when he has trouble in breathing but is ignored when he is constipated or has diarrhea, as an adult he is more likely to develop asthma than colitis.

Simple, reward-type learning is the basis for two of the five factors listed. We learn bad habits in reducing anxiety, and we learn certain diseases because they may provide secondary gains. Learning may also be related to the "choice" of different organs for expressing emotions. In other words, bad habits and even diseases can be learned "solutions" to the problem of anxiety.

All these factors can occur in diseases which damage the body itself, but only the last two—emotional expression and secondary gains—are related to the purely psychological diseases. Now that we have a general idea of how anxiety affects our bodies, we can see how many different kinds of diseases it causes and analyze the specific causes of a few diseases. We shall begin with the psychosomatic diseases because they are more common and more serious.

The word "psychosomatic" comes from two Greek words, *psyche* (mind or soul) and *soma* (body). A psychosomatic disease is therefore one in which the mind causes *actual damage* to the body. Because there are so many psychosomatic diseases, we shall classify them by systems—the respiratory system, the circulatory system, and so on—and list only a few diseases for each system.

THE DIGESTIVE SYSTEM

Peptic ulcer. Peptic ulcers are the clearest example of psychosomatic disease. Anxiety causes or aggravates them by stimulating excessive secretion of stomach acids which attack the stomach lining and cause irritation and inflammation.

Because people who have peptic ulcers are rather similar to each other, we learn a great deal about a man if we know he has a peptic ulcer. He probably has very strong desires to lean on people and have them make his decisions for him. A few ulcer patients directly display this desire, but because this desire is unacceptable in our society, especially among executives, most patients repress and overcompensate for it by being extremely independent and aggressive. This saves their images but hurts their health.

We can see how these dependency desires and anxiety about them cause ulcers by remembering the importance of feeding in infancy, the period when we were all completely dependent on other people. Several other actions are related to the feeding process. We swallow, and our stomachs churn and secrete acid to digest our food. In adults anxiety can cause swallowing and, more important, it can stimulate the flow of stomach acids. These acids cause peptic ulcers.

Diarrhea and constipation. Surprisingly, anxiety also causes problems at the other end of the digestive system. It can cause either chronic or acute diarrhea or constipation. Most people who chronically suffer from either diarrhea or constipation are tense and anxious, and many people have bowel problems in periods of heavy stress.

The psychoanalysts say that these and other problems are caused by poor toilet training. In fact, they say that there is an "anal personality type" and "anal personality characteristics." An "anal person" is one who won't let go of anything. He holds tight to everything— his feces, his money, his emotions, and so on. The psychoanalysts also say that a person who is chronically constipated probably has other anal characteristics as well: He is probably tight with his money, avoids risks, and does not express much emotion. The theory does not contend that people who suffer from chronic diarrhea have the opposite personality characteristics.

However, this is a very controversial topic, and many psychiatrists and psychologists have rejected the theory. In any case it is an interesting way of looking at personality, and you may find that it provides you with some insight into yourself or your associates.

Ulcerative colitis. Anxiety is unquestionably a cause of ulcerative colitis; but we don't clearly understand the causal relationship, nor can we clearly identify an "ulcerative colitis personality type." People who have this disease tend to be intelligent and superficially unemotional, but the relationship is far from perfect. Attacks frequently occur during periods of stress, especially stress caused by failure, loss of self-esteem, or separation from a meaningful person. Furthermore, anyone who has a tendency to suffer from diarrhea when he is placed under stress is a potential ulcerative colitis patient.

Although ulcerative colitis is more rare than peptic ulcers, it is also much more serious. Severe cases are very painful, may necessitate disfiguring operations, and can even cause death.

Chronic gastritis. Chronic heartburn, "indigestion," gas, stomach rumblings, and the like are often caused by anxiety and other emotions. Although they rarely incapacitate executives, they certainly reduce efficiency and make many executives very uncomfortable.

Poor appetite. Anxiety causes some people to overeat, but ruins other people's appetites. Some people are chronically poor eaters, whereas others lose their appetites during stressful periods.

THE CIRCULATORY SYSTEM

The circulatory system is the one that executives really worry about. They may be afraid of ulcers, but they are terrified of heart attacks. They have seen too many of their friends and associates die from such attacks, and every department has a few men who have had one and must "take it easy" to prevent another.

This concern about heart attacks shows up in many places—in locker-room conversations about the value or danger of exercise, in cocktail lounges where executives wonder out loud whether they should have another cocktail or cigarette, at lunch when they order low-calorie and low-cholesterol specials. But their attention may be focused on the wrong things. Their basic problem may not be exercise, cigarettes, calories, or cholesterol; it may be anxiety.

We are just beginning to understand how much damage anxiety does to the heart and circulatory system, but the evidence clearly suggests that *anxiety is a major cause of heart attacks and other cardiovascular diseases.*

Although we do not fully understand how it operates, we know that anxiety directly causes certain kinds of heart attacks and high blood pressure and cholesterol levels (which may then lead to heart attacks or cerebral hemorrhages). It also strains the heart by making people eat, drink, smoke, work, and exercise too much.

Heart attacks. Anxiety lowers the heart's efficiency and increases its workload by changing the pulse rate, stroke volume, cardiac output, peripheral resistance, and arterial blood pressure. It also reduces the heart's efficiency, primarily by interfering with the coronary circulatory system and mechanisms which control the heart's rate and rhythm. In addition, it increases the speed and ease of blood clotting, which probably increases the chances for coronary thrombosis. Its long-term effects are therefore to increase the chances for several kinds of heart attacks.

Cholesterol levels. Recent research shows quite clearly that psychological stress dramatically raises cholesterol levels. As there is a strong relationship between cholesterol and heart attacks and many executives are on low-cholesterol diets, this research is much too important to ignore.

In addition to the detrimental effects of *chronic* anxiety, *acute* anxiety causes many heart attacks. Many heart attacks occur during or shortly after a period of great emotional stress caused by the loss of a job or the death of a friend or relative. Both chronic and acute anxiety, therefore, are major causes of heart attacks.

Less serious heart ailments. In addition to causing heart attacks, anxiety causes a wide variety of less serious heart ailments. It can cause pain, palpitation, murmurs, spasms, and shortness of breath. These symptoms frequently occur immediately after an event which makes a person feel anxious about his heart—for example, failing a physical examination, or a heart attack suffered by a friend.

High blood pressure. Both psychological and organic health problems can cause high blood pressure. Regardless of its cause, if it persists, it strains the heart and blood vessels and can cause heart attacks and cerebral hemorrhages, both of which can be fatal.

Psychologically caused high blood pressure ("essential hypertension") often occurs in people who feel anxious about expressing their aggressions. Like all people they feel angry and hostile, but they usually don't express their feelings, and they may not even be aware of them. They hold in their feelings and present a calm, controlled exterior. This image may be good for their careers, but it is hard on their bodies. They would probably live longer if they honestly expressed their feelings.

Headaches. Some of the most painful headaches (migraines) are caused by anxiety which increases the blood pressure in the head. Severe headaches are often a warning that other parts of the cardiovascular system are in poor condition. Merely taking pain-killers is therefore very foolish.

These headaches can be caused by the same psychological problem that causes some cases of essential hypertension—failure to express anger and hostility. In fact, these headaches frequently occur after an incident which makes a person angry even if he doesn't know he is. Expressing this anger may relieve the pain.

THE MUSCLES AND SKELETON

Rheumatoid arthritis. This rather painful disease is relatively rare among executives and among men in general; but some executives do suffer from it. People with rheumatoid arthritis may have problems in personal relationships; they tend to be cold and inhibited and may even be unable to become emotionally involved with other people. They may also have strong desires to depend on people but deny these desires and overcompensate by being very independent, self-sufficient, self-sacrificing, domineering, hostile, and resistant to external control.

THE RESPIRATORY SYSTEM

Tuberculosis. Anxiety greatly affects the onset, development, treatment, and recovery of tuberculosis. Because prolonged anxiety wears out the body, it can directly lower resistance to the tuberculosis bacillus. It can also lower resistance indirectly by causing overwork, poor sleeping and eating habits, and excessive drinking and smoking.

Nearly all tuberculosis treatments include deliberate attempts to reduce the anxiety and stress of adult responsibilities. All of a patient's physical and psychological needs are satisfied for him and he is required to accept passively a dependent role. Some patients resist this role, but others accept and enjoy it. A few people even express relief when they learn that they have tuberculosis because they know that they will be taken care of in a sanitarium and will be free from the stress and anxiety of life. The patients who can relax and be openly dependent usually recover more rapidly than those who remain tense and reject the dependent role.

Tuberculosis also provides us with some insight into personality. This disease usually develops in people who have rather strong dependency desires, although they may repress or hide them under a tough, independent facade; and they frequently do not know how to handle hostility effectively. Some can't express hostility at all, whereas others tend to go to the other extreme and lose their tempers over minor issues.

Asthma and allergies. Asthma and allergies are caused by both psychological factors and physical sensitivity to certain substances. A recent experiment showed how much influence psychological factors can have on asthmatic attacks. Asthma patients were told they would inhale a new cure for asthma. They then inhaled a substance to which they had previously been allergic, and about half of them experienced an immediate improvement in their condition. They were later told that they would inhale the substance they were allergic to; actually, it was a drug that they normally used to control their symptoms. Nearly half of them developed symptoms immediately.

Although there is no doubt that psychological factors are important in many cases of asthma and hay fever, their importance varies from case to case, and asthma and allergies can occur in a wide variety of personality types. The knowledge that a person suffers from asthma or allergies, therefore, does not tell us much about the person himself.

However, because asthma or allergy attacks are more serious and frequent during periods of stress, they can often tell us something about the kinds of things which disturb a person. For example, if he frequently has an attack when he must make a speech or go on a trip, we should be able to understand what these attacks mean. This same general principle applies to many other psychosomatic disorders.

The common cold. Anxiety can even make people catch more colds! Colds are "resistance diseases." We almost always have cold germs in our systems, and we usually contract a cold when our resistance goes down or the number of germs goes up. Anxiety can lower resistance directly by wearing us out, and indirectly by ruining our sleep or making us work, eat, drink, or smoke too much.

THE SKIN

Very little is really known about the relationship between anxiety and skin problems, but research indicates that anxiety and other emotions affect many annoying disorders—acne, psoriasis, warts (which have sometimes been removed by hypnotic suggestion), dry skin, itching, and eczema. There is even some evidence that anxiety can cause baldness!

MULTISYSTEM DISORDERS

In addition to affecting individual systems, anxiety is a factor in at least two disorders which involve several systems—diabetes and cancer. Cancer can occur in many parts of the body, and diabetes involves both the digestive and circulatory systems.

The role of anxiety in either disease is not clearly understood, but there is little doubt that it is a factor. Cancers spread more rapidly and are harder to control in anxious patients. Anxiety can affect diabetics (especially people who do not know that they are diabetics) by making them eat too much or eat the wrong things. It may also directly affect the pancreas or blood vessels, but this relationship is currently unclear.

We have seen, then, that anxiety is a major health problem, perhaps the most serious one we have; if we include mental patients, it certainly is. We now know that it affects a huge number of diseases in which the body is actually damaged. These diseases range from the major killers such as heart disease and cancer to petty annoyances such as colds and warts. And, as we probe more deeply, we will certainly find that it affects other diseases as well.

In fact, most doctors have stopped treating the body and the mind, the psyche and the soma, as separate systems and regard them as an indivisible unit. General practitioners, internists, even surgeons take courses in psychological and psychoanalytic theory and learn how to deal with the emotional causes of physical diseases. They also learn how to diagnose and treat purely psychological "diseases."

PURELY PSYCHOLOGICAL "DISEASES"

Anxiety and other emotions can cause almost every symptom known to medical science. Medical records contain hundreds of cases of purely psychological "pregnancies," "heart attacks," "paralyses," and so on. There is a story that one person had his appendix "taken out" so many times that a disgusted surgeon tattooed "no appendix here" on his stomach.

There is little point in trying to list all the symptoms that anxiety can cause, but a great deal can be learned by analyzing a few of the more common ones. Our analysis will show that a person learns to have certain symptoms and that these symptoms solve the problem of anxiety for him. They give expression to his emotions and provide many secondary gains.

Hypochondria. Many people confuse hypochondria with malingering. They think that a man who goes from doctor to doctor, describing his symptoms, is the same as the man who takes sick leave to go fishing. Neither is physically sick and they are both trying to solve a problem; but the resemblance ends there. The malingerer is deliberately and consciously faking, but a hypochondriac really believes that he is sick, and he really does have the symptoms he describes. His symptoms are caused by his emotion, but they are not imaginary. His heart does flutter. His back does ache. He does feel nauseated.

The hypochondriac clearly illustrates the two basic principles of psychologically caused symptoms. First, his symptoms express his feelings: He feels inadequate, unable to meet the challenges and demands of his life, and he expresses this feeling by being physically inadequate.

Second, his symptoms solve some of his problems: He feels inadequate and wants attention and sympathy; and his symptoms provide him attention and sympathy and reduce the demands he has to face. In other words, he learns that the sick role solves his problem, and he prefers the sick role to the normal one. Since being "sick" solves their problem, most hypochondriacs strenuously object to any suggestion that their symptoms are purely psychological and refuse to see psychiatrists. If they realized that their symptoms were purely psychological, their symptoms would lose their value. They would not be able to play the sick role, and the sick role solves their problem.

Impotence. The same two factors operate in psychologically caused impotence (and most impotence is caused or aggravated by psychological factors). "Impotence" is, of course, a general term which covers a wide variety of sexual problems, temporary or permanent, severe or mild. It includes the complete inability to have sexual relations, premature ejaculation, and lack of interest in sex. Any of these problems can be temporary or permanent.

192

Temporary impotence can be caused by overwork, resentment or dislike of the partner, resistance to adult demands and responsibilities, and many kinds of anxiety, including anxieties about job and career problems. For example, in the chapter on failure we saw that being fired causes temporary sexual problems for many men. Temporary impotence expresses a man's feelings of inadequacy and, in some cases, his feelings toward his partner. He rejects her and the adult male role at the same time, and in doing so provides himself with some satisfaction.

Chronic psychological impotence expresses the same feeling and is also a rejection of the adult male role, but in this case, causes are completely within the person. Temporary impotence can be reaction to external stresses, but permanent impotence is caused by severe anxiety about being inadequate. The chronically impotent adult feels that he is not much of a man, and his behavior proves it. He may try to overcompensate for these feelings by presenting an overly masculine façade—tough, authoritarian, independent—and these overcompensations may make him become a very successful executive. But he is obviously not a successful man, and both he and his wife know it.

Backaches. Backaches, especially aches in the lower back, are rarely caused by physical conditions. Usually, they are the effect of prolonged, unrelieved tension, and they may be a symbolic expression of the person's resentment about excessive burdens. The executive who complains about chronic backache may be indirectly expressing his resentment about being overworked or pushed too hard. When he says: "My back hurts," he may really be saying, "Get off my back!"

Psychic blindness, deafness, dumbness, and paralysis. One of Freud's major discoveries was that many cases of blindness, paralysis, and similar diseases were purely psychological and could be cured by purely psychological treatment—hypnosis, suggestion, and permitting people to talk freely about themselves. Again and again he was able to use these methods to cure cases which had been unsuccessfully treated by traditional methods.

He found that such diseases were frequently caused by guilt about sexual feelings or actions and were attempts by the person to "pay off his conscience." A woman may feel guilty about masturbating and punish herself by developing a paralysis in her hands. Or a man may feel guilty about peeping and develop blindness.

Because these problems are now very well understood and people feel much less guilty about their desires, the problems rarely occur today. But there are occasional cases of "traumatic blindness" in which a person develops blindness after seeing something very shocking—an automobile accident, a plane crash, a friend's death. These cases are especially common during wars, and veterans' hospitals are full of people with such problems.

Although both types of psychic blindness and paralysis are very rare among executives, they do occur occasionally. The primary purpose of describing them here is that they clearly illustrate how the body can symbolically express psychological problems. The person who saw something shocking develops blindness, not paralysis, whereas the person who did something he is ashamed of develops paralysis rather than blindness (except in the case of the peeper, who became blind). And, if the act was committed by one particular part of the body, that part—not the whole body—is "punished."

PART FOUR

Solving the Problem

12

Popular Solutions

CORDELL HULL, SECRETARY OF STATE DURING WORLD WAR II, WAS
of a temperament that made him grow very impatient with
policy makers who couldn't be bothered with details or practical
problems. On one such occasion he made his point by saying that
we could end submarine attacks on our convoys by boiling the
entire Atlantic Ocean. "When the subs came up to cool off," he
declared, "we could bomb them and solve the problem permanently. And, if people ask me how we are going to boil the ocean,
I tell them not to bother me; I'm a policy man and don't have time
for little details."

Because anxiety is such a serious problem, people with all kinds
of backgrounds and beliefs have tried to solve it; but many of these
solutions fall into the "boiling the ocean" category. They would work
if they could be carried out, if men were or could become basically
unselfish, if executives' goals and values were more humanistic, if
our society and organizations were not so demanding. In short,
most of the proposals made have not worked, and we are as anxious
as ever, simply because they ignore the "little details."

So many people have faith in these proposals, and desperately
want to believe that easy solutions are possible, that perhaps we
should not say they are doomed to failure. People hope that we will
have peace on earth, that we will someday live without fear, that we
will rise above our biological heritage and be noble and godlike.

They want these things so badly that they close their eyes to the facts and rely on faith. It is, of course, their right to ignore facts, but as scientists and executives we cannot afford to do so. We work with facts, not faith; with reality, not hopes; and the facts show that the proposed solutions have simply not solved the problem of anxiety. Unless we have the courage to face the facts, to admit that there are no easy or complete solutions, that man and society will never change very much, our work will be an exercise in futility; and we will end up as anxious and uncomfortable as we began.

We shall therefore begin our search for a better solution by analyzing some of the ambitious failures. "Failures" may be too strong a term, because they have helped some people; but, if we compare their results with their intent, it is clear that they have failed. After this analysis we shall examine certain proposals which are much less ambitious but more useful.

Attempts to Change Human Nature and Ethics

Probably the most common and most useless attempts to reduce anxiety have taken the form of exhortations to change human nature and improve our ethics. Billy Graham and other clergymen urge us to love our neighbor. Speakers at graduation exercises tell us to be courageous and independent. The right entreats us to respect the law, while the left demands justice for the oppressed; and the American Civil Liberties Union pleads for tolerance of all points of view.

These admonitions make the speakers feel that they have done something, and a few people in the audience always nod their heads and agree with them, but they accomplish very little. Man hasn't changed very much in thousands of years. Herodotus began to write history by analyzing a war, and wars have dominated history ever since. Men killed, robbed, and exploited each other then and they do so now. And every one of the grand schemes for changing man's basic nature—from Christianity to capitalism, psychoanalysis, and communism—has had negligible effects.

Thousands of years of history have proved that man's basic nature cannot be changed. Man is an essentially selfish animal who acts for his own interests. We may change his behavior by changing his perception of his interests or by making "unselfish" behavior rewarding, but we cannot change his essential selfishness. If a man helps someone else, he does so for the satisfaction or relief *he* gets, not for the benefit of the other person. We can therefore help men to be more noble by making nobility more satisfying, but exhortations about morality have all the impact of King Canute's order that the tide stop coming in.

To use another analogy: Asking men to change their basic natures is as useful and sensible as an engineer's arguing with friction. Engineers don't like friction; it complicates their calculations and burns up their machines, but they have to live with it. And we have to live with human nature *as it is*. If we don't understand what it is, if we don't base our work on the harsh realities of human nature, we shall fail—utterly and inexorably.

This is not a very noble or inspiring position. Some people may even find it offensive and prefer to exhort men to rise above themselves. But we have better things to do than argue with friction—we have a problem to solve.

SMALLER SOCIAL UNITS

People with widely differing philosophies have advocated breaking society into smaller units. The political conservatives want to reduce the size of the Federal Government and bring control back to the local and state levels. The black militants want neighborhood boards of education in New York and other cities. The Chinese Communists have experimented with small communes. The Utopian Socialists have lived in small integrated communities. Educators have proposed breaking up the huge, impersonal universities. Executives have decentralized their companies. And the Federal Government has its Antitrust Division to prevent monopolies.

Occasionally one of these plans works, at least for a while, but the general trend is clearly in the opposite direction. Governments get bigger even when they are run by conservatives; for example, budgets and bureaucracy increased in California under Reagan and in Alabama under Wallace. Unions get bigger and merge with each other; so do universities. Mergers are fantastically popular in the business world; most executives are deeply committed to organizational growth, and many corporations are recentralizing their operations.

Calls for breaking society or organizations into smaller units therefore fall into the "arguing with friction" class. They ignore the harsh reality that the very forces which made our organizations large are still operating today. We have a vast population, and it grows larger every moment. People may fear big government, corporations, and unions, but they want the things that these huge organizations provide—and they want more of them. They want not less but more social security, more medicare, more cars, more everything, and big organizations provide them all. Size not only gives organizations the resources they need to provide these goods and services, but it also increases the corporations' chances for survival and the power and privileges of the men who run the corporations.

Organizations will therefore become bigger because people want the things that they provide, because organizations have a growth dynamic of their own, and because the men who run them want more power and privileges. Size is another fact of life that we must accept and include in our plans, whether we like it or not.

PERMISSIVE CHILD REARING AND EDUCATION

For decades psychologists and educators have advocated permissiveness: The theory is that we should give our children more freedom, reduce status differences between them and ourselves, not resort to arguing, avoid punishing them, and so on. Their ideas have undoubtedly helped many children, but they have not had the overall impact on society that was predicted.

The college students of today were brought up more permissively than their parents, but very few people could argue that they are less anxious. The causes for their anxiety are not clear, and it is foolish to claim, as some extremists do, that permissiveness has fostered hippies. But permissiveness has certainly failed as a social policy although not necessarily as an individual policy. Like most grand schemes, it promised more than it could deliver; it was sold

200

to the public as an all-purpose antidote for anxiety, but obviously it has not reduced the general level of anxiety in our society or our young people.

However, the failure may have been caused by parents and teachers, not by permissiveness itself. It may have been improperly applied, and some parents and teachers have certainly used the techniques without accepting the underlying philosophy; but inadequate teachers and parents are another unpleasant fact of life. Regardless of where the fault lies, permissiveness has definitely not resulted in a less anxious generation.

ECONOMIC SECURITY

Since many of men's fears are related to economic problems, economic security should have reduced anxiety. Perhaps it has; people should be less anxious when they are economically secure, and our society might be even more anxious without social security, unemployment compensation, medical insurance, welfare, vested pensions, and the like. But the evidence is not encouraging.

Americans and the people in most other countries are more secure economically than man has ever been; but people are still anxious, and riots and other evidences of extreme anxiety and irrationality have not been confined to the poor and insecure. In fact the opposite is often the case. Negro rioters have often been better off economically—though not psychologically—than nonrioters, and college students are for the most part a privileged group with much higher family incomes than the national average.

We are not arguing that social security, unemployment compensation, and similar benefits should be abolished; they have unquestionably helped millions of people, but we must not confuse their contribution with the solution to our general anxiety.

CHANGING REWARD SYSTEMS

The theories and proposals so far discussed apply to everyone; they are attempts to change men or society in ways that would benefit the general public. Now we turn to proposed changes in organization.

One of the least known but most reasonable of these changes proposes to change the reward system so that men can advance *within* their specialties. This proposal, if acted upon, would end the problem of having to give up enjoyable work and professional identity for the higher status and pay of administration. Men would be rewarded for being good professionals—engineers, scientists, copywriters, or salesmen—instead of becoming poor or dissatisfied administrators.

Unfortunately, very few firms have acted on this proposal even though it has been made repeatedly over the past 20 years, and there is little reason to believe that it will be widely accepted in the future because it violates too many beliefs and principles.

First, it conflicts with the pyramidal principle and the traditional conception of people's worth. Supervisors are almost universally regarded as more valuable than people who just do things—even if the things they do require great skill. To pay them the same amount would therefore seem unfair to many executives. Second, most managers prefer to ignore the entire problem even though they know they have ruined some professionals—engineers and scientists especially—by promoting them. Facing this problem would require the managers to reconsider their entire conception of what men are worth and what they should want; and they much prefer to believe that supervisors are worth more than professionals, that professionals can become supervisors if they try hard enough, and that the only legitimate career goal is "moving up." Third, the system would require basic changes in bureaucratic procedures and evaluation programs, and bureaucratic systems are notoriously resistant to change. Fourth, even if this system were accepted in a company, it would affect relatively few people—primarily, very highly skilled engineers and scientists.

A related change which could affect many more people is the attempt to re-establish achievement orientation as the dominant management attitude, while de-emphasizing the desire to move up. This goal is implicit in the extensive and widely publicized work of Dr. David C. McClelland and his associates on achievement motivation, but they have rarely discussed it explicitly. Even more important, they have not devoted much attention to the problems of changing organizational reward systems so that they emphasize good performance rather than position and promotion. Unless these changes are made, achievement will continue to mean promotion or at least be measured by it.

A few firms do emphasize performance rather than promotion, but they are generally rather small. As a company grows larger, it inevitably grows more bureaucratic, and the keystone of the bureaucratic system is that pay, status, and other rewards are determined by position. Size therefore leads almost inevitably to pay scales, classifications, ranges, and so on. However, at least one company which ignores this principle has had very good results.

Edward Ryan, president of Ryan Homes, very emphatically states that he rewards performance instead of position, and many of his men are paid more than their immediate supervisors. His system has caused some real problems, but it has had some very important benefits: Men are generally more interested in performance than position and get their satisfaction from accomplishment rather than promotion. In fact, demotions—which rarely occur in most companies—are not at all uncommon, and many men have accepted them and stayed with the firm. This system has created a very healthy climate for individuals, yet the firm has had a remarkable growth rate the past ten years (over 30 percent a year).

Unfortunately, this system wouldn't work in most companies. It could give people more satisfaction and sense of accomplishment and might even improve performance, but it violates too many traditions and would encounter very strenuous resistance. Because it violates the entire bureaucratic tradition, few executives would tolerate having subordinates who were better paid than they.

HUMAN RELATIONS

A very different kind of attack on bureaucratic tradition has been made by the industrial psychologists, who have had a much greater impact on management. They have argued that traditional practices tend to frustrate individuals' needs, especially their need to grow, and that this frustration causes apathy, malingering, work restrictions, strikes, and other undesirable behavior. Even more important, the industrial psychologists have produced extensive data to support their argument. From the classic Hawthorne experiments to the present, they have repeatedly shown that traditional practices lowered productivity and caused turnover, absences, and strikes, while their own approach had the opposite effect.

The Hawthorne experiments were particularly important because they took place in the early 1930's when unions were growing very rapidly. Human relations techniques seemed to be one way to slow down unionism and reduce the problem of restriction of output (which the Hawthorne research illustrated so dramatically). Managers were also impressed by the huge increase in productivity that occurred when workers were allowed to participate in decisions.

The human relations movement gained momentum in the tight labor market of World War II and has become more powerful ever since despite vigorous attacks on it. Autocratic leadership is on its way out in many firms, and most executives follow human relations principles or at least accept them.

Although management accepted human relations techniques for eminently practical reasons, the goals of their adherents have changed through the years. The early advocates completely accepted management's goals and treated workers as objects to be controlled. Mayo and his associates were essentially sophisticated "union busters," who papered over real conflicts to prevent workers from joining unions or acting for their own interests.[1] Coch and French showed managers how to overcome resistance to change by letting workers *feel* that they had participated in decisions which were already made.[2]

But the human relationists have slowly changed their goals, and many modern specialists sincerely care about both individual and organizational goals—for example, McGregor, Argyris, Likert, and Haire. Some critics still argue that they are all manipulators, but it appears that their intention was—and is—to help individuals become more independent and satisfied. There are, however, several questions about the effects of the human relationists' work.

[1] For a thorough discussion of this issue see Loren Baritz, in *The Servants of Power.* Science edition, John Wiley & Sons, Inc., New York.
[2] L. Coch and J. French, "Overcoming Resistance to Change," *Human Relations,* Vol. 1, 1948, pp. 512–532.

Principles and techniques. There are many differences among the human relationists, but most of these specialists advocate the following principles and techniques:

1. *A different model of man.* Managers have traditionally viewed their subordinates as lazy men who want money but as little responsibility as possible. They therefore have to be controlled from above. Most human relationists feel that men are basically active, have many goals, want responsibility, and can control themselves. Their different conception of man is intimately related to the techniques they advocate. If their conception is correct, then traditional leadership practices will be generally ineffective, and in fact these practices have repeatedly demonstrated their ineffectiveness.

2. *Emphasis on noneconomic rewards.* Human relationists generally feel that men have many needs and can be motivated only by the needs which are not satisfied. Since most economic needs are satisfied in our society, they suggest that supervisors motivate their subordinates with noneconomic rewards (status, recognition, opportunities to express themselves, enjoyable work).

3. *Employee-centered leadership.* Human relationists advocate listening to subordinates' problems, trying to see things from their point of view, avoiding punishments, not supervising closely, letting people know the standards by which they are judged, and generally encouraging frank communication. Although these recommendations have been attacked as "soft," extensive research indicates that employee-centered supervisors get more production than production-centered ones.

4. *Broader participation in decisions.* Instead of the boss's making all the decisions, subordinates should participate in decisions which affect them. This participation may result in better decisions, but research has shown that its primary benefit is in increasing their motivation to carry out the decision.

5. *Broader delegation.* In management theory, delegation is an old and revered concept which the human relationists have simply broadened. They advocate freedom for subordinates to choose their own methods, along with only general supervision and appraisal by results. These policies would give subordinates a greater chance to act creatively and independently.

6. *Changed goals and attitudes.* The modern human relationists go beyond techniques and consider the goals and attitudes of the superior. They advocate a more humanistic attitude toward subordinates, one which regards them as intrinsically important, as ends in themselves, not just means of increasing production or advancing their superiors' careers. Bosses should not shirk their responsibility to the firm but must also recognize their responsibility to their men and try to develop them *because their growth, dignity, and satisfaction are worthwhile goals in their own right.*

Benefits. If all the modern human relationists' suggestions (including the ones about superiors' attitudes) were followed, everyone could benefit. Research is not extensive (and most of it refers to workers, not executives), but it generally shows that this approach increases organizational effectiveness: Production rises, and turnover and absenteeism decline. Independence, creativity, frustration, and anxiety have not been adequately measured, but indexes of general satisfaction usually rise. And several conditions related to anxiety could be improved if all these suggestions were followed: People would feel less frustrated and have more of their needs satisfied; they would have more genuinely human contact with their bosses and more opportunities to express and develop themselves; they could be more creative and independent, obtain the satisfaction of genuine accomplishment, and influence the decisions which affect them.

Limitations. Unfortunately, the benefits of the human relations approach usually do not occur because supervisors do not accept all the recommendations; they accept the techniques but reject the philosophy. They let people think they are participating but don't allow them to have any real influence on decisions. They listen to subordinates' problems but don't really care about them. They delegate authority but retain real power. These supervisors *seem* to care about their subordinates, but they don't respect their intrinsic worth and they regard them as beings to be manipulated for their own purposes. Some superiors have accepted the human relations philosophy and given their subordinates genuine freedom and respect; but, as the history of the human relations movement clearly shows, its general effect has been an increase in domination and a decrease in actual freedom.[3]

The inability to change some superiors' attitudes brings us right back to the general failure of all attempts to change human nature by exhortation. If 2,000 years of Christianity have not made men unselfish, how utterly naïve it is to assume that superiors will ever change their basic attitudes merely for the good of their subordinates! If one trait characterizes executives, it is the desire for power, yet the human relationists show them how to increase their control over people and expect them to let people have more genuine independence. Their naïveté on this issue is related to their basic inability or refusal to recognize that some conflict is inevitable between individuals and organizations, between superiors and subordinates. Even the men who have explicitly and repeatedly discussed these conflicts keep trying for an impossible idea, the complete integration of the individual and organization, the nirvana in which both individual and organization achieve maximum satisfaction. For example, Warren Bennis has said: *"Effective leadership depends on mediating between the individual and the organization in such a way that both can obtain maximum satisfaction."* [4] This sort of thinking makes it hard for men to recognize and act for their own interests; and, if they can't do that, they certainly can't be independent.

Furthermore, the conflicts between individuals and their organizations are greatest where decisions about their careers are concerned, but very few human relationists have considered this area or suggested that people participate in such decisions. All of their work seems to be oriented downward; they work only on techniques for influencing subordinates and have ignored the problems of upward influence, even though men care much more about their superiors than their subordinates. The net effect has been that most executives are much better at handling their subordinates than at influencing their superiors and have problems in controlling their own lives and careers.

[3] Loren Baritz, *op. cit.*
[4] Warren Bennis, "Revisionist Theory of Leadership," *Harvard Business Review,* January–February 1961, pp. 26–40.

The human relationists have also caused a very different problem—greater uncertainty. Autocratic leadership is unquestionably frustrating, but it does let people know where they stand. Many human relations techniques have the opposite effect: They confuse some men and make them unsure of where they are and what they should do. Men may dislike implementing decisions that they haven't influenced, but not everyone wants the responsibility of making decisions, especially decisions at higher levels. Close supervision can be frustrating, but it does provide clarity. The old-time firing techniques were rough on the ego, but at least men knew where they stood; today, they may be dead and not even suspect it.

These are not just theoretical questions or issues that refer primarily to the rank and file. In one organization where management tried to apply the McGregor approach, the workers enjoyed their new freedom, but the executives disliked theirs and asked their supervisors to be more directive! This difference was apparently caused by the fact that most workers had routine jobs, while the executives already had to cope with a great deal of uncertainty and didn't want any more of it.

Although it has not had the benefits for individuals that were anticipated, the human relations movement has been far from a complete failure. In terms of its primary goal, increasing organizational effectiveness, it has been quite successful. It has also changed a few men's attitudes and given their subordinates more independence. Even if it has increased the amount of manipulation, it may be better to be skillfully controlled than overtly dominated. It is harder to fight back against manipulation, but domination is more visibly frustrating and the restrictions on freedoms are usually much narrower. We therefore cannot be sure of the net impact of the human relations movement on anxiety until research focuses directly on this problem, and no such effort is likely in the near future.

OTHER SOLUTIONS

Thus the grand schemes for changing society, organizations, and human nature have not been very successful. Now let us look at a few less ambitious but more effective proposals.

Relaxation. Since a man cannot be anxious and relaxed at the same time, many doctors tell their patients to relax. This recommendation may help, but most people can't follow it because their anxiety is stronger than their ability to relax.

Numerous doctors and several books have tried to solve this problem by *teaching* people how to relax. They describe and illustrate techniques that relax the body. Some of these techniques are quite effective and can relieve anxiety, related emotions, and their harmful effects. Similar methods are in fact used to make childbirth less painful ("natural childbirth").

Some doctors and psychologists go further and systematically associate frightening stimuli with relaxation to desensitize the patient and make him less anxious in certain situations. Desensitizing (which is described in Appendix A) has been very effective in dealing with anxiety and related feelings.

Unfortunately, we do not know how well people can learn these techniques from books. There is no solid evidence, but some people have claimed that the books are useful. Even if the simple relaxation techniques can be learned, their usefulness will be somewhat limited because they just reduce anxiety without affecting its causes. However, since anxiety has so many serious effects, a method of reducing it which does not have the unpleasant side effects of most defenses is certainly worth considering.

Controlled expression of emotions. A related and even more common way of lowering tension is to express anxiety, anger, frustration, and other feelings in safe ways. Instead of hitting his boss or barking at his wife, a man should chop wood, hit a golf ball or punching bag, yell at an umpire, or watch a violent movie. Such activities as these let him drain off tension but don't cause the problems that result from most defenses.

In addition to being the most common recommendation for reducing tension, this is also the oldest: More than 2,300 years ago Aristotle noted that watching a tragedy "purged the soul" by creating and then exhausting pity and fear. The viewer drained off his tensions and became free of their effects.

Despite its antiquity, to drain off emotions in ways that do no harm to anyone is still a good method of relieving tension and should be learned and practiced. Simply expressing emotions, of course, will not solve the problems that caused them, but it will reduce the tension and its harmful effects.

Open expression of emotions: the T-group movement. If we go a step further and make it legitimate to express our feelings to each other, we get the same relief but also deal with some of the underlying problems. Some of our anxiety occurs because we don't understand or accept our own feelings, don't know how people really feel about us, and regard our personal relations as superficial and insincere. Openly expressing our feelings to each other can help us solve all these problems and build stronger and more authentic personal relations.

The T-group movement is based on these assumptions and a few scientific discoveries.

The T-group method. Nondirective interviewing, the basic technique for getting people to talk about their feelings, was first used with individuals. Superiors or interviewers would listen patiently while workers talked about whatever they pleased. The worker was in control of the conversation, and the superior did not criticize the worker even if he contradicted himself. The superior's job was to understand and accept whatever the worker said or felt and then reflect it back to him. He was essentially a sounding board or mirror that helped the worker express himself and see how he really felt.

Because he was free and felt safe, the worker slowly got around to talking about what really worried him. Sometimes he was quite surprised to hear himself say something revealing because he didn't know his own feelings. Something had been troubling him—irritation with his wife, concern about lack of education, resentment of his boss, or fear of unemployment—but he hadn't really understood it. Once these feelings were out in the open, he could understand and do something about them; and since the superior had accepted them as legitimate, the worker didn't feel as guilty or defensive about them. This combination of letting people express whatever they feel and accepting their feelings as legitimate is the foundation of all the other methods.

Sensitivity training groups (T-groups) among strangers are the most popular method today. These groups were originally conducted by the National Training Laboratories at Bethel, Maine, and other locations, but hundreds of organizations and individuals now offer

210

them. Some intensive programs last a few days or weeks; others meet over several weeks or months. Each meeting is unstructured and has one or two trainers (usually psychologists) and ten or twelve trainees.

The trainers are permissive and respect the trainees' ability to solve their own problems. They allow the group to discuss whatever it wishes in whatever way it feels is appropriate. The emphasis is on learning by doing and feeling, on process rather than content, on emotions rather than thinking. People are therefore free to do as they wish and learn by analyzing their own behavior, motives, and feelings (with or without the help of the trainer).

The trainer encourages them to express feelings that they don't normally give vent to but are accustomed to hold back. As a climate of trust and frankness develops, they become more honest and open. This honesty helps both the sender and the receiver: The sender drains off tension and understands how he really feels, and the receiver sees how people feel about him. This can be very rough on defensive people who have false images about themselves, but it can also be very helpful. The net result of the process can be more deeply human and authentic relationships, ones which contain little hypocrisy.

The same general method has been used with executive teams at work or during intensive courses at universities, resorts, and other "cultural islands." The cultural-island programs get the participants away from everyday pressures and make it easier to relax and speak frankly, but they can create some re-entry problems (which are also severe for other kinds of T-groups). The participants can't be as frank when they come back as they were while they were away. In fact, being frank can cause real problems. Since basic attitudes can't change very much in a few days, most participants soon slip back into their old habits. Groups at work have more problems in getting started, but the members can slowly apply their new habits and attitudes to the job.

Executive teams can deal with more important and irritating problems than groups of strangers, but generally they have more difficulty in being frank with each other. They know that they will have to live and work together and so may be afraid of hurting each other or making themselves vulnerable. And—since knowledge is power—some people will deliberately say very little about themselves while learning how to handle their associates in future political battles.

In addition to T-groups some psychologists have used role playing or other exercises, either alone or as a supplement to the training groups. Audio and visual tapes have also been made to let people see themselves as they appear to others. But the heart of most programs is still the small training group.

Benefits. Most T-groupers are quite idealistic and are at least as concerned with individuals as organizations. They therefore focus more directly on changing people's attitudes toward themselves and other people. There are, of course, some manipulators, but most of them sincerely care about good human relations, personal growth, identity problems, insecurity, and defensiveness and regard the improvement of human relations and satisfaction as intrinsically important goals.

However, T-group advocates generally have the same blind spot as the other human relationists about individual-organization conflicts, and they have kept trying for that impossible integration in which both get maximum satisfaction. They claim that their techniques can help develop integration in several ways. Participants learn to understand themselves and their feelings, accept their feelings as legitimate, and become less defensive and anxious. They also increase their sensitivity to group processes, other people, and the impact they have on them. They are therefore more aware of their real choices and more independent, effective, and satisfied.

Limitations. T-groupers do indeed marshal an impressive list of claims, but they haven't delivered yet. Research in this area is very poor and ambiguous, but it does not support their assertions, especially about improved performance and organizational effectiveness. At the present time there is no solid evidence that T-groups and similar programs improve organizational effectiveness. A few case studies do suggest some improvement, but case studies are notoriously subject to bias and misinterpretation.[5]

Here, however, we are much more concerned with individuals,

[5] All the data and conclusions here are from Campbell and Dunnette, "Effectiveness of T-Group Experiences in Managerial Training and Development," *Psychological Bulletin*, Vol. 70, August 1968.

and the evidence on them is ambiguous but a little more encouraging. Participants generally feel that a program has been worthwhile and educational, but they usually feel that way about any program. They often have more insight into themselves when they have completed the program, but similar improvements occurred in control groups who simply filled out self-description questionnaires twice. They may also be more sensitive to other people, but this apparent increase in sensitivity may be "merely the acquisition of a new vocabulary."

The most important issue is attitude change, and here the data are inconclusive but encouraging. Several studies have found that a significant number of participants developed more considerate and less domineering attitudes toward leadership or became more open, tolerant, and understanding on the job. This is, of course, the key issue for our purpose because goals and attitudes are much more important than sensitivity itself. Developing a man's sensitivity without changing his attitude can merely make him into a more effective manipulator. Since these data suggest that genuine changes in attitudes do take place, T-groups and related activities may well be more effective at solving the problem of anxiety than exhortations and the other human relations techniques.

However, we must not be overly optimistic. Fewer than half of the participants change, and a few change in the opposite direction. Furthermore, although the T-groupers' *training* system causes some executives to develop more humanistic attitudes, their *business* system works in the opposite direction and greatly reduces the impact of their programs.

Motivation is crucial for growth, but some T-group organizations' procedures guarantee that many participants won't have the proper motivation. Personal change and growth will usually not occur unless a person *wants* to grow and accepts responsibility for growth. But their business procedures bring in people with very different desires.

They sell their courses to organizations on the grounds that they will improve organizational effectiveness. The organizations then select the participants, who do not ask to go and who may go for a very different purpose than advancing their own personal growth. They often go to improve their leadership and manipulation skills

213

and organizational effectiveness rather than to learn about themselves. Some even regard the program as an assignment.

They may work as hard on this assignment as they do on their regular jobs; but they are working to satisfy their bosses, not some inner need, and are more interested in learning skills than new attitudes. Furthermore, a few participants are so unprepared or unfit for this type of program that it really hurts them. Their defenses are stripped away, and their anxiety overwhelms them. They leave the program with serious scars, and several such people have ended up in mental hospitals—a result that the program directors very carefully keep secret.

Open expression of feelings therefore seems to be a risky but rather effective solution, one which directly helps some participants and indirectly helps their associates and subordinates. Some participants become less defensive and more understanding and accepting; and, when they return to their jobs, they create healthier climates and help other people.

It seems, then, that proposals which focus directly on individuals have usually been more useful than the grand schemes. Simple ideas such as learning how to relax, developing better ways of expressing emotions, and legitimizing the expression of feelings have probably done more for individuals than all the inspiring attempts to change society, organizations, and human nature.

The next chapter continues in this "think small" tradition. Instead of proposing a grand scheme for changing the world, it outlines a simple strategy for living more effectively as an individual.

> *"Man's aim is to be himself and ..*
> *the condition for attaining this goal is*
> *that man be for himself."*
> —Erich Fromm.

> *"If you want to make the world a*
> *better place, start with yourself."*
> —Folk saying.

13

Enlightened Individualism

THE PRECEDING CHAPTERS HAVE BEEN DELIBERATELY WRITTEN TO discourage. We have tried to show that anxiety is a central and inescapable problem of our times and that no complete or perfect solution is possible. The problem continues to exist and may even become more severe because the forces which caused it will continue, and many of them will grow even stronger. Organizations are becoming larger and more bureaucratic; social change is more rapid every day; conformity pressures are increasing; individual power is declining.

The grand schemes have not considered these forces and the harsh realities of human nature. They have tried to solve the problem for everyone by changing society, organizations, or man, but they have had very little impact. The bitter inescapable truth is that no solutions on a grand scale are possible, and anxiety continues to be a central problem of our era. You must therefore realize that *no one else will solve your problem; you will have to do it yourself.*

It is certainly not an easy problem to solve. External pressures and your own defenses and habits drastically reduce your freedom of action; and even though the external pressures are the most visible obstacle, the real barriers are within yourself, in your attitudes, habits, fears, and defenses. Although inner problems are harder to recognize, they are within your control. You can't change society or your organization, but you can change yourself.

Our proposal is therefore based on a very simple assumption: *You must accept these pressures as a fact of life, realize that you can't change the world, and look for your own solution to the problem of anxiety. To do this you must free yourself from your inner prison, from the fears and defenses that undermine your independence.* As you free yourself, social and organizational pressures become less important. They are still there and are still powerful, but they don't mean as much. As you become free of your inner prison you expand the walls of the outer one; you understand the pressures and their impact on you and can resist them or choose the place where the pressures are not so irritating. You can find meaningful work, build real bonds with the world, and control your own life.

You can accept the limitations of your power, realize what you can change and what you cannot, and select a job and life style that are the most appropriate for you. Defenses make men ignore these limits and try fruitlessly to change their environments. Self-understanding helps a man realize that he can't change things very much, that the most reasonable strategy is to select an environment that satisfies him.

The elements of our proposal are therefore *individual responsibility, education, personal relations, meaningful work,* and *choosing the right environment.* You must accept the responsibility for your own life, understand yourself and the world you live in, develop authentic personal relations, and find meaningful work. The easiest as well as the most reasonable way to do this is to select an environment rather than try to change one. This is hardly an original or complicated proposal, but it is quite hard to carry out.

EDUCATION

A liberal education is an essential part of any lasting solution, but very few executives have this advantage. They have received excellent practical training from their colleges and companies, but this is no substitute for a liberal education. Training prepares a man for his work but not for his life. It provides the skills that make a man an effective executive but does not give him the understanding he needs to be an effective human being.

A well-trained but poorly educated man has skills but does not know what to do with them. He knows how to do things, but he does not know what he should do. He does not know who he is, or what he wants, or where he is going. He therefore lets other people select his goals for him and surrenders control of his life to his superiors, his organization, and anonymous authority. They tell him what he should want, what goals he should have, and because he has nothing better, he accepts their goals and devotes his life to them.

Occasionally he realizes that he is not in control of his own life, and this knowledge is profoundly disturbing—so disturbing that he usually pushes it out of his mind and works even harder for these imposed goals and becomes even more obsessed with success, profits, production, and so on. But the doubts remain because his humanity, his need to grow, and his hunger for independence cannot be denied. So the cycle of doubts and defenses continues.

Education is the only way out of this cycle, the only adequate foundation for a lasting solution for the problem of anxiety. It works on the causes of anxiety by answering the nagging questions, reducing our uncertainties, and strengthening our identities. It helps us relate to ourselves, our work, and other people; puts aging, success, and failure into perspective; and develops the inner resources and strength that we need to cope with our frustrations and distresses. It is, as Gilbert Highet wrote, "The best way to develop the countless potentialities for growth which everyone possesses." [1]

Although education does all these things, it is not a substitute for practical training; it helps a man to live, but does not help him to earn a living. Since he must do both, he must work on both. He must develop the skills and techniques he needs at work, but he must also develop his other potentialities.

Although education can develop these potentialities, it cannot be rigorously defined. No one can ever *have* an education. It is a

[1] Gilbert Highet, *Man's Unconquerable Mind*, Columbia University Press, New York, 1954, p. 76.

process, not a product, an approach to knowledge rather than knowledge itself. "Education" is, as Albert Einstein affirmed, "that which remains if one has forgotten everything he learned in school." It is openness to experience, a spirit of inquiry, perspective, independent judgment, a hunger to understand the world, an ability to see yourself and the world honestly.

Although this definition is not very satisfying, it is the best we can offer now. It should become clearer as we describe a strategy for educating yourself.

A strategy for self-education. The fact that you have read thus far in a book which has so little practical value suggests that you do want to educate yourself, but to do so requires much more than just reading a few books. It is a lifetime task which has immediate and very visible costs but deferred and unmeasurable benefits.

The task requires an enormous amount of time, but it does not necessarily advance your career; it certainly does not advance it as much as an equivalent investment in practical training. It can be an enjoyable process, but some pain is inevitable. It takes away your illusions about yourself and the world, weakens your defenses, and creates immediate uncertainty and anxiety. You become more open to your experience, more aware of your feelings and problems, and less able to deceive yourself. If you keep on with it, you will ultimately be stronger, more sure of yourself, and more able to cope with stresses, frustrations, and anxiety; but this benefit comes only after a period of vulnerability, uncertainty, and anxiety.

That is the price you have to pay, and you are the only one who can decide if it is too high. You can't educate yourself without cost, nor can you do it and preserve your defenses and illusions. As you understand your defenses they lose their value, and you feel the anxiety they help you to avoid. As you learn what you really want you realize how much of your life you have wasted on goals that other people chose for you. As you learn how you affect people you lose some of your self-image. As you learn about the world your illusions crumble and you become aware of your uncertainties.

At times these costs may appear to outweigh the benefits, but the costs are temporary and the benefits are permanent. And you can't have the benefits without paying the price. Education exacts its price, but without it you cannot break out of your inner prison and relate yourself to the world.

Planning. Because education is so demanding, planning is essential. You don't have enough time to do everything now, and you can't simply add education to your already busy schedule. You will not have the time unless you decide that your education and personal growth are as important as some of the things you are doing now and explicitly plan to spend that time on your education.

It probably won't do much good to say you will cut down on watching television or evening work so that you can spend more time on your education. Your education makes no immediate demands, and television, work, and all your other activities are constantly clamoring for your attention. Deadlines come up; special television programs look inviting; someone invites you out for the evening; and you just never get around to your education. If you are really serious about educating yourself, you should treat it as a serious responsibility and set aside certain specific hours for reading, discussion, self-analysis, writing, and similar activities. The following suggestions may help you plan your education more effectively.

1. Don't be too ambitious. If your plans are too ambitious, you won't be able to carry them out and will probably get discouraged and drop the whole idea. It is much better to make modest plans and follow them.
2. Balance your plans. You need to learn about three things— the world, yourself, and your role in the world—and should plan to spend definite hours on each of them. You should also balance your plans on many other dimensions: reading versus discussion, fiction versus nonfiction, and so on.
3. Set aside specific hours for each kind of educational activity. Don't just say you'll read three hours a week and spend two hours in serious conversation. Plan to spend Tuesday evening reading and Thursday afternoon from five to seven in a discussion group, for example.
4. Spread your education over several days each week. Concentrating your education in one day has about the same effect as taking no exercise all week and then playing 36 holes of golf on Sunday. You get tired, don't enjoy it, and don't get the maximum benefits from it.

219

5. Follow your schedule, but not too rigorously. If something comes up that is really more important, do it; but be sure to make up the time. An overly rigid schedule can take the fun out of education, and you need to enjoy it to keep at it.

Enjoyment. Time wouldn't be such a problem if education were more enjoyable, but the natural desire of Americans to learn has been stifled by years in a coercive educational system. European executives find time to continue their education because they enjoy it. They have learned that education is exciting and self-fulfilling, whereas Americans have found it dull and mechanical.

The American system of higher education is based on several mistaken assumptions. Professors usually won't admit it, but it is generally assumed that students don't want to learn, are too stupid to read original works, and are too lazy to read on their own initiative. They are therefore forced to sit in classrooms for 15 or 20 hours a week, read specified pages of simplified and poorly written textbooks, and take frequent examinations to make sure that they have done their homework.

European university students don't read textbooks; they read *books.* They don't read some dull summary of Freud, or Keynes, or Plato, nor do they have "ponies" which give the plot of—for example—*Jane Eyre, War and Peace, Madame Bovary,* or *Tom Jones;* they read Freud, Keynes, Plato, and most of the world's great novels. They don't read *Hamlet* aloud, one line at a time; they see the play and analyze it.

European students can do these things because they don't have to spend 15 hours a week warming a chair while some professor tells them what is in the books they haven't read and the plays they haven't seen. They can read these books for what they mean instead of trying to remember specific facts and trivia, because they are not subjected to "pop quizzes" and multiple-choice exams. They are given very infrequent and very broad exams which measure their understanding of what they have read and their ability to integrate this understanding. Their system emphasizes individual responsibility, reading, and understanding, whereas ours emphasizes coercion, lectures, and memory. The net result is that most Americans can do things better than their European counterparts but are bored by their education and stop studying as soon as they graduate, while many Europeans enjoy and continue their education throughout their entire lives.

It is, of course, hard to change the attitudes and habits you have built up from years in the system, but one simple rule can help you enjoy and continue your own education: *If you don't enjoy a particular book, article, play, or discussion, drop it.* No professor is standing over you now, and there is no need to spend your time on activities you don't enjoy. There are thousands of fine books to read and plays to see, and millions of people to talk to. If a book doesn't arouse your interest in the first few pages, put it down. If a discussion group bores you, drop out and find another one. Learning and enjoyment go together, and some of the world's most important and influential books and plays are also the most enjoyable.

In fact these works have been influential *because* people enjoyed them. A book or poem which is not read or a play which is not seen cannot have any impact. Shakespeare did not write his plays for the aristocracy; he wrote them for everyone, including illiterates; and they are as alive today as when they were written, because people in all eras have enjoyed them. Dostoevsky, Flaubert, Lawrence, Conrad, and most other great writers supported themselves in exactly the same way as Harold Robbins, Mickey Spillane, and Erle Stanley Gardner—by selling their books and stories. But long after most of the modern writers are forgotten, people will be reading the great ones.

If you expose yourself to great books, poems, plays, and paintings, you will probably enjoy them a great deal more than you enjoy the trash you read and watch on television, and it is very easy to get this exposure. You don't have to go to college, or buy a set of great books or reproductions of great paintings or symphonic records. Shakespeare's plays are performed frequently in every major city, and other great playwrights' works are staged occasionally by university and amateur groups or shown on educational television. Every public library contains hundreds of great books, and most cities have an art museum and a symphony or other orchestra. If you want to be a little more organized in your search, there are several guides to help you. You can also buy a book of original articles in any area—literature, economics, political science, psychology, other sciences—and browse through it, reading only what you enjoy. Then, when you find an author or topic that you particularly enjoy, you can try one of his books or longer articles, or use his footnotes to find other material.

The important thing is to expose yourself to great works and select only what you like. If you do this, your education will be enjoyable and exciting and it will be much easier to keep to your plans. If you try to force yourself to read or do things that you don't enjoy, you will probably become bored and stop trying. This advice is, of course, an argument against taking formal study courses; if you were enrolled in a course—in literature, say, or political science —your instructor would prescribe your reading.

Reading. Reading is obviously a basic part of any educational program, but many Americans—including a great number of college graduates—do not know how to read. The spectacular commercial success of reading schools is clear evidence that many adults know that they don't read very well.

Again, our educational system is at fault. It teaches students the wrong habits and emphasizes reading for facts rather than understanding. Students learn to read and remember facts which they can give back on multiple-choice exams; but they don't learn what an author meant, how he made his argument, or how his work agrees or disagrees with other books. If you have the same problem, you should admit it and learn how to read (preferably, by taking a reading course).

In addition to reading for enjoyment and understanding, you should deliberately strive for balance in your reading. If you look about you, you can find histories which are as fascinating as today's newspapers, essays which read like editorials, and poetry which is as lively as prose.

You should also strive to balance fact, theory, and opinion. You need facts, but you also need help in understanding them; and historians, psychologists, economists, and other specialists have written books about their disciplines. Many of these books—especially college texts—are very poorly written, but a few are so good that they make the best-seller lists. Two works in this class are *The Af-*

fluent Society, by John Kenneth Galbraith, and *Between Parent and Child,* by Haim Ginott.

You should also balance your reading by finding authors who disagree with you, instead of following the common habit of reading only authors who reinforce your own opinions. The men who disagree with you can't be completely wrong, and in any case they have facts and opinions that you need to understand our world. Liberals should read *The National Review, The Conscience of a Conservative* (by Barry Goldwater), and other conservative publications, while conservatives should try *The New Republic, The Nation, Why We Can't Wait* (by Martin Luther King, Jr.), and *The Arrogance of Power* (by J. William Fulbright). Following the same principle in other areas will expose you to ideas that you have never considered and build a stronger understanding of yourself and the world we live in.

A few people object to periodicals that express a political viewpoint, because they want authors to be "objective" and "impartial." This desire reveals a complete misunderstanding of objectivity and suggests that such people do not understand our legal and political systems. These systems, the foundation of our liberties, are based on the *adversary principle* under which two or more *biased* people present their arguments and leave the decision to an objective judge, jury, or voter. We have three branches of government to create checks, balances, and opposition; two major political parties to debate each other; defense and prosecuting attorneys to present each side of a case. Our system requires a great deal of time and money, and some people call it inefficient; but it is our best defense against tyranny and the surest road to sound decisions.

Judges, juries, and voters make the best decisions when all sides are presented by advocates, and you will get the best education if you follow the same principle. The author's job is to present an argument; yours is to weigh it. If you give up this task, if you let only a few editors decide what you should read, you will never understand what is going on.

Discussion. Genuine give-and-take discussion can be as valuable as balanced reading, but this kind of discussion is rather rare. Instead of talking frankly and open-mindedly about serious issues, most people talk about the weather, sports, gossip, and their jobs. Even when they do talk about politics, foreign policy, or other serious issues, they generally talk to people who agree with them, or else they close their minds and try to convince those who disagree.

However, if you do want genuine discussion, it is not hard to find. In large cities the libraries and newspapers can refer you to groups which discuss almost any topic: foreign policy, great books, marital problems, child rearing, or race relations. If you can't find what you want in discussion groups, your local high school, college, or university may have noncredit courses or luncheon meetings with speakers and discussion periods. As a last resort you can look for instructors who allow this kind of discussion, and take credit courses under them. In most credit courses, however, the emphasis is on the examinations rather than on discussion and true learning.

Counseling. All the activities mentioned are useful, even essential, but they cannot do as much for you as a systematic analysis of yourself. You do have to understand the world to relate to it successfully, but it is much more important to understand yourself. You have to understand your own goals, needs, and defenses, and counseling can help you to do so. Unfortunately, many people who do want to understand themselves will not even consider counseling.

These people may sincerely believe that they should solve their own problems, or they may be afraid to admit that they want or need help; but they avoid counseling or anything that even looks like counseling. If they aren't hurting themselves or other people, this may be the best policy for them. Counseling can help, but it is expensive; it does not help everyone, and it actually harms some people. They lose their defenses but don't get anything better; and in the end they feel all the anxiety they had kept buried.

On the other hand, if you are harming yourself or other people, feel unsure of who you are and what you should do with your life, or really want to get acquainted with yourself, counseling is certainly worth considering. If your problems are more serious—if you drink too much, always feel tense and irritable, take tranquilizers regularly, can't get along with your wife or associates, have an ulcer, or show any other signs of serious anxiety—you should give it very thoughtful consideration.

This advice may offend you by violating your beliefs about individual responsibility and your own psychological health. You may want to solve your own problems and to believe that you can do it. The desire to solve your own problems is laudable, and accepting responsibility for your life is essential; but it is very hard to see through your own defenses without help. Your defenses have persisted because they solve a problem for you; they help you cope with the stresses of your life, and you will not discard them as long as you need them. You may therefore need a place where they are less necessary, where you feel safe enough to let them go. Counseling can provide that kind of place. In fact the counselor's primary job is to create an atmosphere in which his clients feel safe enough to drop their defenses.

Even when the client has attained a feeling of safety, it is very hard for him to drop his defenses. He has depended on them for such a long time that he will let go very slowly and very reluctantly. This is why counseling usually requires such a long time. After a few interviews any counselor can describe a client's personality and problems, but it would not do any good. The client must control his own education and proceed at his own pace. *He* decides how quickly he discards his defenses, how honestly he faces himself, how much truth and anxiety he can stand.

Learning about yourself is very slow and difficult with a counselor, but it is much more difficult without one. Therefore, if you really want to understand yourself or if anxiety is a significant problem for you, your responsibility may not be to treat yourself but to accept honestly your need for help and pay what it costs in time, money, wounded pride, and temporary anxiety. If you do want to consider seeing a counselor or joining a counseling group, see Appendix A for suggestions on selecting one.

If you want to consider some of the issues that are normally covered in counseling but prefer to avoid counseling itself, you might complete the Goal Analysis Questionnaire in Appendix B. It has helped some executives analyze themselves in a systematic way, but it is just a step in the right direction and is not nearly as valuable —or as threatening—as working with a counselor or counseling group.

Observation. Reading and talking are not enough even if you talk with a counselor or counseling group. You have to open your eyes and look at what is happening around you—*all* around you, not just at your job or among your narrow social circles. What do Negroes really want? What is happening in Washington or City Hall? Where is this country going? Where do you fit into it? These questions are not easy to answer, and the answers are often very unsettling; but you cannot afford to ignore them. You live in a complex, interdependent world, and you cannot afford to run away from it. The only recourse is to understand it.

Reflection and writing. Questions of this type require a blend of observation, reading, discussion, and reflection. Reading, discussion, and observation provide the raw material of an education, but reflection and writing make sense of them. They gather isolated facts and opinions and put them into some perspective, some conceptual scheme that shows their interrelationships. Reflection can, of course, occur without writing; but the discipline of writing, the attempt to organize material and communicate with someone else, helps us to learn what we really think, to recognize the gaps and inconsistencies in our knowledge and opinions, and to tighten our reasoning. The more we discipline ourselves, the better we write and the more we learn. The first draft may help us understand our own opinions; but when we critically analyze and revise that draft, we realize how little we know and develop new insights.

Therefore, if you really want to understand yourself and the topics you read and talk about, *write, criticize,* and then *rewrite.* Send letters to the editor, write to your friends—even to yourself— but put those ideas on paper! When you read a book, write down the main points; challenge the author; and try to relate his work to other things you know. If something is unclear to you, try to explain it to someone else in a letter. You will win the satisfaction of expressing yourself and dramatically increase your understanding.

Value and limitations. Education is an indispensable foundation for lasting solutions to the problem of anxiety. It opens a man to his experiences, develops perspective, and helps develop the strength he needs to discard his defenses and relate himself to the world.

But education is not to be had for nothing. It takes time and energy that can be used for other purposes, creates appetites that are often hard to satisfy, and may even increase temporary anxiety and uncertainty by destroying illusions and weakening defenses.

Because the price is so high, many executives are unwilling to pay it, and they never really try to educate themselves.

We live in a practical society which values production much more than education, doers more than thinkers; and executives are one of the most practical groups in our society. They want more tangible benefits than psychological security, relatedness, and the pleasures of the mind—more proof that they are getting their money's worth. But no proof is possible. We cannot put anything on a balance sheet which clearly justifies the time, energy, and pain a man must invest in education, nor can we prove that education necessarily helps a man. Education is therefore exactly the sort of investment that most men do not want to make, one with high costs and unmeasurable benefits.

Education is also an incomplete solution to the problem. It lays the foundation, but there are several other things you have to do: build solid personal relations, take the responsibility and control for your own career, and find meaningful work. Since each of these actions increases your costs and none can be justified economically, our proposal will not appeal to most executives.

We are not trying here to appeal to most executives, nor are we trying to change the executive culture. We simply want to help a few individuals who are not satisfied with that culture. If you have read this far, you may be one of these individuals.

PERSONAL RELATIONS

Education helps you to know who you are and relate yourself to the world, but you must also develop satisfying personal relations and meaningful work. We have already seen how hard this is to do because our culture emphasizes the extrinsic rather than the intrinsic aspects of both work and personal relations—their effects on productivity, profits, efficiency, and careers—rather than the satisfaction they provide.

This emphasis is certainly a legitimate one. You do have a job to do, and failure to do it will have very unpleasant consequences. But you also have a basic need for meaningful relations with people, and there is some incompatibility between this need and the emphasis on doing your job. You may enjoy your relations with your subordinates, superiors, and associates, but you know that these relations exist for business purposes, not to satisfy your needs for relatedness. Exclusive concentration on these purposes may therefore make you an effective executive, but it can also keep you from developing the sort of relations you need to escape from "the prison of your aloneness."

Intrinsically satisfying relations. To escape from this prison you need some relations which exist primarily for themselves, some in which the emphasis is on the relationship itself rather than its effects on your career and daily work life and in which the satisfaction comes from expressing and being yourself and sharing thoughts and feelings with others.

But purpose alone is not enough. The purpose is the most important characteristic of any relationship, but other qualities also influence how well it satisfies your needs. Generally, relationships become more satisfactory as they become more honest and open, as each person lets down his defenses, expresses himself openly, and accepts the other person as he is. In this kind of relationship there is a dual benefit; each person obtains a feeling of oneness with the other while gaining a greater sense of his own individuality and identity.

Developing satisfying relations. It is far from easy to develop this kind of relationship. It may require changing some basic attitudes and habits, and it always involves some very real risks. You must commit yourself, and commitment makes you vulnerable. You open yourself to another person and invest something of yourself in him, and he may reject or hurt you. Since the costs and risks are so high, the first and most important step in developing these relationships is understanding how much you need them. Without this understanding you may be unwilling to pay the price or take the risks. Hopefully, this book has helped you realize the consequences of not developing this kind of relationship.

Even if you do have this understanding and desire, it still takes time to develop them. Most people commit themselves very slowly and carefully. They do not want to go further than the other person; so each takes small steps toward the other and waits for him to take a step in turn. Unfortunately, since each is unsure of how far the other person will go, both people will often hold back, each waiting for the other one to go first. This waiting can keep the relationship at a superficial level.

Although you may want to speed up the process, you should realize that people move slowly because they *have* to move slowly; if you make too large or too sudden a commitment, you may just frighten them away. You can therefore improve matters by taking the first step but can probably go further if you keep the steps small and don't get too far ahead of the other person.

You are, of course, the sole judge of how far you go, but the further you go the more honest you are; and the more of yourself you share with people the more satisfying your relationships will be. Regardless of how far you want to go, you may find the following principles useful. They are only a few of the valuable insights contained in Carl Rogers' book, *On Becoming a Person*.

> *In my relations with persons I have found that it does not help, in the long-run, to act as though I were something I am not.* It does not help to act calm and pleasant when actually I am angry and critical. . . . It does not help to act as though I were a loving person when actually, at the moment, I am hostile. . . . What I am saying here, put in another way, is that I have not found it to be helpful or effective in my relationships with other people to try to maintain a facade; to act in one way on the surface when I am experiencing something quite different underneath.

> *I find I am more effective when I can listen acceptantly to myself, and can be myself.* . . . The curious paradox is that when I accept myself as I am, then I change. . . . We cannot change, we cannot move away from what we are, until we thoroughly *accept* what we are. Then change seems to come about almost unnoticed. Another result which seems to grow out of being myself is that relationships then become real. . . . If I can accept the fact that I am annoyed at or bored by this [person], then I am also much more likely to be able to accept his feelings in response. . . . It is when I do accept all [my attitudes] as a fact, as a part of me, that my relationship with the other person then becomes what it is, and is able to grow and change most readily.

I have found it of enormous value when I can permit myself to understand another person. It is necessary to *permit* oneself to understand another. . . . Our first reaction to most of the statements which we hear from other people is an immediate evaluation, or judgment, rather than an understanding of it. . . . Very rarely do we permit ourselves to *understand* precisely what the meaning of his statement is to him.

I have found it enriching to open channels whereby others can communicate their feelings, their private perceptual worlds, to me. Because understanding is rewarding, I would like to reduce the barriers between others and me, so that they can, if they wish, reveal themselves more fully.

I have found it highly rewarding when I can accept another person. I have found that truly to accept another person and his feelings is by no means an easy thing, any more than is understanding. Can I really permit another person to feel hostile toward me? Can I accept his anger as a real and legitimate part of himself? Can I accept him when he views life and its problems in a way quite different from mine? . . . All this is involved in acceptance, and it does not come easy. I believe that it is an increasingly common pattern in our culture for each of us to believe, "every other person must feel and think and believe the same as I do." We feel it is very hard to permit our children or our parents or our spouses to feel differently than we do about particular issues or problems. . . . Yet . . . this separateness of individuals, the right of each individual to utilize his experience in his own way and to discover his own meanings in it—this is one of the most priceless potentialities of life. Each person is an island unto himself, in a very real sense; he can only build bridges to other islands if he is first of all willing to be himself and permitted to be himself.

The more I am open to the realities in me and in the other person, the less do I find myself wishing to rush in to "fix things." . . . I am much more content simply to be myself and to let another person be himself. I know very well that this must seem like a strange, almost an Oriental point of view. What is life for if we are not going to do things to people? What is life for if we are not going to mold them to our purposes? . . . The

230

paradoxical aspect of my experience is that the more I am simply willing to be myself, in all this complexity of life, and the more I am willing to understand and accept the realities in myself and in the other person, the more change seems to be stirred up. It is a very paradoxical thing—that to the degree that each one of us is willing to be himself, then he finds not only himself changing; but he finds that other people to whom he relates are also changing.[2]

These principles are not easy to apply; they require real discipline and restraint, but they can help you develop the kind of relationships you need. Furthermore, they are completely general; they can be applied to any relationship—on the job or off it, with your wife or children as well as with your friends.

Indeed, it may be even more important to use them in your relations with friends and family than on the job. They are the people who can really give you a sense of relatedness, and you may not be nearly as effective at relating to them as you are at getting people to do their jobs.

If you do want to apply these principles, three very readable books can help you. Carl Rogers' *On Becoming a Person*, already quoted, is the most general and complete discussion. Chris Argyris' *Interpersonal Competence and Organizational Effectiveness* (Irwin) applies these principles to organizations. Haim Ginott's best seller, *Between Parent and Child* (Macmillan), applies them to relations with children, but the book is so clear and readable that it can help you in other relationships as well.

CAREER PLANNING

As we have seen, education and personal relations are essential parts of any lasting solution, but they usually will not be enough. Your career is very important to you, and you will probably have to plan and control it yourself. It is not easy to do so; you have to spend long hours analyzing yourself and your situation, learning new skills, and overcoming some very severe pressures. These pressures are so strong that many executives leave most of the decisions to their superiors.

[2] Carl R. Rogers, *On Becoming a Person*, Houghton Mifflin, Boston, 1962.

If you yield to these pressures and fail to plan your career, you will harm yourself in several ways: (1) You will know that you do not control your career, and this knowledge will make you feel powerless and anxious. (2) You will devote part or all of your career to goals imposed by other people and will therefore feel somewhat alienated from yourself and your work. (3) There are some real conflicts between you, your superiors, and your organization, and their decisions will generally be based on their interests, not yours. These consequences are usually ignored, but they are so important that we shall discuss each one in some detail.

In Chapter 5 we learned that feelings of powerlessness generally lead to anxiety; this anxiety is greater for very independent people and very important issues. Executives are generally independent and concerned about their careers. But most organizations insist that they stifle this basic need and passively accept their superiors' decisions about their careers. The net result has to be anxiety and resentment.

You may bury your own anxiety and resentment and accept these policies as legitimate. You may even be relieved by them, because they take away your responsibility for your career. You don't have to make these decisions; you just do your job and leave the decisions to your superiors. But you cannot escape this responsibility, and trying to run away from it will create much greater problems than accepting it. The responsibility is there; the freedom is yours, and you cannot escape it. You cannot suppress your individualism, uniqueness, and independence; they are a part of you, and trying to suppress them will only make you feel helpless, alienated, and anxious.

These feelings will come, regardless of the benevolence of your superiors. Even if they make exactly the decisions you want (a most unlikely possibility), you will still know that your career is in their hands. You may try to escape this knowledge by burying yourself in your work, protesting that they are fair men with your best interests at heart and ignoring the real conflicts between you, but you will always know that they control your career, and you will never escape the consequences of this knowledge.

Furthermore, leaving the decisions to your superiors means that you must devote much of your life and work to goals which they have chosen for you, goals which you may not want. You may try not to think about it, but you will always know that you are working for things that you do not really want; and this knowledge inevitably leads to alienation and anxiety. You can no more suppress your basic goals than you can suppress your individualism and need for independence; they are part of your basic humanity and cannot be denied.

Many executives may feel a little uncomfortable with the preceding paragraphs; the statements in them are too abstract and philosophical and depend on assumptions that these executives may not share. Let us therefore discuss more concrete reasons for controlling your own career. You, your superiors, and your organization have many common interests, but there are also some very obvious and very important conflicts between you. You want more money; they want lower costs. You want variety; they need standardization and routine. You want to live in certain places, but they have slots to fill. You want time with your family, but they have jobs to be done.

Furthermore, even if your superiors are very fair and generous men, even if they care about your needs, goals, and ambitions, they will usually be more concerned with the organization's needs than yours. Their responsibility is to the organization, and their own careers and ethics demand that they put the organization's needs before yours, even if they don't want to.

They may also be unaware of what you really want. Extensive research indicates that most superiors overestimate their subordinates' desires for money and underestimate their other desires. Therefore, even if they are concerned with your goals, they may try to help you reach goals that you really don't care about.

In brief, whether your superiors understand and care about your goals or not, leaving these decisions to them will lead to frustrating some of your needs. If they are generous men who understand you, this frustration may not be severe, but some frustration is inevitable. Leaving these decisions to them must also cause feelings of alienation, helplessness, and anxiety because you will know that you are working for goals you reject and do not control your own career. It is therefore essential that you accept the responsibility for your own career and make—or at least influence—the decisions about it.

Meaningful work. We are not suggesting that you "game" your way to the top, nor are we advocating a socially irresponsible form of individualism. On the contrary, we feel that ignoring social responsibilities and concentrating solely on your advancement will aggravate the very problems that you are trying to solve. We therefore propose that you plan your career so that you satisfy all your needs, including your needs to be independent, to grow, to relate to other people, and to do meaningful work.

"Meaningful work" is not necessarily the most financially rewarding and prestigious; it is work that *you* find intrinsically satisfying, that gives you a sense of accomplishment and social contribution. This kind of work satisfies your deeper needs and can help you relate to the world and yourself, while work which provides only money and prestige can leave you feeling useless and alienated. Exclusive concentration on traditionally defined success is therefore not in your own best interests, and you will probably be healthier and happier if you find work that gives you a sense of satisfaction, accomplishment, and contribution, even if it does not pay as well.

Women have an edge on men here. Child rearing does not confer very great prestige on women, and they often grow tired of it; but it is intrinsically satisfying, and they do know that they are doing something worthwhile. Men obtain greater prestige and other external rewards and may find their work more exciting, but most of them wonder occasionally how much they are really accomplishing or contributing.

Since our complex society makes it very hard for many people to see the results and value of their work, you may never be able to completely escape from this dilemma. But, if you can control your own career, you can select projects you like or choose companies that provide products and services which you respect and then find enjoyable, challenging, and useful jobs in them. Doing so is not easy; it requires extensive analysis and planning, but the right kind of job for you can provide a sense of security and satisfaction that you cannot obtain in any other way. It can also help you reach your other goals, because people generally work more effectively at activities that they enjoy and for goals that they value.

To find this kind of job has never been easy and may be particularly hard today because of all the trends we have discussed, but two trends are rather encouraging. First, after a long period of changing the external aspects of jobs, a few companies are experimenting with ways of making them intrinsically more satisfying. (American Telephone and Telegraph, with the help of Professor Herzberg, is the most notable example.) Most of these experiments have focused on the worker level, but this kind of thinking is changing some executive jobs as well.

The second trend is even more important: A growing number of senior executives are rising above the traditional obsession with immediate profits and are developing broader conceptions of profits and their social responsibilities. They still recognize the crucial importance to our system of making profits but are developing a larger and longer-term perspective and are concerned with the future of our society as well as their companies. They are therefore working on some of our most important and difficult problems: race relations, air pollution, training and hiring the hard-core unemployed, and rebuilding our cities, for example. This concern with social problems offers new opportunities for service and satisfaction, and the executive who wants to contribute to these problems can do so as part of his regular job instead of working part-time at politics and civic affairs.

These remarks do not mean that we do not value the contribution of traditional business activities, nor are we suggesting that this sense of satisfaction, achievement, and contribution can come only from working on certain kinds of problems. We do realize the contributions and satisfaction of traditional business activities and wholeheartedly endorse working for them—*if they satisfy you.* But if you are not proud of your company's products and services, if you do not enjoy your work or get a sense of accomplishment from it, you should probably start looking for a place where you will get these satisfactions. You have to be the judge, and you cannot let anyone—your bosses, anonymous authority, or this book—tell you what you should enjoy or produce. The key question is not what someone else thinks of your work, but what you think of it yourself.

If you enjoy your job and honestly believe that you are accomplishing something worthwhile, by all means stay with it; but don't keep the same job if it bores you or makes you feel defensive or useless. Far too many executives have to rationalize about their work, and life is too short and too precious to waste on distasteful activities and trivial problems.

Not everyone, unfortunately, can find the right kind of job or move to it. Some men lack the necessary skills, and others are locked into their present jobs by financial or other pressures. If you cannot change jobs yet dislike the one you have, you may have to find your feelings of accomplishment and satisfaction off the job. But you cannot afford to do without them. If your job provides only money and status but you cannot change it, you will be much better off if you work in politics, charities, youth groups, and the like than if you spend your time on golf, television, and cocktail parties. You do have a need to accomplish and contribute something, and your life will be meaningless and empty if you don't satisfy it. It is, of course, best to satisfy it at work, but if you can't, you have to do so somewhere else.

A word of caution: Don't jump to the conclusion that you are locked into your job until you have thoroughly examined your situation. You may have much more freedom and power than you think, and you may be able to find more satisfying work in your own or another company. Changing jobs is a skill and a fairly simple one, but most executives never learn it. If you read certain books [3] and the section on strategy in this book, you may find that you can change jobs more easily than you thought.

The moral issue. Although we have explicitly stated that a man cannot get the satisfaction he needs from life unless he contributes to society, some people may still feel that our position is unethical, that men should work for the good of their organizations and leave the decisions about their careers to their superiors. This ethic is expressed in many ways: in derogatory comments about "company politicians," in satirical plays such as "How to Succeed in Business Without Really Trying," in constant reminders of the need for company loyalty, and in a wide variety of more subtle ways.

Since many executives share this ethic and may be inhibited by it, we shall show why an executive is justified in controlling his own career. The first and most important justification is that the consequences of not doing so are very serious but this ethic ignores them.

Second, independence and individualism are a central part of

---

[3] Auren Uris, *The Executive Job Market,* McGraw-Hill, New York; Carl Boll, *Executive Jobs Unlimited,* Prentice-Hall, Englewood Cliffs, New Jersey; Allen Rood, *Realizing Your Executive Potential,* McGraw-Hill.

the American tradition and have helped us to build an outstanding society and economy. Conditions have changed and our old forms of individualism do not apply to men in large organizations, but we must modify this tradition instead of discarding it. Because so many men work in large organizations, we must emphasize individualism *within* organizations, but we certainly cannot afford to reject the tradition and values which have built our society.

On this point one must agree with Whyte that we have gone so far in the direction of cooperation that we need more individualism, for the sake of the organizations as well as for the individuals in them.

> Precisely because it *is* an age of organization, it is the other side of the coin that needs emphasis. We do need to know how to cooperate with the organization, but, more than ever, so do we need to know how to resist it. Out of context this would be an irresponsible statement. Time and place are critical, and history has taught us that a philosophical individualism can venerate conflict too much and cooperation too little. But what is the context today? The tide has swung far enough the other way, I submit, that we need not worry that a counteremphasis will stimulate people to an excess of individualism.[4]

Third, working hard may lead to greater rewards, but the correlation between performance and rewards has never been perfect. Some men perform well but are not rewarded adequately, whereas others gain more than they deserve. Furthermore, as noted earlier, your superiors may not even know what you really want; therefore, even if they do try to reward good performance, they may not give you what you really want.

Fourth, the current ethic is essentially a one-way loyalty system. Individuals are expected to be loyal to the organization, but the organization has no reciprocal loyalty requirement—as it has, for example, in Japan. Top management is expected to drop unnecessary men; indeed, it would be violating its other responsibilities if it did not do so, and many executives have been dropped after 20 years of loyal service. We are not objecting to management's right

[4] William Whyte, *The Organization Man,* Simon and Schuster, New York, 1956, pp. 12–13.

to drop them; in fact we are strongly opposed to paternalism. But we do think that it is unreasonable to expect complete loyalty from the individual if there is so little from the company.

Fifth, it is still regarded as ethical for a man to strive for the maximum return on his capital, but executives' primary capital is their earning capacity. If it is ethical to strive for the maximum return on their money, why is it unethical to strive for the maximum return on their careers? Is money more important than lives? If not, why should men have more freedom in investing their money than they have in investing their lives?

Sixth, the moral position taken in this book is both broader and narrower than the current one. Each man should strive to maximize satisfaction from his career, but he can do so only by finding work that contributes to society; it is contribution to *society* that is important, not contribution to the organization. Each individual must therefore decide whether his work contributes to society and satisfies his needs. If it does not, he should either change jobs to get the satisfaction and sense of contribution he needs or else develop meaningful activities off the job, because he cannot afford to just work for the organization and leave the moral questions to his superiors. The moral responsibility is his, and he cannot abdicate it without impoverishing himself.

Fear. Even if a man feels justified in trying to control his career, he may be afraid to do so. Some men are afraid to accept the responsibilities, whereas others are afraid of their superiors' response to any independent action. Although they may be justified, fears about superiors' reactions are often exaggerated. Most people don't know how their superiors will react and simply assume that they will react negatively, but these assumptions can also be a defense that keeps them from realizing that they are more afraid of the responsibilities than of their superiors. If your fears about their reaction are actually a defense, they can be overcome only by honestly looking at yourself. If they are not a defense, you may find that they are based on inadequate data and faulty assumptions. Therefore, if you do not know how your superiors will react to your independence, you might try them out with a mildly independent action—such as asking for a slight change of duties—and observe

238

their reaction. They may brush you off or put you down, but many subordinates have been surprised to learn that their superiors accepted their suggestions and actually welcomed their independence and respected them for it. Once they realized this, they were able to begin a more ambitious program of career planning.

But perhaps your fears are justified; perhaps your superiors will hold your independence against you. If so, the sooner you find another job in your current company or another, the better off you will be. You cannot afford to live in fear, nor can you stifle your need for independence without paying a terrible price. Anxiety, anger, and other emotions can cause ulcers, heart attacks, and many other diseases, and no job is worth your health or your life. Therefore, unless you are absolutely locked into your current job (a very rare occurrence), you should try to exert some control over your career.

Strategy. Now we can move from *why* to *how*, from the ethical justification and psychological necessity of controlling your career to a strategy for career planning. This strategy can help you obtain and use the power you need to control your career and may also reduce the problem of fear by showing you that you are not so dependent on your superiors and organization. The general approach is very similar to the professional approach to management, but is somewhat broader: It is based on the same general assumptions, but more goals are related to your career; it is more systematic, and more tactics are regarded as legitimate.

This strategy is simple in outline and is based on education (in the broadest sense of the word), but it requires extensive analysis of yourself and your situation and is time-consuming and rather hard to implement. It also involves some risks, but they are not nearly as great as the risks of not having any strategy at all (the usual situation).

You will eventually want to lay out your entire strategy, plan your tactics in greater detail, and procure important background information—for example, on salaries in different industries and mobility patterns in different specialties. The following section simply outlines the eight major steps in the strategy.

1. *Analyze your own goals.* An intelligent career strategy obviously requires a clear understanding of your own goals. If you don't

know what you want, you obviously can't get it. If you don't understand your own goals, you can't work toward them. Unfortunately, relatively few people ever carefully analyze their own goals; they simply accept the goals that other people say they *should* want instead of determining what they *do* want. Then, if they do succeed in reaching these goals, they may find that their success is meaningless and empty because it does not provide the satisfaction they anticipated.

The American emphasis upon material success creates many such problems. We are told that we *should* want to get ahead, that we *should* want a lot of money, that we *should* try for the top. For some people these are meaningful goals but not for everyone. And they are not enough for anyone. You may want to get to the top, but you also want other things—enjoyable work, time with your family, compatible associates, a certain kind of schedule, a sense of accomplishment and contribution. Your own habits and the culture you live in may cause you to suppress some of these other goals, but you cannot afford to do so. You must therefore analyze your goals very thoroughly and work for the goals you really have, not for the ones other people try to impose upon you.

Because our culture is so complex and the pressures against self-analysis are so great, you probably will not be able to completely understand your goals without help from a professional counselor, but the Goal Analysis Questionnaire in Appendix B may help you arrive at a clearer understanding of your goals and the chances you have of reaching them. You can increase the questionnaire's value by discussing your answers with your wife, a friend, or even your minister. Even if you do not discuss it, this questionnaire can take several hours and may be rather disturbing, because some answers will be rather inconsistent or appear illogical. But, since inconsistency is a part of human nature and self-knowledge is never easy to acquire, there is no reason to be embarrassed or upset. Everyone has some inconsistencies, and bringing them out in the open will help you to deal with them and act more effectively.

2. *Analyze your assets and liabilities.* It is not enough to understand your goals; you must also understand the assets which will help you reach them and the liabilities which will hold you back. You wouldn't try to make a company's future plans without a clear

understanding of its assets and liabilities, and you obviously can't plan your own career without a similar understanding. Unfortunately, analyzing your personal assets and liabilities is much more difficult than analyzing those of a business. A business generally has standardized accounting procedures for measuring its assets and liabilities, and they can be made directly comparable to each other by converting them into dollars. A person's assets and liabilities, on the other hand, are usually very hard to measure and cannot be compared directly with each other. It is nearly impossible to say —for example—how much intelligence compensates for the lack of a college degree, or how much a proven record of success compensates for the fact that a man's age is over 50.

Even though you cannot make a completely accurate estimate, you can greatly increase your understanding by asking yourself a large number of specific questions and looking for patterns in the answers. Since most of us have rather biased opinions of ourselves, the help of another person (particularly that of a trained specialist) can be invaluable, but it is not absolutely necessary.

Ask yourself the questions in the following list; and, again, don't be embarrassed or discouraged if you can't give complete or logical answers. Even an incomplete or somewhat illogical answer can improve your self-understanding.

- How intelligent are you? (The important comparison for intelligence and all other assets and liabilities is not with the general population but with the people with whom you are competing for jobs, promotions, and raises. You are probably not competing with average men and must therefore compare yourself with your competitors rather than the general public.)
- How does your income progress compare with the progress of other people in your firm?
- How does it compare with other people your age in other firms?
- Do you have favorable contacts in your firm?
- Do you have favorable contacts in other firms?
- How do your social skills compare with those of your competitors?
- Do you have all of the necessary credentials for the jobs you want (degrees, certificates, proper experience, the right social and religious background, and so on)?

- If not, can you acquire these credentials?
- How valuable is your experience to your firm?
- How valuable is your experience to another firm?
- How valuable will it be in the future?

Your answers to these and many similar questions should help you decide how realistic your ambitions are and what steps you must take to make the best use of your assets and minimize the effects of your liabilities.

3. *Analyze your opportunities.* Normally, the word "opportunity" refers primarily or entirely to chances for advancement, but here it will be used to refer to your chances of reaching your goals, regardless of what they may be. If you want to move into top management, "opportunity" refers to your chances of doing so; if you want a job with lower pressure or more satisfying work, more regular hours, and less company travel, "opportunity" refers to your chances of reaching these goals.

We advocate making as objective an analysis of your real opportunities as possible. Determine as carefully, systematically, and unemotionally as you can the opportunities you really have to reach your goals in your own or another firm. It is usually very hard to make this analysis because most firms are rather less than candid about the opportunities which they really offer; they try to create the impression of a better situation than really exists. Fortunately, there are sources of information other than interviews with recruiters, personnel managers, and superiors: published data, stock analysts, friends, management consultants, and personal observations. The use of these other sources of information in a systematic way can result in a much clearer understanding of your real opportunities.

The Goal Analysis Questionnaire raises some questions about your opportunities to satisfy certain goals, but you need to go much further. The technique you used in analyzing your assets and liabilities will be effective in this effort: Write down a number of questions and look for patterns in the answers. The questions listed here should then help you focus your answers and act on them. Ask questions such as these:

- How rapidly is your industry growing?
- How profitable is your industry, compared with other industries?

242

- How well does your industry pay, compared with other industries?
- What would be the effect upon your industry of a great decrease in military or governmental spending?
- How does the growth of your firm compare with the rest of the industry?
- How well does your company pay?
- How many new products has your firm introduced in the past ten years?
- Do you respect your company's products or services?
- Do you like your schedule?
- Do you like the area you live in now?
- Do you like the area you will have to live in if you advance in the company (that is, if you are transferred to the home office)?
- How many people have moved upward from your unit or present job to higher management?
- Is your boss promotable?
- Does your immediate superior want to help you get ahead?
- Do your other superiors want to help you get ahead?
- How many people who are important to your future do you normally contact on your job?
- How much has your income increased since you joined the firm?
- How many *real* promotions have you had?
- How high do you think you have a reasonable chance of going in your firm?

The answers to these and many similar questions should help you answer the following *key questions:*

- Should you stay in your present job?
- Should you look for another job with your current firm?
- Should you look for a job in another firm?
- Which firms or industries should you consider?

4. *Learn the rules of company politics.* For centuries political scientists have recognized the distinction between techniques for acquiring power (the art of politics) and techniques for using it wisely (the art of government). As even the most casual examination of any government clearly reveals, the masters of politics, not the masters of government, have most of the power. Unfortunately,

this distinction has rarely been made in the business world, despite the abundant evidence that many executives acquired their jobs for reasons other than their competence and performance.

Of course, doing your job well will probably help your career, but it will not guarantee that you will get the job that you want or that you will be properly rewarded for your work. In fact, good performance may not have much effect on your career at all, because it is usually very difficult or even impossible to say how good a job a manager is doing. A worker's performance can often be rated on several fairly objective criteria such as number of units produced per hour or amount of scrap, but a manager's performance can very rarely be judged as accurately or objectively. Therefore a manager's pay, performance ratings, advancement, and all other aspects of his career are very dependent upon his superiors' opinion of him and his work—opinions which are influenced by many factors besides performance. In a word, a manager's career depends upon politics.

You may dislike the fact that your career depends upon politics, but you cannot escape it. Politics exists in every department and in every organization, particularly at the managerial and executive levels. The only way you can completely avoid politics is to leave executive life.

The question, then, is not *whether* you become involved in politics but *how* you become involved and in what kind of politics. Here again there is no substitute for a thorough analysis, both of yourself and of your situation. You have to decide what kind of political role you are willing and able to play and what effect your particular style of politics will have on your career in your current or another job. To do so you have to understand yourself and the rules of the political games in your own or any organization you are considering joining. There are several sets of rules in each organization or department—rules for getting ahead quickly, rules for surviving quietly, and so on. After you understand these rules, you have to decide whether you want to play according to their dictates or whether you should go elsewhere to find a game more to your liking. Once you understand the games and have selected one, you can play it more effectively. You can obviously do better if you know what the rules are, how points are really scored, how evaluations are really made, how people really get ahead.

To understand the politics in any department or organization you must determine two things:

1. Who are the people with the real power (especially the power to influence your career)?
2. How do they make their decisions (especially decisions related to your career)?

Once you know which people have the power to influence your career and how they decide to use that power, you can evaluate your own situation and take steps to improve it. You can leave; "play it cool"; build good relationships with the right people; and so on.

5. *Learn and use bargaining tactics.* Bargaining is only part of politics, but it is so important that it will be discussed separately here. Most executives know how to bargain for the company—with suppliers, customers, or unions—but do not know how to bargain for pay, promotions, duties, or transfers. However, the tactics are essentially the same, and the underlying principle is identical: *Bargaining is based not on morality but on power, and power depends on the number of options available to each party.*

Since the firm generally has many more options than you do, your bargaining power is going to be very limited unless you can develop other alternatives. Sometimes these alternatives are offers from other companies, but you may receive the same benefit from "offers" from other parts of your own company; and these offers are not very hard to get.

Until very recently there were no guides to help executives obtain offers and bargain with their companies, but several books on job hunting have appeared in the past few years. One author [5] has written a book and an article on bargaining tactics in which he goes much further than anyone else in describing how to bargain with a current employer. He also describes bluffing techniques to be used when there is no other alternative. Many executives have been shocked and outraged that a man would advocate using the same techniques with his superiors that his superiors use with unions, customers, and suppliers.

[5] A. Z. Carr, *Business as a Game*, New American Library, New York, 1968. See also A. Z. Carr, "The Ethics of Bluffing in Business," *Harvard Business Review*, January–February 1968.

Although the logic of their position is questionable and the ethic is clearly inconsistent, you cannot afford to ignore it. You will therefore have to be very subtle when you bargain with your employers. In fact the idea is to bargain without appearing to do so, to let them know that you have other options and will leave if you are not satisfied, but not to confront them with a situation in which they must *openly* bargain with you. If they have to bargain with you openly, their pride may make them act to your disadvantage.

These subtle bargaining techniques can be used more easily on some issues than on others. They can help you win raises or promotions, but they are still more effective in obtaining changes in duties, location, and responsibilities. It is usually easier to obtain an offer or other expression of interest from another division of your company than it is to get a firm offer from another company, and your superiors don't feel as outraged about your "disloyalty" as they would if the offer came from outside. Therefore, if you like your company or have strong reasons for staying with it but dislike some aspects of your present job, develop alternatives in other parts of the company. If these alternatives are better than your present job, you can switch jobs. Whether they are better or not, you can use them to bargain—though subtly—with your superiors.

However, if you want a radical change in your situation, or a promotion or a large raise, you will probably have to get an offer from another company (preferably, in writing). You need a concrete offer for your superiors to match, and you can usually get a better deal from another company than from any part of your current company. You can bargain harder with the other company because hard bargaining with a potential employer is perfectly legitimate, and the potential employer knows that you have the alternative of staying where you are. (A few people give away this advantage by saying that they are definitely leaving or even that they are being forced out, but most executives act with more perception of the situation.) Then, when you do receive this offer, you can either accept it or use it to get concessions from your superiors that they would never offer without it.

6. *Develop visibility.* Although you can get some offers by applying for jobs and using the other standard techniques for job hunting,

the really attractive jobs go to men who don't ask for them. In fact, you cannot apply for them any more than you can apply for membership in certain clubs. You must be invited, and invitations depend on visibility. Developing visibility is therefore essential if you want to reach the very top, and it is also very useful if you have other goals: It increases the number of offers you will get from other parts of your own firm as well as from other firms. These offers may be attractive enough to tempt you, and unsolicited offers raise people's opinion of you and subtly bargain for you even if you do not use them directly. And you can, of course, use them in bargaining. A strategy for developing visibility is therefore essential. Unfortunately, relatively little has been written on this topic.

7. *Plan your career.* Although learning these techniques and performing these analyses can be time-consuming and even annoying, they are eminently worthwhile, for they enable you to do something that very few men ever do—to plan and control your own career, decide where you are going and how you will get there. Successful businessmen nearly always plan for the future of their firms, but very few men plan their careers. They take a job and then let inertia and their emotions take over. They may stay at that job long after they should have left or change jobs prematurely or for irrational reasons. They rarely have an overall concept of where they are going and how they will get there. They are therefore only rarely successful, if success is defined in terms of reaching all their goals, not merely their monetary and advancement goals.

If you want to reach all of your goals, you have to make careful long-range plans. These plans can be made only after you have completed the suggested analyses, because you need the information that they provide. Once you have completed these analyses, plan your career in three major phases.

First, set realistic long-term goals. You should decide what you want to be ultimately. Once you have a clearer idea of your personal goals, assets, liabilities, and opportunities and understand the harsh realities of company politics, what job do you want as the culmination of your career?

Second, set intermediate-term goals and plans which are consistent with your long-range goals. You must decide upon the step-

247

ping-stones to your long-term goals. What experience, training, credentials, connections, and so forth do you need to reach your long-term goals, and how can you acquire them? Again, realism is crucial. Don't try to do too much too fast, or you may become discouraged and do nothing. And don't try to do too many things that you regard as unpleasant but necessary to reach your long-term goals. If the intermediate sacrifices are too great, the long-term goals themselves may be unrealistic or unreasonable. Set a reasonable schedule for advancing yourself toward your long-term goals, making sure that the intermediate points are within your abilities and worthwhile in and of themselves.

Third, plan your immediate future so that it fits in with your longer-term plans. Your next job, if you are now a fairly young man, should be picked not for its salary or its "opportunities for advancement" but for the chances it provides for getting the experience, training, and connections that you need to reach your long-term goals. The job which is superficially attractive to you because it has a high salary or offers the opportunity for immediate advancement or is located in a desirable place may be a mistake from the standpoint of your long-term career. Your immediate plans should be made because they fit into your longer-term plans, not because they are attractive at the moment.

Note that the planning strategy advocated here is exactly the opposite of the strategy that most people follow (if theirs can be called a strategy). Most people do not plan further ahead than their next job, if they plan even so far in advance. They take a job because it looks attractive and then see what they can do with it. We advocate looking as far into the future as you can and deciding where you want to be at the height of your career and what steps lead to it. In that way your life and your jobs and your career fit into some intelligent overall plan, and you retain control of your life rather than simply respond to circumstances.

8. *Periodically analyze your progress and make necessary changes in your career plan.* Many people would regard the creation of a career plan as the final step in formulating a career strategy. Unfortunately, in most cases it is not the last step; even the best of plans can't provide for all possible contingencies. Conditions change and people change. The job which looked like a stepping-stone to

bigger things turns out to be a dead end; the goals which seemed so important once become less attractive as you approach them. You must therefore periodically examine your progress and goals and make whatever changes appear necessary.

There is another even more important reason for periodically thinking about your career plans. Although this discussion of the steps in forming a career strategy has listed them one by one as if each were independent and could be dealt with in a fixed order, the process is not nearly so simple as that. Instead of a simple sequence from goal analysis to asset and liability analysis, to opportunity analysis, to political analysis, to career planning, to analysis of progress, there is a rather circular process. As you understand your real opportunities and the techniques and sacrifices needed to reach your original goals, the goals themselves may change to some extent, causing further changes in your opportunities or in the techniques needed. Therefore, the overall goal of this program is not simply to provide the answers to the questions raised here but to help you become more aware of yourself, your goals, your opportunities, and what you must do to reach your goals and live the kind of life you want. Then, and only then, can you truly be your own man, making the important decisions about your life rather than passively accepting the decisions of your superiors.

A FINAL WORD

Anxiety is inherent in the human condition; it is a result of the pressures of our complex society, and we can never escape it completely. To ignore it or deny it will simply increase its impact on us. And its primary impact is to undermine our most basic right and most basic human quality—our ability to choose. It can bind us to our alternatives or prevent us from choosing the ones that will really satisfy us.

The best solution to the problem of anxiety is, therefore, to understand it, for understanding it will develop the power to choose. The first three parts of this book analyzed the causes and effects of anxiety; the last two chapters have discussed ways to reduce its effects and exert the ability to choose. Specific techniques such as relaxing can help minimize the effects of anxiety, but for a lasting solution we must educate ourselves, develop satisfying personal relations, do meaningful work, and plan our careers. These four essential activities are all interrelated, and improving one improves the others. As work becomes more meaningful we become more able to share ourselves with other people; as we become more educated, we become more able to act independently and plan our own careers.

It is true, however, that even though they are interrelated none of these activities is easy to engage in. They all conflict with the pressures of our culture and our own attitudes, habits, and defenses. They require us to do things that we prefer to avoid; we would rather not look at ourselves and the world we live in, or discard comfortable illusions, or make ourselves vulnerable to other people, or accept the responsibilities for our own lives and decisions. No one can overcome all his resistance in these matters or fully implement the suggestions made in this book, but even a slight use of the suggestions can help you. Since we have focused only on individual problems, each of these actions is within your own control. You cannot change society, nor can you solve the problem of anxiety for other people; but you can take some of these actions if you really want to do so.

And so we come to the end of this book. But we end on a note very different from the one on which we began. We began by discussing the negative aspects of anxiety—its power to make people act irrationally. We end by noting that anxiety has a constructive side as well. It can make men irrational and defensive, but if it is properly understood, it can also motivate them to reach their full potential, to engage in the uniquely human acts of learning, loving, and creating.

Appendixes

Appendix A

Choosing a Counselor

WHETHER YOU WANT HELP WITH A SERIOUS PROBLEM OR SIMPLY WANT to understand yourself better, you can choose from many types of counselors. Probably, the first person to consider is your physician or clergyman. He may not be as well trained as a psychologist or psychiatrist, but many people in these two professions have studied counseling, and they have certain natural advantages as well. You can raise the issue with them gently, whereas you would have to spell out your problem for a specialist. You may have more confidence in them or relate to them more easily. Ministers are much less expensive than specialists, but medical doctors are at least as expensive as psychiatrists and are usually too busy to give you the time you need.

If you prefer a specialist, you can select a psychiatrist or psychologist. Psychiatrists have M.D. degrees and medical training, whereas psychologists have Ph.D.'s and psychological training. Because they are doctors of medicine, psychiatrists can perform physical examinations, have a clearer understanding of psychosomatic diseases, can prescribe drugs, including tranquilizers, and cannot be compelled to reveal what their patients have told them—that is, communications are "privileged." Some states have also given psychologists the right of privileged communication. Because all specialists respect your confidence, privileged communication is not very important, but it may make you feel more comfortable as a client.

Psychiatrists and psychologists use so many methods that a man's degree does not say very much about his approach. Some psychiatrists use approaches developed by psychologists, and vice versa. However, all psychoanalysts use some form of psychoanalytic treatment. The word "psychoanalyst" is not legally defined—nor is "psychologist," in some states—and anyone, even a quack, can call himself a psychoanalyst (or psychologists, in unregulated states).

Most men with psychological training are M.D.'s, and only M.D.'s can be members of the major associations. Freud objected to this rule, and several psychologists have taken psychoanalytic training, call themselves "lay analysts," and offer essentially the same services.

There is no evidence that psychiatrists are more effective than psychologists, but most psychiatrists and other M.D.'s believe that psychologists should not do counseling and should confine themselves to psychological testing and similar activities under the supervision of a psychiatrist or an M.D., even one who has no psychological training. Your doctor will therefore probably refer you to a psychiatrist if you ask for a recommendation. The reasons for this policy are primarily economic and have had the intended effect of keeping psychiatrists' fees considerably higher than those of psychologists.

Counseling fees are generally regarded as tax-deductible, and some group insurance policies pay part of the fee (usually, with the restriction that the counselor be an M.D.). Some companies also employ counselors or retain them at company expense for their executives and other employees, but most executives are reluctant to use these people or even to apply for insurance benefits. They fear that their conversations may not be kept confidential or that their associates will learn that they are seeking help and will lose respect for them. Unfortunately, these fears are occasionally justified; but the situation is gradually improving, and the entire relationship is usually kept confidential.

Regardless of whom you see or your reasons for wanting help, counselors are expensive. Fees range from $15 to $25 per hour for psychologists and $20 to $35 for psychiatrists. Men who are well known in their profession often charge more, and some specialists raise their fees for wealthy people because they believe that the fee has to "hurt" in order to force the client to take counseling seriously. There is no evidence either for or against this belief, and many people feel that it is simply a rationalization for higher fees.

But money is not the major cost. Counseling generally takes a great deal out of a man and can be an acutely painful process. Most people expect the specialist to solve their problems and are disappointed when they have to do most of the work themselves. They want quick and easy answers, but there aren't any. They want instant relief from their discomfort, but they frequently become more uncomfortable during the process. They lose their defenses and temporarily feel the full impact of their underlying anxiety. If they continue the relationship, they may become far less anxious and have much better ways to deal with their anxiety; but many people become discouraged and leave in worse shape than they began. Furthermore, some people are harmed no matter how long they work with the counselor. This problem is especially acute for psychoanalysis, the longest and most expensive system: Some people spend a number of years and thousands of dollars but in the end are more anxious and ineffective than before. The psychoanalysts, who have almost infinite patience as long as someone else pays for their time, usually refer to these people as "premature terminations," even if the patients have had three or four years of treatment!

In other words, counseling is a costly and risky undertaking. It will be expensive and demanding, and results are uncertain. You therefore should think very carefully before beginning. On the other hand, if you have spent years wondering what to do with your life, or want to do something about your drinking problem, or are destroying your career, health, or family, or simply want to know yourself better, the risks and costs may be justified. Only you can make that decision, and it has to be made wholeheartedly. Your motivation and commitment are crucially important. Without them nothing happens; you will merely spend some money and have superficial conversations with the counselor. But if you do have that desire, if you are willing to pay the price, you will find that the journey into yourself is the most fascinating trip that you could ever make. It is painful; it requires more real courage than a trip to deepest Africa; but it can be infinitely rewarding.

THE GOALS OF COUNSELING

Regardless of their method or training, all counselors have the same fundamental goal: helping people to become less anxious and more effective, satisfied, and independent. They try to help you feel less anxious and handle your anxieties in less defensive, destructive ways. This may require you to learn new kinds of behavior, become more aware of the options available to you, or be more able to exercise these options; but the net effect is greater independence, greater awareness of the forces that control you, less need for rigid and defensive behavior, and more ability to resist these forces and make genuine choices and decisions.

Most counselors work on the client's understanding and feelings about himself and other people. They believe that people behave ineffectively because they don't know what they really want or feel guilty about their own feelings and desires. They therefore aim for greater openness, greater ability of the client to understand what he really wants and feels, and more acceptance of his own goals and emotions.

This goal is intimately related to the goal of better personal relationships. A person who rejects himself will reject other people, and poor relations with other people will lead to feelings of worthlessness and self-rejection. To help a person understand and accept himself will therefore help him relate to other people. Some counselors go a step further: They also focus directly on better ways to understand, communicate, and live with other people.

A few counselors pay relatively little attention to self-understanding and focus directly on anxiety and defensive behavior. They feel that both are learned in the same way that other feelings and actions are learned, and use conditioning techniques to reduce anxiety and teach people better ways of handling it. Their method is not nearly as well known as psychoanalysis and client-centered counseling, but it has been rather successful.

Common Elements

All counseling relationships are one-sided; the counselor has extensive responsibilities to the client, but the client has no responsibilities to the counselor other than paying his bill and keeping appointments. The counselor is genuinely concerned with the client's growth and satisfaction but expects no reciprocal concern; he is there to solve the client's problems; his work focuses exclusively on helping him; and the counselor's problems and personality are rarely discussed.

Counselors usually work by discussing topics that the client cannot talk about with other people—his basic goals, fears, values, attitudes, feelings, beliefs, and desires. Some counselors supplement the discussions with various kinds of exercises and treatments—hypnosis or tranquilizers, for example—but most of the time in the sessions with the client is spent in talking. During these discussions the counselor is very permissive and accepting; he does not criticize or reject the client for what he says or feels.

Because no other adult relationship permits this degree of one-sidedness or gives the client such unconditional acceptance, the client feels safe enough to discard some of his defenses and try out new ways of thinking about himself and the world. He can also learn by doing things that he

256

can't do freely in other relationships: express anger directly, or lean on the counselor, or discuss things he is ashamed of, or be completely selfish and ego-centered, or try new ways of relating to himself and to other people. That is, he is free to work out his own problems in an atmosphere that allows him to make and learn from his own decisions.

Psychoanalysis

Psychoanalysis is the best known, most ambitious, slowest, most expensive, and least validated form of counseling. Psychoanalysts generally refuse to help a man solve the problems that he complains about (impotence, alcoholism, indecisiveness, depression, and so on). They regard these issues as mere symptoms of underlying problems and will accept the man only if he agrees to commit himself to years of treatment which can cost thousands of dollars. They feel that this commitment is necessary because they aim not to solve his "superficial" problems but fundamentally and permanently to alter his basic personality so that he can develop his full potential and live a more satisfying and productive life.

Because it is so slow and costly and so often ineffective, orthodox psychoanalysis is offered by relatively few practitioners today. Most modern psychoanalysts are neo-Freudians: They accept some of the basic theory and method but have made so many changes that Freud would probably not regard them as psychoanalysts. Freudian methods and theory have also influenced counselors of almost every other school, but these people do not call themselves psychoanalysts.

Theory. As stated in earlier chapters, Freud emphasized childhood experiences and divided personality into three parts: the id (the largely unconscious demanding part), the superego (the largely unconscious forbidding part, the "conscience"), and the ego (the largely conscious rational part). The id wants complete and immediate satisfaction for all its demands, but the superego prohibits acting or even wanting to satisfy these demands. That is, everyone has socially unacceptable desires, and most people feel guilty about them.

Furthermore, these desires and prohibitions are very rigid and unrealistic. They are absolute and unyielding and do not allow for the demands and limitations of reality. The ego's goal is therefore to compromise between the id, the superego, and reality so that the person can live with himself and the world. If it is strong enough, it can usually make the necessary compromises, but sometimes certain childhood experiences have prevented it from developing and becoming strong enough to do

257

the job. The person therefore suffers from guilt and anxiety and acts in rigid, repetitious, and self-destructive ways.

Much of this guilt refers to sex and aggressive feelings, especially toward one's parents. According to Freud, boys wanted to sleep with their mothers, girls with their fathers. Since the spouses stood in their way, the children were jealous and wanted to kill them. Both of these desires are extremely powerful, and they arouse enormous guilt and anxiety. Freud called the combination of desires, taboos, and guilt the "Oedipus complex" and argued that the desires were deeply repressed, while the guilt and anxiety remained powerful at the unconscious level and were the basic cause for most neuroses.

The basic task of psychoanalysis was therefore to strengthen the ego so that it could exert more control over the id and superego and the person could act more realistically and effectively. Since the problem began in childhood, the person had to reconstruct his childhood and bring the Oedipal conflict and other repressed material back into conscious awareness. Once this happened, the ego could exert some control and free itself from the crippling effects of unconscious conflicts.

Methods. Psychoanalytic counseling is therefore concerned with repressed childhood feelings and experiences. Since the client does not want to remember these things, it takes years to reconstruct his childhood and see how his problems began. The resistance to remembering things is overcome by using *free association:* The person lies on a couch and says anything that comes into his mind. Most of his remarks are irrelevant, but occasionally he says something "meaningful" about himself or his childhood. Most of his remarks are very indirect and their feelings are carefully disguised, but the analyst understands the language of the unconscious and can interpret them. His interpretations show the client what his remarks "really" mean, what he is indirectly saying about himself.

The counselor also analyzes *dreams.* Because defenses are weaker while we sleep, dreams can express deeply buried desires and fears. These feelings are expressed very indirectly and symbolically, but the analyst can often see beneath the surface. For example, a man can express his hostility toward his wife by dreaming of trying unsuccessfully to save her from an automobile accident, or he can express his feeling of being overburdened and inadequate by dreaming of climbing an endless mountain. Free association is often combined with reports of dreams to increase insight.

The analyst also interprets the client's *resistance,* his evasion of certain topics or his refusal to recognize obvious facts about himself. Resistance is a defense against anxiety and indicates that a person is trying to avoid something that he fears. The analyst points out these evasions and helps him realize why he is avoiding certain issues or facts.

Finally, he analyzes the client's *transference*. The client develops very strong feelings (positive, negative, or both) toward the analyst and acts as though the analyst were some important person from his past— usually, a parent or a lover. As the transference develops he expresses the same feelings to the analyst that he had toward that person and behaves in the same ineffective way. The analyst then interprets his behavior to show him how he really feels toward the original person.

In all phases of the treatment the patient brings things up from his unconscious, and the analyst interprets them. The result is that the person can understand and control problems and feelings that were previously unconscious and out of his control. Or, as Freud put it, "At the expense of the unconscious the ego becomes wider by the work of interpretation which brings the unconscious material into consciousness." * When the most important problems and feelings—the Oedipal conflict especially—have been brought into consciousness and solved, the patient is free from the anxiety and defensiveness they caused and can live a more satisfying and effective life.

Values and limitations. In addition to being extremely expensive and time-consuming, orthodox psychoanalysis has never been validated. Nearly all psychoanalysts have no scientific training and strenuously resent attempts to investigate their effectiveness. They demand essentially that their work be taken on faith, and the scientific community has been extremely critical of this attitude. Because of their resistance and the serious problems of measuring improvement, we have only a few studies, and they have not been well conducted. They do, however, suggest that in a statistical sense, *orthodox psychoanalysis is slightly worse than useless:* The improvement rate is higher for people who get no treatment than it is for those who undergo psychoanalysis. The psychoanalysts have hotly criticized these investigations and pointed out several flaws in them, and they have argued that statistics are meaningless because their goals are so ambitious; but they have not produced any solid data in support of their position. At this time, therefore, there is very little explicit justification for spending thousands of your dollars and years of your life in orthodox psychoanalysis.

The neo-Freudians. Because of their dissatisfaction with some aspects of Freudian theory and methods, most modern psychoanalysts are neo-

* Sigmund Freud, *A General Introduction to Psychoanalysis*, translated by Joan Riviere, Washington Square Press, New York, 1960, p. 463.

Freudians: They accept some of his ideas but differ with him on important issues. These differences vary from person to person, but most of them emphasize current problems and play down childhood conflicts and Oedipus complexes. They want to help people see how their current behavior is self-destructive, and they usually don't spend much time on its childhood causes.

They have also rejected Freud's emphasis on id-superego conflicts and concentrate directly on culture, alienation, relatedness, meaning, and identity. Although not completely discounting conflicts between desires and prohibitions, they feel that most problems are caused by cultural conflicts and ambiguities and our general inability to make sense out of our lives or relate to ourselves or other people.

Since interpersonal relationships are so important to them, they emphasize the interpersonal aspects of the client-counselor relationship and create a more realistic and equal relationship between themselves and their clients. The client does not take a completely passive and dependent role, lying down, free-associating, reporting dreams, and acting out feelings, nor does the analyst make all the interpretations. The client generally sits opposite the counselor and talks to him in a more controlled, give-and-take fashion. He is also encouraged to interpret his own remarks and behavior and relate them to the problems he has with other people.

Because there are so many varieties of neo-Freudian counseling, no overall evaluation of its effectiveness is possible now. The logic of their position is more attractive than Freud's—but logic is no substitute for data, and the data are not yet available. Some neo-Freudians' basic attitudes and methods are similar to those of the client-centered counselors, and this approach has been rather successful. However, these data are still indirect and cannot be regarded as conclusive evidence of their effectiveness.

Client-Centered Counseling

Theory. Client-centered counselors are also interested in childhood development and conflicts between desires and prohibitions, but they don't go nearly as far as the psychoanalysts. They note that people learn in childhood that certain feelings are not allowed; but these feelings are an inescapable part of human nature. People therefore feel guilty about the feelings and reject or deny part of themselves.

This denial and rejection continue into adulthood and protect them

260

from some anxiety, but create serious problems. They feel that the self they present to the world is not their real self, that their real self is something bad that must be kept hidden. They feel lonely because they know that they present a pseudo-self and people don't really know them. They are therefore alienated and isolated from themselves and other people. They don't know or like their real selves and think that other people feel the same way.

Their goals are as false as their feelings. They have accepted the goals that other people say they should have, instead of choosing their own; but when they have done so, their activities become meaningless. They are not in control of their own lives, and they work for things they don't really want.

These imposed goals and denied feelings combine in each person's *ideal self*, his belief about what he should be. He thinks he should be a much better person than he is—harder working, self-sacrificing, less interested in sex and self-indulgence, more ambitious, less dependent, more decisive, more intelligent. As he can't measure up to this ideal, he rejects himself as worthless, stupid, lazy, and immoral.

However, because these feelings are so unpleasant, he tries to escape them. He may simply try not to think about himself, or build his ego by bragging, or take refuge in many other defenses. The result is that he becomes increasingly confused about who he really is, but he is afraid of finding out.

The counselor's task is therefore to help him overcome these fears so that he may explore himself and learn who he really is and what he really wants to do. Once he has learned this, he develops more respect for himself, can accept himself as a decent human being, work for his own goals, and control his own life.

Method. The counselor tries to understand how the client feels about himself, to go beneath the surface of what he is saying, to the attitudes and feelings he has about himself and the world. In other words, he tries to see the client as the client sees himself.

To reach this understanding the counselor must avoid evaluating, criticizing, or rejecting the client and what he says. His goal is to understand the client's feelings, not to judge them. When the client touches upon a topic he fears or expresses a feeling he rejects in himself, he finds that it is understood and accepted as legitimate. He therefore understands and accepts this feeling and no longer has to deceive himself about it. As the process continues more and more of his feelings and experiences are explored, and he learns to understand and accept them. He therefore sees himself more clearly, feels he is a better person, depends less on his defenses, and becomes free to choose his own goals and act in their interest.

Values and limitations. Client-centered counseling is much faster and less expensive than psychoanalysis, but it is generally slower and more expensive than counterconditioning. However, direct comparison with either method is somewhat misleading because their goals are very different. Psychoanalysts' goals are somewhat similar to those of client-centered counselors, but more ambitious. They both aim for greater self-acceptance, clearer self-identification, and greater personal freedom, but the analysts go much further and want to reorganize a man's personality. The counterconditioners are much less ambitious than either of the other two; they simply want to solve some specific problem that is bothering a man—jealousy, a phobia, or excessive drinking, for example.

Although their goals are rather similar, the attitudes of the client-centered counselors and psychoanalysts toward research are very different. The analysts generally resist all attempts to measure their effectiveness, while the client-centered counselors have a tradition of very active research. This research indicates that their work is usually quite helpful. It does not help everyone, but after counseling many clients accept and feel more comfortable with themselves, understand their defenses and rely less on them, are more able to tolerate frustration, and are generally more mature. Counseling can also improve job performance; but some clients actually quit their jobs or don't work as hard after counseling as they did before it. Although their superiors would probably disagree, this can be a healthy sign; these clients formerly worked for goals that they thought they should have but are now free to pursue their own.

Some people unfortunately receive no benefit at all from counseling, and a few are actually harmed by it. Their defenses become less effective and they become more anxious and uncomfortable. As we cannot identify these people before they begin counseling, anyone considering counseling should realize that it involves significant risks.

COUNTERCONDITIONING

Theory. The counterconditioners have a much simpler theory and approach. They base their work on learning theory and focus directly on anxiety and behavior. They think that anxiety and ineffective behavior are learned in the same way as other things—by association or reward—and can be unlearned in the same way. If a person feels anxious in a safe situation, he has learned to associate something in that situation with pain or fear.

A classic experiment illustrates this principle: Some people think that children's fear of furry animals is instinctive, but Professor John B. Watson proved that it is learned by association. When rats, rabbits, and dogs were placed next to children who had never been exposed to them, the children showed no signs of fear. They smiled and generally reached out to touch the animals.

This kind of fear can be developed by associating animals with something painful or frightening. One child had not previously been afraid of a white rat. But each time he reached for it, Watson frightened him by striking a metal bar behind his head. After a few associations the child became very afraid of the rat even if no sound was made. He would cry and crawl away from it as soon as it was put next to him. He also became afraid of fur muffs, rabbits, and other furry objects that he had formerly played with. His fear had generalized; he had become afraid of objects similar to white rats even though the objects had not been directly associated with the frightening sound.

This same process occurs in adults. We have learned to be afraid of things that were once associated with pain or fear, and our learned fears generalize to similar objects and situations. So many things have either been associated with pain and fear or are similar to associated objects that anxiety can be aroused by an enormous variety of objects and situations. And—as shown throughout this book—regardless of how it is aroused, anxiety usually causes defensiveness and ineffective behavior.

The counselor's job is therefore to find out what things frighten his client and to make them less frightening. He then *desensitizes* the client so that the things that used to frighten him no longer make him anxious. He does this in a very simple way.

Method. Anxiety is a physical response (which, however, has psychological components), and some physical responses are incompatible with each other. For example, a man cannot straighten his arm and bend it at the same time. The muscles can go in only one direction. Anxiety and relaxation are incompatible in the same way; we cannot be relaxed and anxious at the same time.

In counterconditioning the counselor relaxes the client and then does something which would normally cause mild anxiety. Because the relaxation response is stronger than the anxiety response, it slowly becomes associated with the formerly frightening stimulus. As this association develops the person feels less anxious.

Another experiment with children and animals illustrates this principle. A young boy was extremely afraid of animals and other furry objects. The research team counterconditioned this fear by feeding him and then placing a caged rabbit in the same room. The rabbit was so far away that the relaxation and comfort he felt were greater than his anxiety. Each day they moved the rabbit closer, proceeding slowly because the relaxation response had to be stronger than his anxiety. At the end of treatment he was not afraid even when they placed the rabbit in his lap, and he had also lost his fear of other furry objects.

The same general principle is used in counterconditioning with adults, but different methods are used to relax the client and present the frightening stimulus. By means of the answers to careful questioning the counselor makes a ranked list of the things that make the client anxious. He then relaxes the client, often by using hypnosis, and tells him to think about the least frightening thing. If he can remain relaxed, they move on to the next situation. They continue this process, stopping for deeper relaxation whenever the anxiety response is strong enough to override his relaxation. Ultimately, the person no longer feels anxious in these situations.

The same general strategy can be used to help overcome ineffective behavior. Ineffective behaviors are learned in the same way as effective ones—by being rewarded. They can be unlearned by associating a mild punishment with them or by letting them occur without being rewarded. For example, the most effective treatment for bed wetting, a common childhood problem, is to have a loud buzzer wake the child whenever he urinates and completes a circuit in a wired bed beneath the sheets. Several cures for alcoholism are based on association of drinking with punishment. The alcoholic is given a drug which, when combined with alcohol, makes him feel nauseated. This method works in about 60 percent of the cases of alcoholics who *want* treatment—a very high recovery rate.

Values and limitations. The counterconditioners, who are very thorough researchers, have clearly demonstrated the value of their work. It has been extremely successful at curing certain kinds of anxiety and other feelings such as phobias, shyness, and jealousy. It has also been used rather successfully with more complicated feelings (general anxiety, even identity problems). And it has been quite helpful in getting rid of ineffective, destructive behaviors such as alcoholism.

It is also much speedier and less costly than any other type of counseling. Speed is achieved by focusing directly on the fears and behaviors themselves and ignoring their causes or their meaning to the client. The psychoanalysts would spend months or years in finding out why a man feels as he does, and he might feel the same way even after understanding the causes of his feelings. The client-centered counselors

264

would help him understand what his feelings mean to him. But the counterconditioners aren't interested in either of these issues (nor are most clients); they just want to get rid of the fears or destructive behaviors (and that's all a client usually wants).

Shedding their fears will permit men to live more freely and effectively. However, counterconditioning may not have as much impact or benefit as the other two methods. It may get rid of specific fears and destructive behaviors but not solve underlying problems or prepare the client for as rich or rewarding a life. The counterconditioners reject the position stated here; they assert that there are no underlying problems, that the problems are the visible fears and behaviors. They also claim that their approach is more beneficial as well as faster and less expensive than other forms of counseling. Unfortunately, current data do not clearly indicate just how effective their approach is at solving the larger problems, but the data are encouraging.

GROUP COUNSELING

There are several kinds of group counseling, but most of them are rather similar to T-groups in their basic goals and approach: Members are free to say and do as they wish, and they learn by analyzing their own and each other's behavior. This general approach has been used with strangers, families, executive teams, and several other types of groups.

T-groups are the most popular type of group counseling, and the line between them and therapy is rather blurred. In fact, the T-group system at the University of California at Los Angeles is almost indistinguishable from therapy. There is a distinctive line between most other forms of T-groups and therapy, however: T-groups are generally used with people who do not have serious problems; the discussion focuses on the "here and now" and general group processes, and the members have a fairly equal relationship with the trainer. Group therapy is generally for people with more serious problems; more time is spent on members' previous history or problems with nonmembers (wife, superiors, children, and so on), and the therapist is somewhat above the group.

The great benefit of group counseling is that members can do more than just discuss their problems; they can learn how they affect each other and try out new behaviors in a permissive, low-cost environment. If the new behaviors don't work, they can go back to their old style without losing much. In other words the group offers a realistic but permissive place to learn about themselves and their ways of acting; and since the group is more similar to the outside world than a one-sided relationship with a counselor, they can transfer what they learn more easily to the "real world."

People also have much more control over their own behavior and much more responsibility for it in groups than in other forms of counseling. The group is permissive, but other members are not nearly as permissive as a professional counselor. They have their own needs and problems and will tell a member when he offends or hurts them; each member therefore learns how he affects people and must also accept some responsibility to the rest of the group. Group counseling is also much less expensive because the counselor's fee is shared by several people. (Furthermore, if you want to attend a T-group or similar program, your company may be willing to pay for it—and this payment will not entail the same embarrassment as a fee for a psychiatrist or clinical psychologist.)

There are too many kinds of group counseling to permit an overall evaluation, but the limited data we have on T-groups do indicate that they help individuals. The data about benefits for organizations are much less encouraging, but that is not our concern here.

CONCLUSIONS

To choose a counselor is far from easy. There are several major types and literally dozens of "schools" within each type. But this brief description should give you some idea of the sort of counseling which would be most useful to you. If you do contact a counselor, discuss your doubts or questions about him or his approach *before* you begin working with him. To do so is not bad manners; in fact, it is the first step in building an honest relationship with him, and this kind of relationship is one indispensable ingredient of successful counseling. Without it counseling will probably be unsuccessful; with it you will probably gain a great deal, regardless of his approach. In other words a man's theory and method are not nearly as important as whether or not you can relate to him. Your own emotional reaction to him may therefore be the best guide for deciding whether to work with him. This reaction, however, will probably be influenced by his approach. Some approaches are simply more compatible with your personality.

Appendix B

The Goal Analysis Questionnaire

T HIS QUESTIONNAIRE IS NO SUBSTITUTE FOR COUNSELING, BUT IT MAY increase your understanding of yourself and your goals. The more completely, thoroughly, and thoughtfully you answer these questions, the more benefit you will receive from this analysis. We suggest that you think carefully about each answer, write it down on a *blank* piece of paper, and go on to the later questions. As you answer the later questions, think about your earlier ones and change them if you wish. After you have answered all of the questions on blank paper, think about them and write your answers on the form.

Don't be disturbed if it takes several hours to complete this form. These questions, particularly the "Why?" questions, are not easy to answer, but the information and clarity you will gain from answering them should be worth the effort.

I. CAREER GOALS
    1. *a.* If you could have *any* job you wanted, what job would you take? _____

       b. Why? _____

2. *a.* How important is making a lot of money to you? _____

   b. Why? _____

     _____

3. *a.* How much income per year do you *need* to live at the standard of living you desire?

     1. Now. _____   3. In 10 years. _____

     2. In 5 years. _____   4. Ultimately. _____

   b. How much income do you *want?*

     1. Now. _____   3. In 10 years. _____

     2. In 5 years. _____   4. Ultimately. _____

   c. If there is a difference between what you *need* and *want,* *why* is there a difference? What does this "unnecessary" money mean to you?

     _____

     _____

     _____

4. *a.* How much income does *your wife* want you to earn?

     1. Now. _____   3. In 10 years. _____

     2. In 5 years. _____   4. Ultimately. _____

   b. If there is a difference between your wants and hers, *why* is there a difference?

     _____

   c. What are the probable effects of this difference? _____

     _____

5.   What kind of work do you really want to do? Ignore income differences. Answer in your own words, but be as explicit and as specific as possible.

     _____

     _____

     _____

6. *a.* Do you really want to do executive work (not lead an executive's life)? That is, do you really want to accomplish things by motivating, directing, and controlling other people, or would you prefer a job in which you advised people or worked on your own?

     _____ *b.* Why? _____

     _____

     _____

7. *a.* If you really want to do executive work, *at what level* would you like to work? Ignore income differences and focus your attention on the duties, responsibilities, pressures, and so on of different levels (for example, top management, middle management).

_____

b. Why? _____

_____

8. *a.* In what size firm would you prefer to work (in assets)?
1. Over $1 billion.
2. $100 million–$1 billion.
3. $10 million–$100 million.
4. $1 million–$10 million.
5. Under $1 million.
6. Your own business of any size.

b. Why? _____

_____

c. If you are not presently working in a business of that size, *why* aren't you doing so? _____

_____

9. *a.* In what industry would you like to work? _____
b. Why? _____
c. In what industry are you working? _____
d. If there is a difference, why are you working in your present industry?

_____

10. *a.* For what company would you like to work? _____
b. Why? _____
c. In what company are you working? _____
d. If there is a difference, why are you working for your present company?

_____

11. *a.* In your own words, state the kind of company you would prefer working for.

_____

b. Why? _____

_____

c. In your own words, state what kind of firm you *are* working for.

_____

    d. If you are not working for the kind of firm you want, *why* aren't you doing so? _____

_____

12. *a.* Would you rather work for a "tough" or a "democratic" firm?

    b. Why? _____

    c. Which type of firm do you work for now? _____
    d. If there is a difference between *a* and *b, why* are you working there? _____

13. *a.* Would you rather work in a "flexible" or a "bureaucratic" firm?

    b. Why? _____

    c. What kind of firm are you working for now? _____
    d. If there is a difference, why are you working there? _____

14. *a.* Would you rather work for a "tough" or a "democratic" boss?

    b. Why? _____

    c. What kind of boss do you work for now? _____
    d. If there is a difference, why do you work for him? _____

15. *a.* Would you rather work in a company where most decisions are made by individuals or in a company where they are made by committees? _____
    b. Why? _____

    c. What kind of company do you work for now? _____
    d. If there is a difference, why do you work there? _____

16. *a.* What kind of work would you like to do *now?* _____

    b. Why? _____

    c. What kind of work are you doing? _____

    d. If there is a difference, why are you doing your present work?

      _____

17. *a.* Would you rather have a secure job or one in which you could "sink or swim"? _____

    b. Why? _____

    c. What kind of job do you have now? _____

    d. If there is a difference, why do you keep it? _____

18. *a.* Would you rather work independently in an unstructured situation or have clear guidelines from above? _____

    b. Why? _____

    c. What kind of job do you have now? _____

    d. If there is a difference, why do you keep it? _____

19. *a.* Where do you want to live and work? _____

    b. Why? _____

    c. Where are you living and working? _____

    d. If there is a difference, why? _____

20.   What is wrong with your present job? _____

21.   What do you want out of your next job (in your current or another firm)? _____

II. SACRIFICES AND THE PRICE OF SUCCESS

  1. *a.* Are you missing pleasures or satisfactions now because of your career ambitions? _____

    b. What are they? _____

    c. Why are you missing them? _____

    d. How important are they to you? _____

    e. When do you expect to enjoy them? _____

    f. Why will you be able to enjoy them then, when you can't now?

      _____

271

2. *a.* What price are you *willing* to pay to get ahead? (Answer in your own words.) _____

_____

_____

   b. What price is your wife *willing* to pay? _____

_____

_____

   c. What price will you *have* to pay? _____

_____

   d. What price will she *have* to pay? _____

_____

3.   Are you willing to risk your health to get ahead? _____

4.   Are you willing to risk disrupting or damaging your family life? _____

5. *a.* Are you willing and able to "play politics" to get ahead? _____
   b. Is your wife willing to do so? _____
   c. Can you maintain your self-respect if you do so? _____
   d. Can she maintain her respect for you if you do so? _____

6. *a.* Are you willing and able to "cut corners" (act in unethical, semilegal, or illegal ways) to get ahead? _____
   b. Is your wife willing to do so? _____
   c. Can you maintain your self-respect if you do so? _____
   d. Can she maintain her respect for you if you do so? _____

7. *a.* Are you willing and able to drop old friends as you move upward? _____
   b. Is your wife willing and able to do so? _____

8. *a.* Are you willing and able to change your style and pattern of living as you move upward? _____
   b. Is your wife willing and able to do so? _____

9. *a.* How many hours per week do *you want* to work? _____
   b. How many does *your wife want* you to work? _____
   c. How many hours a week will you *have to* work to reach your goals? _____
   d. Do you *prefer* a regular schedule of hours or an irregular one? _____

   e. Does your wife prefer a regular or an irregular schedule? _____
   f. Will you *have to* work a regular or an irregular schedule to reach your goals? _____

10. *a.* Where do you want to live? _____

 b. Where does your wife want to live? _____

 c. Where is the home office of your present firm? _____

 d. Where will you have to live to advance in your present firm?
_____

11. *a.* Are you willing and able to relocate whenever and wherever your firm directs? _____

 b. Are you willing to relocate for promotions or raises? _____

 c. Is your wife willing to do so? _____

12. *a.* Are you willing to spend a substantial amount of time away from home on company travel? _____

 b. Does your wife mind your being away from home?_____

13. *a.* Are you willing and able to engage in necessary "business socializing"? _____

 b. Is your wife willing and able to do so? _____

14. *a.* Are you willing and able to "butter up" important people to advance your career? _____

 b. Is your wife willing and able to do so? _____

III. OVERALL GOALS AND PLANS

Reread all of your previous answers and think carefully about them. Then carefully answer the following questions:

1. There are many factors to be considered for any career choice (duties, title, income, superiors, locations, firm, travel, and so on). On a blank sheet of paper list all of the factors which *you* feel are important *to you* (and to your wife if you sincerely intend to allow her wishes to influence your decisions). Then arrange them in order of their importance *to you* on that sheet. When you have completed putting them in order, write them in the spaces below. (1 = most important.)

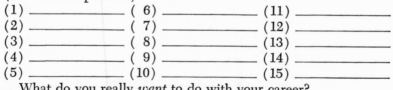

(1) _____ (6) _____ (11) _____
(2) _____ (7) _____ (12) _____
(3) _____ (8) _____ (13) _____
(4) _____ (9) _____ (14) _____
(5) _____ (10) _____ (15) _____

2. What do you really *want* to do with your career?

 a. Now. _____
_____

 b. In 5 years. _____
_____

c. In 10 years. _____

d. Ultimately. _____

3.   What *are* you going to do?
    a. Now. _____

    b. In 5 years. _____

    c. In 10 years. _____

    d. Ultimately. _____

Index

Index

About the Author

ALAN N. SCHOONMAKER holds a B.A. in psychology from Monmouth College and a Ph.D. in industrial psychology from the University of California at Berkeley. He has taught industrial psychology and organization theory at U.C.L.A. and Pittsburgh and Carnegie-Mellon Universities. Currently, he is research adviser to the Belgian Productivity Center. He counsels executives on their career problems and has served as a consultant on management development to the International Business Machines Corporation, the Bell Telephone Company of Pennsylvania, the Republic Steel Corporation, the Aetna Insurance Company, the Aluminum Company of America, Ernst & Ernst, the Xerox Corporation, the Westinghouse Electric Corporation, Ryan Homes Inc., The Young Presidents Organization, and the Japanese Productivity Center.